CULTURAL RELATIONS

BETWEEN

THE UNITED STATES AND THE HISPANIC WORLD

Volume One

CULTURAL RELATIONS BETWEEN THE UNITED STATES AND THE
HISPANIC WORLD

THE UNITED STATES AS SEEN
BY SPANISH AMERICAN WRITERS

(1776 - 1890)

by

JOSE DE ONIS

University of Colorado

SECOND EDITION

GORDIAN PRESS
NEW YORK
1975

Originally Published 1952
Reprinted 1975

144421

Library of Congress Cataloging in Publication Data

De Onís, José.
   The United States as seen by Spanish American
writers, 1776-1890.

   (Cultural relations between the United States and the
Hispanic world ; v. 1)
   Reprint of the 1952 ed. published by the Hispanic
Institute in the United States, New York; with new
introd.
   Bibliography: p.
   Includes index.
   1. Latin America--Relations (general) with the
United States. 2. United States--Relations (general)
with Latin America. 3. United States in literature.
4. Spanish American literature--History and criticism.
I. Title. II. Series.
F1418.D45 1975   301.29'73'08   74-26684
ISBN 0-87752-184-0

INTRODUCTION TO THE SECOND EDITION

The present volume, *The United States as Seen by Spanish American Writers*, is one of a series of four, entitled *Cultural Relations Between the United States and the Hispanic World*, which we plan to complete and publish by 1976 to commemorate the Bi-centennial of the Independence of the United States. This work is of a general nature, giving the reader a synthesis of the cultural relations between these two regions during a period embracing 120 years, from the latter decades of the XVIIIth Century to the beginning of the XXth, with particular concentration on the XIXth Century Liberal Revolution and its immediate aftermath. One chapter deals extensively with Domingo Faustino Sarmiento, without doubt the outstanding Hispanic personality to be encountered in the history of these relations.

The second volume, *The Liberal Revolution in the Hispanic World*, is more specialized. It is a work composed of monographs, some twenty-five studies, each based on an individual author or on a particular problem of inter-cultural relations. The major writers treated in these monographs are: Antonio de Alcedo y Bexarano, Francisco Iturri, Benjamin Franklin, Valentin de Foronda, Thomas Jefferson, Manuel Torres, Cabrera de Nevares, Manuel Bartolome Gallardo, William Cullen Bryant, Jose Maria Heredia, James Fenimore Cooper, Timothy Flint, Father José Antonio Martinez, Fanny Calderón de la Barca, Domingo del Monte y Aponte, Mary A. Maverick, Jose Marti, Engenio María de Hostos, and Herbert E. Bolton. In this volume we have tried not to duplicate work by previous critics in the field, particularly that of Stanley T. Williams in *The Spanish Background of American Literature*. This will explain the absence of some important personages from the list, e.g. Prescott, Ticknor, Washington Irving, Longfellow. Nonetheless, they are included in the various texts and in some instances play an important, though secondary, role in their development.

The third volume, *Herman Melville and the Hispanic World* is made up of nine essays of an interpretive nature. The importance of Melville's interest in the Hispanic World cannot be overestimated. This interest, as brought out in this study, is a primary factor in determining the sources of his creative genius—not an external added element, but an organic, vital part of his work. This volume also presents an interesting contrast between Herman Melville (1819-1891) and his contemporary Domingo Faustino Sarmiento (1811-1888). Both lived during the greater part of the XIXth Century and both were subject to similar influences. But whereas the Argentinian Sarmiento—the finest exponent of positivism, progress and democracy in the Hispanic World—was all faith and optimism, Melville—his contrasting counterpart in North America, a much more complex and disturbing figure—questions many of these same concepts and values. The two complement each other and constitute a paradoxical unity indispensable for the comprehension of their era.

The fourth and final volume, *Literature of the Disenchantment*, composed of fourteen monographs and essays, based on the writings of XIXth and XXth Century authors evaluating the accomplishments of the Liberal Revolution and North American cultural influence in general, represents the end of an era and the coming of a New Age.

The order followed in this work is chronological, starting with the beginning of inter-American cultural relations during Colonial days in volume one and bringing them up to the present in volume four. There is some overlapping of subject matter as we go from one volume to another, but seen in perspective there is a logical sequence and a progressive flow of narrative. Some authors appear in several of the volumes; each new case however is presented from a fresh point of view and is supported by a new set of documents. We have intended in the exposition of the four volumes, that there be a minimum of duplication. If this has not always been possible, it is because of the inevitably complex nature of the materials involved. The area covered in these cultural relations could be compared to a triangle, with the United States as the apex and Spain and Spanish America as the complementary angles. All three must be considered in the various relationships if we are to have a complete understanding of the problem.

J. de O.

PREFACE

The historian of cultural relations between peoples faces a task beset with pitfalls. Theories and beliefs as to the relative value of traits represented by the people he deals with limit the universality of his work: ethnocentrism tends to infect him, despite good intentions. The author of the present work is fortunately the possessor of a cultural heritage which has delivered him from some of these difficulties. Educated in this country, a citizen (and sometime a soldier) of the United States, he is also a descendant of a notable Castilian family and has therefore naturally absorbed much of the Hispanic tradition and point of view which his studies have subsequently intensified. He can understand more fully than most of us the dialectic of attraction and repulsion, admiration and disdain, friendship and hostility in terms of which the story of inter-American relations must be told. Further, he combines the sensitivity of the Latin with the industry attributed by many to the "Anglo-Saxon." The value of this book, therefore, lies both in its serenity of temper and in the laborious compilation of data from widely-scattered sources.

The chronological limits of his work may be explained and justified by criteria somewhat different from those followed by the author himself, though in harmony with the latter. The interaction of Latin America and the United States has taken place in a period marked by two revolutions: the liberal revolutions of the end of the eighteenth and the early nineteenth centuries and the collectivist revolutionary movements of the present age. In the first of these the United States was the example *par excellence* of revolutionary accomplishment and the cynosure of all true adherents to the causes of personal liberty, equality of opportunity, and representative government. In the second, the United States represents conservatism (the idea of conserving the gains achieved through its own earlier revolution). To most foreigners, the United States in our era stands primarily for engineering proficiency, know-how, and ability to organize successfully and to carry to completion great material tasks. Concomitantly, it also stands for a society offering high material rewards to labor, skilled and unskilled. Its appeal, therefore, is no longer to the impatient. restless, visionary, embittered men and women from whose ranks revolutionaries are recruited.

No sharp chronological division, of course, can be made between the older and the newer vision of the United States abroad. Some scholars would make the break at the era of the American Civil War. Professor de Onís ends his story a little later, yet most of it lies within the earlier period. In short, he has chronicled inter-American cultural currents in the era of gestation of revolution, in the revolutionary era itself, and in a subsequent era of attempted consolidation of the consequences of revolution. Sarmiento represents the last link in a chain going back to 1776. Martí is the harbinger of a new tendency with innumerable presentday adherents in which those who still deplore the liberal revolts of a past century join hands with those to whom that movement seems not to have gone far enough, and which has undergone modifications and turns which the gentle Cuban with the burning and prophetic soul would by no means have followed. It is to be hoped that the present study will have a sequel in this latter story, and that in it, as in the pages which follow, there will be evidenced the ability to transcend the prejudices of nationalism and the presentmindedness of the rootless observer of the contemporary.

                                                    CHARLES C. GRIFFIN

Vassar College

CONTENTS

INTRODUCTION

Much has been written on the subject of the relations between the United States and Spanish America, but this writing has not been primarily concerned with intellectual or cultural relations as such, nor with the study of the respective attitudes of these countries toward each other as seen in their literatures. The topics studied have dealt in most cases with the political, economic, and diplomatic problems that the American nations have experienced.

Perhaps the most notable exception to this are the two studies by John Englekirk, the first of these dealing with the influence of Edgar Allen Poe in Hispanic Literature, the second with Whitman in Spanish America.[1] There are also a few other articles by North American critics studying the individual relations of Spanish American authors with the United States. Among these are Marshal E. Nunn's study of Rubén Darío's attitude toward the United States;[2] Watt Stewart and William French's article on the influence of Horace Mann on the educational ideas of Domingo Faustino Sarmiento;[3] Madaline W. Nichols' "A United States Tour by Sarmiento in 1847";[4] Edith F. Helman's "Early interest in Spanish in New England";[5] and James F. Shearer's "Pioneer publishers of textbooks for Hispanic America: the house of Appleton."[6]

Of a more general nature are Harry Bernstein's two studies on the cultural relations between New England and Spanish America;[7] Manuel Pedro González's short treatise on the intellectual relations between the United States and Spanish America;[8] Clarence H. Haring's book, *South America looks at the United States* (New York, 1928); and Irma Salas' article, "Las relaciones culturales entre Chile y los Estados Unidos".[9] Bern-

---

[1] *Edgar Allan Poe in Hispanic literature,* Instituto de las Españas, New York, 1934; "Whitman in Spanish America," *Hispania,* November, 1942.

[2] "Rubén Darío y los Estados Unidos," *América,* Habana. I, 1939, 61-64.

[3] "The Influence of Horace Mann on the Educational Ideas of Domingo Faustino Sarmiento," *The Hispanic American Historical Review,* XX, 1940, 12-31.

[4] *The Hispanic American Historical Review,* XVI, 1936, 190-212.

[5] *Hispania,* August, 1946, pp. 339-351.

[6] *Hispania,* February, 1944.

[7] "Las primeras relaciones entre New England y el mundo hispánico: 1700-1815," *Revista Hispánica Moderna,* V, 1939, pp. 1-17; "Some Inter-American Aspects of the Enlightenment," *Latin America and the Enlightenment,* New York, 1942, pp. 53-69.

[8] "Intellectual relations between the United States and Spanish America," *The civilization of the Americas,* Berkeley, 1938, pp. 109-137; "Las relaciones intelectuales entre los Estados Unidos e Hispano-América," *Universidad de la Habana,* VIII, no. 24-25, 84-110.

[9] *Boletín de la Unión Panamericana,* Washington, 1940, pp. 570-576.

stein's two articles are primarily concerned with the relations of New England and the Hispanic World during colonial times. González's essay, published first in English and later revised in Spanish, in spite of its comprehensive title, deals almost exclusively with the intellectual relations between the United States and Cuba. Haring's book is more representative of the whole of Spanish America and, although it has to do mostly with political developments, has several chapters in which the attitude of contemporary Spanish American authors is discussed.

Information concerning literary relations between the United States and Spanish America may be found in books such as Ferguson's *American literature in Spain* (New York, 1916); Coester's *The literary history of Spanish America* (New York, 1929); García Godoy's Studies in Spanish American literature; and Henríquez-Ureña's *Literary currents in Hispanic America* (Cambridge, Mass., 1945).

As concerns the political, economic, and diplomatic relations between the two Americas, many studies have been made, for the most part by North American historians. Political movements are not in themselves of any direct literary influence, any more than are economic developments. Nevertheless, it must be remembered that the circumstances under which people live do exert a definite influence upon the type, quality and tone of their literary production. This fact is particularly true in Spanish America, where writing and politics have always gone hand in hand.

Among the students of political relations are numbered some of the outstanding historians of our time: Harry Edwing Bard, William S. Robertson, Víctor Andrés Belaúnde, William R. Shepherd, and Herbert E. Bolton. Bard initiated research in this field in 1914 with his book *Intellectual and cultural relations between the United States and the other republics of America.* This was followed in 1915 by Charles Lyon Chandler's *Inter-American acquaintances,* a book containing a wealth of information. In 1923, William S. Robertson published his book *Hispanic American relations,* which has been until recently the most complete of its type. Mention should also be made of Víctor Andrés Belaúnde's work *Bolivar and the political thought of the Spanish American Revolution* (Baltimore, 1938), which has contributed to the study of this subject by giving us the Spanish American point of view.

On the United States' inter-American diplomatic relations there have been studies, for the most part, by the disciples of Shepherd, of Columbia University, and Bolton, of the University of California. The many articles and lectures on Spanish American history by these two historians have inspired younger men to do further research in this field. Among the best known in this group are Fred J. Rippy, Arthur Preston Whitaker, Charles C. Griffin, Philip Brooks, James B. Lockey, John Rydjord, Lawrence F. Hill, William D. McCain, Henry Clay Evans and E. Taylor Parks.

In Spanish America we find information concerning the diplomatic relations between the United States and Mexico in Lucas Alamán's *Historia de México* (Mexico, 1849-52). Concerning relations with Venezuela there is Parra Pérez's *Historia de la primera república de Venezuela* (Caracas, 1939); and pertaining to the relations with Chile at the time of its struggle for independence we have Collier and Cruz's book *La primera misión de los Estados Unidos de América en Chile* (Santiago de Chile, 1926).

For the period prior to 1823, we have used Antonio de Alcedo y Bexarano's *Biblioteca americana,* a bibliographical dictionary in manuscript form of authors who wrote about the American continent during Colonial times;[10] Obadiah Rich's two bibliographies, the *Bibliotheca americana nova,* a catalogue of books relating to America, in various languages, during the eighteenth and nineteenth centuries (London and New York, 1835-46), and the *Bibliotheca americana vetus* (London, 1845), that covers the period from the discovery of America to 1700. Rich also had a catalogue of his own collection of manuscripts on America printed in London, 1848. For this period we also have consulted Joseph Sabin's *Dictionary of books related to America* (29 vols., New York, 1868-1936); Maggs' *Bibliotheca Americana,* part VI (London, 1927), that deals with books on America in Spanish; and José Toribio Medina's *Biblioteca hispanoamericana,* that goes from the discovery of America until 1818 (Santiago de Chile, 1898-1907).

For the period that follows the War of Independence bibliographical information was obtained from Carlos M. Trelles' three studies: *Biblioteca geográfica cubana* (Matanzas, 1920), a bibliography on Cuban travellers; *Estudio de la bibliografía cubana sobre la doctrina de Monroe* (Habana, 1922); and "Bibliografía de la segunda guerra de la independencia cubana y de la hispano-yankee" published in *Cuba y América* (Habana, 1902). We have also used Felipe Teixidor's *Viajeros mexicanos* (México, 1939); J. T. Medina's *Biblioteca americana* (Santiago de Chile, 1928); Sturgis E. Leavitt's *Hispanic American Literature in the United States* (Cambridge, Mass., 1932); and Pane's *Two hundred Latin American books in English translation; a bibliography* (1943).

Most of the unpublished documents used in this study were obtained from the García Archives of the University of Texas; the archives of the Department of State in Washington, D. C.; the Archivo Histórico Nacional de Madrid; and the Rich Collection of Manuscripts at the New York Public Library. Published documents were taken from Blanco y Azpurúa's *Documentos para la historia de la vida pública del Libertador de Colombia, Perú y Bolivia,* and from general sources. Several guides to materials in Spanish

---

10 Alcedo y Bexarano had originally intended to publish the "Biblioteca americana" as an appendix to his *Diccionario geográfico-histórico de las Indias Occidentales ó América,* Madrid, 1786-1789. (*Diccionario,* Introd., p. viii.) This manuscript is now part of the Rich Collection in the New York Public Library.

archives relating to the United States, which have been printed or ofl which transcripts are preserved in American libraries, were also used.

Critical studies and bibliographies of French and English books on American travel were also consulted. We found the most profitable ones to be Henry J. Tuckerman's *America and her commentators* (New York, 1864); Allan Nevins, *American social history as recorded by British travellers* (New York, 1923); Frank Monaghan's *French travellers in the United States* (New York, 1933); and Gilbert Chinard's book *Washington as the French knew him* (Princeton, 1940).

It is the purpose of this study to determine the attitude of the Spanish American authors toward the United States during two main periods, namely: the era of the Independence (1777-1822), and the era of the formation of the Spanish American nations (1823-1890). Its object is to analyze the available works pertaining to this subject written by Spanish Americans, to ascertain the attitude of the outstanding, representative authors, as well as the characteristics common to all writers of each period, and to trace the evolution of certain fundamental ideas in the literary and political thought of these two epochs. We have tried to find out and present to the reader what the various authors thought about the United States and why they thought as they did, rather than to prove whether their opinions were right or wrong. Instead of studying each nation individually, we have approached the problem in the light of those general ideological movements that have affected the hemisphere as a whole. This method was adopted because we feel that despite variations of opinion from country to country, due in many cases to geographical, economic and political differences, they all have a common culture. Nor have we limited our investigation to the geographic boundaries of this hemisphere. Whenever possible, we have traced the ideas to their source, which in the majority of cases has been Europe.

The first chapter has been devoted to the study of the main causes for the prejudices and affinities that existed first in Europe between the mother countries and later in America between the colonies, and that have come down to us as an inherent part of the cultures of the different nations that today make up the American continent.

The next two chapters—each devoted to one of the two main periods discussed in this book, the period of Independence and the period of formation—have ben divided as follows: I. The study of the general character of the period; as, for example, the historical elements that directly or indirectly have affected the attitude of the Spanish American authors toward the United States. II. The different points of contact between the two peoples that gave rise to these attitudes such as the presence and activities of North Americans in the countries concerned; the residence of Spanish Americans in the United States; the publication and translation of North American books; the knowledge of European books approving or condemning American ideas and institutions; as well as all other contacts or human media of transmission that might have contributed to the knowledge of the Spanish American authors concerning this nation. III. The study of the attitude of the different authors—travellers, political thinkers, literary critics —as perceived in their interpretations of the different aspects of American life: social relations, political relations, spiritual and creative activities. It was found convenient to divide this section into three parts: the first, dealing with the ideas expressed by the Spanish American travellers who visited the United States and who wrote diaries and memoirs of their experiences here; the second, with the ideas expressed by students of political thought (the bulk of this group is made up of pamphleteer literature, essays and treatises on economic and political sciences); the third is devoted to the United States as interpreted by writers of pure literature and by literary critics.

The fourth chapter deals with a study of the attitude of Domingo Faustino Sarmiento. The prominent part played by this man in the literature and history of Spanish America seemed to warrant giving him special emphasis.

The last chapter, which is only a conclusion to the previous three, summarizes the attitudes of the Spanish American authors and sums up the fundamental traits of the American national character.

It is our belief that if we analyze with care the relations between Spanish America and the United States in the past it will help us create a more substantial foundation for our theory of continental solidarity. An objective study of the United States as seen through the eyes of Spanish American writers will help us to understand ourselves better. As has often been said, "only through the study of human relations shall we ever be able to provide for a lasting foundation of peace and human harmony."

The relations between the two cultures at many periods have been purely negative—in other words, non-existent. This is particularly true of the early periods, when Spanish America was proceeding in its development whereas the North American colonies had not even come into existence.

At every period, the relations of both the United States and Spanish America with Europe have been more important than with each other. The European nation exerting the greatest influence upon the United States has naturally been England; upon Spanish America, Spain. This has been due in both cases to a similarity of background and a common language. The United States had closer relations with France and Spain than with Spanish America, the same being true of the latter.

During the eighteenth and nineteenth centuries the literary relations between the Americas varied in intensity. The period from 1776 to 1810 or 1783 to 1823, if we take end dates, the time during which both the United States and Spanish American colonies gained their independence, relations were close and comparatively frequent. During the better part of the century which followed, the two continents went their own ways of national development. Eighteen hundred and ninety, however, marks the beginning of a new period of closer relationships which has extended up to the present time.

There are Spanish American writers, nevertheless, who claim that although during the last war a common interest in the preservation of our liberty awakened new ties of friendship between the Americas, there is really no basic unity underlying it. Few educated persons in the United States have ever read any of the literature of Spanish America, few know the Spanish language, and the majority of the popular books which are being read and circulated concerning Spanish American countries are written by North American travellers who know little if anything of the history literature, or spirit of the countries they are attempting to describe. They also claim that despite the fact that Spanish Americans give outward signs of friendship they have never been entirely convinced of our good intentions.[11]

We hope that this study concerning the attitude of Spanish American authors toward the United States during the two periods that are least known —the period of Independence (1776-1823), and the period of the formation of the Spanish American nations (1822-1890)—will help answer the question as to whether there really are fundamental traditions common to both Americas which will help lead them to a common destiny.

---

[11] As an example of this attitude see: Luis Alberto Sánchez, *Un sudamericano en Norteamérica,* Santiago de Chile, 1942.

I

ORIGINS OF INTER-AMERICAN RELATIONS

1. Historical Background

The relations of the United States with Spanish America offer problems of peculiar interest. Between them there were at the beginning greater probabilities of friction than friendliness. Generations of European wars; political, religious, and ideological differences had fixed in the minds of the Spanish Americans and in those of the Anglo-Saxon colonists a consciousness of rivalry. Distrust had been deliberately fomented between them by the governments of the mother countries. And since the colonies were generally conservative, sometimes even more so than the metropolis, it seemed only natural that the quarrels started in the Old Continent should continue in the new.[12]

During the early days of colonial history, the Spanish American settlers were constantly reminded of the differences between the two nations by the raids of the pirates and privateering expeditions that came from the north. At first these were mostly English, but in many cases they had their bases in the colonies. One of the main centers for these activities was the island of Trinidad, which grew tremendously wealthy as a result of the loot brought back from the raids upon the coast of Spanish America. These expeditions left a deep impression upon the minds of the Spanish settlers; even today when children misbehave they are often induced to submission by the threat of the coming of *the Drake*.[13]

---

[12] This attitude was not necessarily incompatible with the fact that there was also a view growing in the United States before the Revolution, as expressed in T. Paine's *Common Sense*, that the colonists wished to avoid the quarrels of Europe. For information on the wars between the Spanish and British in America see: Bernard Moses, *The Establishment of the Spanish Rule in America*, New York, 1895; Germán Arciniegas, *Caribbean: Sea of the New World*, New York, 1946.

[13] Later on, in the late seventeenth and eighteenth centuries, the colonies had a good share in these activities. In New England the gold and silver brought back from the Spanish Main was called "spice" and was used to pay for a great part of the goods imported from England. William S. Robertson claims that the peso or Spanish dollar circulated in the thirteen colonies so widely that it, as well as the English pound, was employed as a unit of exchange. *The Diary of Francisco de Miranda, 1783-1784*, New York, 1928, p. 147. It was commonly known at the time that Rhode Island was a free port to pirates who came from all parts. During times of peace, it preoccupied the British authorities that the population of this colony, from the governor on down, encouraged and protected pirates. They fitted pirate ships and provided the crews with food and with whatever other supplies they needed, thus acquiring most of the colony's income. Some of the most notorious pirates in American history retired here or in the near-by country. It is legendary along the coast of southern New England that pirate ships would arrive and land their men, who loaded with spoils would disperse over the country-side. In Massa-

Surprisingly enough, the exploits of such men as these found their way into Spanish literature at a very early date. The best known work of this kind is Lope de Vega's *La Dragontea*, a long epic poem dealing with the adventurous life of the famous English skipper. Lope de Vega had never been in America, but came into contact with the English world when he participated in the ill-fated expedition of the Spanish Armada. Much the same can be said of Cervantes, who at one time made a petition to the Consejo de Indias requesting permission to come to America. The petition was never granted, and instead Cervantes remained in Spain to write among other works *La española inglesa,* a short novel that takes place in England and that deals to a great extent with the activities of the English buccaneers against Spain.[14]

Although Lope de Vega and Cervantes saw the English with animosity, they treat them as romantic characters. In America the attitude was more realistic. A detailed account of the activities of the English, from the year 1567 to 1740, is given to us by Dionysio de Alcedo y Herrera[15] (1690-1777), in his book entitled *Aviso histórico, político, geográphico*.[16] The author himself had been at one time a victim of such an expedition. The boat in which he was travelling was captured by English pirates and Alcedo was

chusetts the situation was very similar. Curtis P. Nettels tells that pirates were encouraged to bring their silver to Boston where it was recast by the Massachusetts Mint. According to this same author, different groups had vested interests in pirates. One well known ship was fitted by no less than the New England Independents, a respected religious group. He also quotes a contemporary observer who in 1684 reported that most of the English plate-ships that had come into Boston during the previous few years, though their owners pretended to have recovered their goods from wrecks, had actually robbed from the Spaniards the greater part of them. "It is well that their government is almost at an end, or Boston would have been the receptacle for pirates in the Western parts." *Money supply of the American colonies before 1720* (University of Wisconsin Studies in Social Sciences and History, no. 20), Madison, 1934, pp. 87-91. In New York piracy reached the very heart of local politics. In Pennsylvania Penn found it necessary to explain that the prosperity of this colony was not due to money from pirate sources. Curiously enough, some of these pirates were Spanish. See: J. Jameson, *Privateering and Piracy during the Colonial period,* New York, 1923; also, J. B. Lockey, *Pan-Americanism: Its beginnings.* New York, 1920, pp. 173-174.

14 According to Joaquín Casalduero this novel suggests the reconciliation between the Spanish and English worlds.

15 In the "Biblioteca americana," a manuscript found in the Rich Collection of the New York Public Library, Alcedo y Bexarano gives a short biography and a complete bibliography of his father, Dionysio de Alcedo y Herrera.

16 *Aviso histórico, político, geográphico con las noticias más particulares del Perú, Tierra-Firme, Chile y Nuevo Reino de Granada, en la relación de los sucesos de 205 años por la cronología de los adelantados, presidentes, gobernadores y virreyes de aquel reyno meridional, desde el año de 1535 hasta el de 1740. Y razón de todo lo obrado por los ingleses en aquellos reynos por las costas de los mares del norte, y del sur, sin diferencia entre los tiempos de paz y de la guerra desda el año 1567 hasta el de 1739 por don ... Dionysio de Alcedo y Herrera,* Madrid, 1740. In 1863 it was reprinted under the title *Piraterías y agresiones de los ingleses y otros pueblos de Europa en la América española; desde el siglo XVI hasta el XVIII, deducidas de las obras de D. Dionysio de Alcedo y Herrera; publícalas D. Justo Zaragoza,* Madrid, 1883.

made prisoner for some time. To him and to the other Spanish Americans of his day the threat of pirate invasions was their main cause of concern, in an existence that otherwise could be described as very peaceful.

Aside from these raids there was very little communication between Spanish America and the rest of the world. For one hundred years after Columbus discovered America no relations whatever existed between the North and South, for the simple reason that there were no important English settlements in North America until about the coming of the Puritans, whereas, during the same period the Spanish colonies were attaining a high degree of civilization.

During the sixteenth, seventeenth and, up to the eighteenth century, such communications as were carried on between the two Americas were effected mainly through Spain. This meant that the contact was limited, for the communications between Spain and her own colonies were restricted to an extreme degree. To Spain her colonies were an integral part of the empire, and not regarded so much as colonies as provinces belonging to the crown, strictly under state jurisdiction. We must also remember that Spain herself, in her efforts to safeguard her religious purity, had almost entirely isolated herself from the rest of Europe. The fact that England was Spain's great enemy also tended to restrict the relations between the two Americas. The English colonists of North America were looked upon by the Spanish Americans as heretics and therefore worthy of abhorrence.

The colonies sometimes played an important part in the wars waged by the mother countries. During the first of King George's Wars,[17] popularly known as "The War of Jenkin's Ear," Norh Carolina, Virginia, Pennsylvania, Maryland, Massachusetts, Connecticut, and Rhode Island supplied several contingents to Admiral Vernon's expedition against the Spanish West Indies and Cartegena. All told there were thirty-six hundred North American soldiers participating. They came from every stratum of society, from aristocrats to thieves. Among them was Lawrence Washington, George Washington's older half-brother. Five companies were recruited in New York alone. Military training was conducted at Annapolis. Freedom was given those in prison who were willing to join the expedition, and they were all promised the right to plunder.[18]

There never was a more popular war. Governor Gooch of Virginia made militant speeches, heaping insults upon Spain and the abominable evils of the Catholic Church—for this expedition had all the fanfare of a religious crusade.[19] (It numbered thirty thousand fighting men, in more

---

17 "King George's War" (1744-1748) opened over the "Asiento", the slave trade concession in the Spanish West Indies. The "War of Jenkins' Ear" between England and Spain (1739) was a prelude to the renewed fighting between England and France. In Europe it was called "War of the Austrian Succession" (1740-1748).

18 Germán Arciniegas, *op. cit.*, p. 298.

19 Herbert L. Osgood, *The American Colonies in the Eighteenth Century*, IV, 101.

than one hundred and twenty ships, the largest fleet that had ever entered the Caribbean.) The Americans gave a good account of themselves, they proved to be brave and loyal; the expedition, however, was not a success. It was repulsed at Cartagena and defeated at La Guayra and Santiago de Cuba.[20]

Despite this defeat, the name of Vernon has come to be dear to most of us. For when Lawrence Washington returned home and built his beautiful estate overlooking the Potomac, he named the place "Mount Vernon" which in time was to become a national shrine. The Colombian historian Arciniegas points out that "the admiral, who had so little faith in the Colonials at least believed in the Washingtons, and it may have been he who opened the way for George Washington to serve with the British troops, thus contributing his mite to the loss of the English colonies."[21]

Colonial troops also participated in the expedition that took and occupied Havana in 1762.[22]

2. Spanish And English Heritage

The attitude of the Spanish American writers very often does not respond to incidents that have taken place recently or even in this hemisphere. The sympathies and prejudices of a people are an inherent part of a living culture, and as such, to be able to understand them, we have to go back to the original sources of their tradition, which in this case are Spain and England.

The main causes for the conflict between these two nations were of a religious and political nature, the first of these resulting from the fact that it was Spain which had taken the leading part in preserving Catholicism in Europe; the second, from the conflicting imperial desires for New World possessions.

The political problem, less spectacular than the religious, was perhaps the more important of the two. On the one side was Spain, already showing signs of decadence, possessing an immense empire—a real source of envy for all other nations—which she was determined to hold at all cost. On the other was England, a young vigorous nation wanting to develop along the same lines as her southern neighbor. In the struggle that followed, America, as a point of contact between the two nations, reflected their opposing attitudes depending on whether the colonies concerned were Spanish or English.[23]

---

[20] Navarro y Lamarca, *Compendio de la historia general de América*, Buenos Aires, 1910-13, I, 403-406.

[21] Arcinegas, *op. cit.*, p. 302.

[22] *Ibid.*, pp. 304-305.

[23] On this subject see: José Gaxiola, *La frontera de la raza*, Madrid, 1917; Alejandro Bermúdez, *Lucha de razas*, México, 1917; Alfonso Robledo, *Una lengua y una raza*, Bogotá, 1916; Juan de Robles, *Las dos razas*, México, 1922.

During the conflict that started in the seventeenth century and ended with the disduption of the Spanish Empire in the nineteenth, Spain and her colonies assumed a defensive attitude. They became isolationist and ortho-dox. In order to protect her interests, Spain promoted international law, very much in the same manner that the English sponsored the League of Nations during the years immediately after the First World War, and she tried to keep the two Americas separated by commercial monopolies. Eng-land on the other hand took an aggressive stand. Because she was at this time in a formative stage of development and eager to further her political progress along the lines of freedom and imperial expansion, she adopted the unusual procedure of discrediting Spain through the use of propaganda. Spain did not reply in kind, probably because she felt it unnecessary since she was already well established in the position of orthodoxy, both political as well as religious.

The course of propaganda as followed by the English was to picture Spain as fanatical, intolerant, bigoted—as seen in the establishment of the Inquisition—,interested only in the discovery of gold, cruel in the treatment of subject Indian peoples. The whole body of this propaganda is known as the "Black Legend," and as historical studies have proven, it is often a distortion of the facts, drawn at times from the self-critical and self-cor-rective documents composed by the Spaniards themselves.[24] It might be said that the poins of conflict were represented by two men: the Duke of Alba and Pizarro. Two portraits—that of Alba killing Protes-tants in the Netherlands, and the other of Pizarro with a naked sword dripping with blood in one hand and a fist full of golden nuggets in the other—could symbolize Spain as interpreted by the English.

Hatred of Spain, however, did not involve a loss of respect for a num-ber of qualities typically Spanish, sometimes exaggerated but nevertheless the subject of such admiration and respect: courtesy, moral fitness, battle pride, and adventurous spirit. Towards Spanish America, on the contrary, disdain as well as hatred was evidenced, due to the fact that there was arising in England at this stage in her development a strong feeling of racial superiority and contempt for people of other races. In order to re-alize more clearly the extent to which North American thinking has been influenced by this English prejudice against Spanish America, one has only to ask the average American of New England or the Middle West what his conception is of the Spanish and Spanish-speaking peoples, and the an-

---

[24] Much has been done by contemporary North American historians to rectify many of the erroneous concepts of the "Black Legend". Among the most prominent we find Herbert Bolton, William R. Shepherd, Harry Erwind Bard, William S. Robertson, Lewis Hanke, Arthur Preston Whitaker, Charles F. Lummis, Charles C. Griffin, J. Fred Rippy, Harry Bernstein, Philip Brooks, and many others that should be mentioned. In Spanish America there was recently published by Rómulo Carbia an excellent study on this subject, *Historia de la leyenda negra, hispano-americana,* Buenos Aires, 1943.

swer will be laziness, fanaticism, "mañana", guitars and general non-com-
prehensiveness. The eminent American historian Herbert Bolton, who was
born and reared in the Middle West, in writing about his early environment
and general outlook, tells that they were "typically Yankee 'American', that
is to say, provincial, nationalistic." He says that his unquestioned, historical
beliefs included the following: "Democrats were born to be damned; Catholics, Mormons, and Jews were to be looked upon askance. We licked England, we licked the Indians; all good Indians were dead; the English
always succeeded; their successors, the Americans, were God's elect; American history all happened between the 49th parallel and the Rio Grande;
we virtuously drove the Mexicans out of New Mexico, Texas, Arizona, California and the rest; and thereby built a great empire." Then Bolton adds
philosophically: "Every one of these concepts is false in whole or in part,
but it took me half a lifetime to discover it."[25]

This deep-seated prejudice of England against Spain, that in part is
still evident in Bolton's analysis of his own attitude, does not destroy the
fact that, despite their points of differences, England and Spain, which constitute the periphery of Europe, have a greater resemblance to each other
than to the rest of the continent.

In the eighteenth century, when England had, at the expense of Spain,
developed and expanded her empire, she welcomed things Spanish even
more, due to this common psychological bond.

It is not surprising that at the beginning of the nineteenth century when
many Americans travelled in Europe, as one of the experiences necessary
to complete their education, almost all those who went to Spain became
Spanish scholars.[26] Longfellow in his letters gives a most interesting account of his European travels. He tells how in all his journeys in France,
Germany, and Italy, he never succeeded in feeling at home with the people
of those nations, and how, when he finally went, with many misgivings, to
Spain (because of the wild tales that were current painting the Spaniards
as brigands and fanatics), he had no sooner crossed the border than he
instantly felt a sense of understanding and fellowship.[27]

3. Knowledge About The United States
In Spanish America Prior To 1776

Prior to the Revolutionary War the British colonies in North America
were not well known. The memoirs of the early settlers such as John
Smith's *Description of New England;* William Bradford's *Plymouth Plan-*

---

25 Taken from a letter written to one of his brothers now living in Appleton, Wisconsin, during the Fall of 1943. The Bolton prejudices mentioned here were not all of
English origin. Some developed in the New World environment.

26 To mention only the most prominent: Prescott, Ticknor, Irving, Motley, Everett,
Longfellow, Lowell.

27 Cf. Iris Lilian Whitman, *Longfellow and Spain,* New York, 1927.

tation or John Winthrop's *Journal* had small circulation in Europe. They were never translated into Spanish. Also there were very few Spaniards who had actually seen the English colonies, for Spanish travellers seldom came North of their own free will. Contacts were for the most part confined to smuggling and predatory raids upon the coast of the Spanish possessions. As we have seen, the Spanish-speaking peoples imposed upon themselves a policy of isolation from the rest of the world, and their attitude toward the British colonies was one of indifference and distrust.

The Spanish papers on the Illinois country mention the presence of Spanish trappers in the north woods of Illinois and Wisconsin about the time of the War of Independence,[28] and Miranda in the diary of his visit to this country, says that he found several Spaniards living here, one of them serving a sentence in the Philadelphia jail. It is not likely, however, that these men ever returned to Spanish countries. Many of them were people who for some reason or other were trying to escape the hand of "the Spanish Law."

Prior to 1776, we have been able to find only one work in Spanish concerning the British colonies in North America. It is an anonymous history of the settlement and commerce of the English colonies, translated from the French. It goes by the title of *Historia del establecimiento y comercio de las colonias inglesas de la América septentrional* and was published at Madrid in 1768. There are also a few dispatches in manuscript form written by officials of the Spanish territories where mention is made of the North American colonies. Perhaps the most interesting of these is Francisco Rui's description of the Illinois country, part of which was published in the *Collections of the State Historical Society of Wisconsin* by Reuben Gold Thwaites.[29]

The information found in these papers is of historical and economic interest, but there is nothing in them that throws light upon the attitude of the Spanish American settlers toward the English colonies.

4. Knowledge About Spanish America
In The United States Prior To 1776

The Spanish colonies on the other hand enjoyed great popularity as a literary subject and had been well known since the coming of the Pilgrims. The letters of the early explorers, dealing with the discovery and conquest

---

[28] Spanish Archives, 1766-1805; Wisconsin Historical Society, Madison. (Photographic copies of official civil dispatches of the governor of Louisiana to the captain general of Cuba, from the Archives of the Indies at Seville, Spain.) Spaniards continued at St. Louis and elsewhere in the upper Mississippi Valley until the ceding of Louisiana in 1803.

[29] "Indians and settlements of Spanish Illinois," *Wisconsin Historical Collections*, XVIII, 299-304.

of America, and the chronicles of the Dominican, Franciscan and Jesuit friars on pre-Colombian civilizations, native languages, geography, animal life, vegetation, and mineralogy had been translated into most of the modern European languages. In England the memoirs of Sir Walter Raleigh and Drake, who had seen Spanish America with their own eyes, were published and widely read by their contemporaries. Works of this type constituted an important section of every good library of that day. Columbus, who as a navigator opened America to exploration and conquest, as an author, "discovered it for the imagination of Europe." Henríquez Ureña claims that he was the source of two ideas that soon became commonplace: "America as the land of plenty, and the Indian as the *noble savage.*" Dr. Johnson said that Columbus "gave a new world to European curiosity." Amerigo Vespucci's accounts of his voyages and Cortés' letters of his conquest of Mexico were equally well known. But of all the book on America, the richest by far and the one that had the greatest influence is Peter Martyr's *De Orbe Novo,* in which the author offered his readers a brilliant pageant in a tropical setting with exotic kings, gold, birds of many colors, and trees of fantastic foliage.[30]

To judge how well Spanish America was known in the world, and this includes the English colonies, we have only to point out that most of the utopias that were written during the sixteenth and seventeenth centuries are set in this hemisphere. Sir Thomas More's *Utopia* has for its setting a vague island visited by an imaginary companion of Amerigo Vespucci. Campanella builds his *City of the Sun* in a tropical country, and gives it characteristics reminiscent of the Inca or Aztec civilizations, Bacon creates his *New Atlantis* in a fantastic land where Spanish is spoken. It is not surprising then, that when Cotton Mather in North America decided to create his own theocratic utopia, *The New Jerusalem,* he should select Mexico for its setting. As critics have pointed out, it seems that the utopian ideal, one of the great inventions of the Greek genius, could not fail to have a new birth in the Renaissance; it was discovered again, along with the New World.

Then there is of course Bartolomé de las Casas' book *Brief relation of the destruction of the Indies* of which it is commonly said that a new English edition was made just before every war between England and Spain. It was used as the foundation for the "Black Legend" by the enemies of the Spanish empire, and is the source of many of the prejudices that are still in existence among us today.

During the late eighteenth century and beginning of the nineteenth, the historians and naturalists Buffon, De Pauw, Raynal, Marmontel, Robert-

---

[30] H. M. Brackenridge in *A voyage to South America,* London, 1820, says that there was a surprisingly large number of excellent works on colonial Spanish America, but admitted the lack of information about its actual state since 1810.

son, Muñoz, Ulloa, Jorge Juan and Carli (whose works dealt to a large degree with Spanish America) were well known in the English colonies, as can be readily seen in Jedidiah Morse's *The American Gazetteer* published in Boston in 1797. The American colonies were also acquainted with some of the Spanish literary masterpieces, especially *Don Quijote*. Miranda found that very often Americans had a good knowledge of Spanish literature. In Charleston, South Carolina, he found a Chief Justice by the name of Burk of whom Miranda said that "he had never found an individual so fervent an admirer of the merits and fine taste of our incomparable Miguel de Cervantes,"[31] and in Providence he met a Doctor Moyes who was "exceedingly devoted to Spanish literature."[32] Not all of Miranda's experiences in this country were so fortunate, for he also found a college president who insisted that the city of Mexico did not exist.[33]

5. Points Of Coincidence Between The Two Americas

There existed from the very beginning a marked similarity between the psychology of the people of the two Americas. This was due to analogous circumstances and not to the influence that either of the two cultures might have had upon the other. America presented essentially the same problems to both peoples. Both were pioneers in a primitive land who had to overcome similar difficulties. And both had to adjust themselves to new measurements of space and time different from those of Europe. Both also felt that they had a religious mission to perform.

The northern colonies were Puritans who came from England in search of a land where they might be free to follow their religious convictions. The Spanish Americans, many of them members of religious orders, took upon themselves the apostolic task of christianizing the American natives, and once this has been accomplished, to maintain them free from corruption, in the broader sense of the word pure, even from the contamination of European Christians. The English colonies of North America were not for the most part concerned with the spiritual salvation of the natives. This was not due to indifference on their part, but to the conviction that the effort would have been futile.

It was through religion that the Anglo-Saxons tried for the first time to approach Spanish America. In 1709 Cotton Mather and Samuel Sewall, both of Boston, conceived the idea of creating in Spanish America (Mexico) a religious utopia where the principles they stood for, and which were meeting considerable opposition in New England at the time, would create a "spiritual renaissance". Mather, the more distinguished of the two, has

---

31 Miranda, *Diario*, p. 21.
32 *Ibid*, p. 113.
33 *Loc. cit.*

been considered by some critics as the foremost Puritan writer in America. In his day he published over 400 books and pamphlets. Hostile critics have pictured him as vain, self-centered, superstitious, intolerant, as an opponent of the democratization of the state and as a cruel witch persecutor. Others have defended him on the grounds that he was a sincere moralist after whom Benjamin Franklin modeled many of his own precepts. His life was a series of disappointments which indirectly were the motivating cause for his interest in Spanish America. An ardent supporter of theocracy, he was greatly disappointed by James II's revocation of the old charter destroying clerical authority in New England. Due to his dissatisfaction and to his naturally eccentric nature, he was given to introspection, very much along the same lines as the Spanish mystics. He dreamed of creating a theocratic state where his lofty religious ideals would prevail. In this he was supported by his friend Judge Samuel Sewall, whose memory is blackened by the stain of having presided over the court that in 1693 sentenced 19 persons to be hanged as witches. They both studied Spanish and made careful plans for the day when New Spain would be the New Jerusalem of Puritan tradition. In order to convey his ideas into Spanish territory he published in Boston, 1699, his *Religión Pura*. Harry Bernstein in his article "Las primeras relaciones entre New England y el mundo hispánico: 1700-1815," says that when the Colombian Carlos Sucre y Borda arrived in Boston in 1709, "Sewall tried to convert him to the project. He loaned him the copy of the Cypriano de Valera Bible, and learned all he could of Mexican life, people, and Aztec culture." Mather's plans never did materialize—as utopias seldom do—but his interest in Spanish America represents a type of contact which is to continue in the nineteenth and twentieth centuries: that of the religious missionary.

Another point of coincidence between the two Americas is seen in the way they both reacted against the unfavorable criticism made of the American continent by Buffon, De Pauw and heir followers.

Buffon, in his *Historie naturelle* put forth the theory that America was an imperfect continent, unsuited to the habitation of man. De Pauw in *Les recherches* went even further—he advanced the theory of America as the impotent continent, that is, the theory that men and animals degenerate here. Gerbi in his book *Viejas polémicas sobre el Nuevo Mundo* (Lima, 1946) shows that these ideas were repeated by many of the European scientists of the day; Raynal, Marmontel, Robertson, Muñoz. They were not accepted, however, by those persons that were acquainted with the American continent from having lived here. There took place, as a result, a heated polemic, that extended over a period covering he later part of the eighteenth and the beginning of the nineteenth centuries. The Spanish American Jesuits, who had been forced to leave their countries in 1761, wrote numerous books denouncing these precepts as false, the most noted being: *Historia antigua de México* by the Mexican author Padre Francisco Javier de Clavigero,[34] and *Historia de Chile* by Padre Juan Ignacio Molina, published in Bologna, 1776.[35]

It was also for the purpose of correcting Buffon and his school that Thomas Jefferson wrote his *Notes on Virginia,* and that Barton had Molina's *Historia de Chile* translated ino English.[36]

The critics Bernstein and Whitaker, who have studied certain aspects of this subject, contend that participation in this controversy—both Americas defending a common cause—created continental consciousness for the first time. They are of the opinion that these discussions were in reality the beginning of modern Pan-Americanism. On the other hand, the Peruvian, Antonello Gerbi, referring to this same question says that "the continental solidarity about which we speak today is a motto of contemporary politics, and its connection with the geological-biological-philosophical thesis is rather remote."[37]

---

[34] First published in Italian, Cesena, 1780-81; translated into English, London, 1787; into German, Leipzig, 1789, and into Spanish, London, 1826.

[35] *Compendio della storia geografica, naturale e civile del regno de Chile,* Bologna, 1776; was first published in Italian, translated into Spanish in 1788, and into English in 1808; it was also translated into French and German.

[36] *Geographical, natural and civil history of Chile,* translated by William Shaler and Richard Alsop, Middletown, Conn., 1808. Jefferson, of course, had other motives beside correcting Buffon for writing his *Notes on Virginia.*

[37] Gerbi, *Viejas polémicas sobre el Nuevo Mundo,* Lima, 1946, p. 118.

II

FIRST PERIOD: TO THE INDEPENDENCE OF SPANISH AMERICA
1776-1822

I. CHARACTER OF THE PERIOD

The War of Independence gave the United States a new personality. Overnight it found itself converted from an obscure colony into a nation that held the interest of the entire world, and for the first time the words "revolution" and "independence" became fraught with a noble meaning. Revolutions of one type or another had always existed, but never before had a colony rebelled against the mother country and won its independence, sponsoring the unusual arguments to be found in the democratic doctrine of "the natural rights of man".

The new state became the hope of the world. As early as 1778 Turgot, the French statesman, wrote in his famous letter to Dr. Price:

This people is the hope of the human race. It may become the model. It ought to show the world by facts that man can be free and yet peaceful, and may dispense with the chains in which tyrants and knaves of every color have presumed to bind them under the pretext of the public good.[1]

The United States had no intention of trying to spread the doctrine of national independence among other countries; nevertheless, she unconsciously influenced them, and they began to look upon her as a model, an example in the political sense. This is particularly true of Spanish America. The Spanish American liberals saw in the United States the same virtues that the Europeans had admired, but in their case the interest was even greater for they were aware of the many similarities that existed between them and their northen neighbors; and seeing how in North America this republican utopia had been possible, they wondered why it should not also take place in New Spain, New Granada or Tucumán.

After 1776, political proclamations in which the United States were held up as a model became quite frequent. We have seen two that can be considered typical. One published in Santa Fe de Bogotá, on the 15th of July, 1810, comparing the behavior of the people of New Granada with that of the citizens of the United States at the time of its independence.[2] The

---

[1] Turgot to Dr. Price, in S. E. Morison and H. S. Commager, *The growth of the American Republic*, New York, 1942, I, 320.

[2] "Representación que la primera junta revolucionaria de la provincia del Socorro de Nueva Granada, elevó a la real audiencia de Santa Fe de Bogotá en 15 de julio de 1810," in Blanco y Azpurúa, *Documentos*, I, 519-521.

other exhorting the population of the Floridas to rise against the Spanish government so that they might become citizens of the United States.[3]

An editorial in the *Political Herald and Review* published in 1785 gave a resumé of political activities in Spanish America, in which it was stated that "the flame that was kindled in North America, as was forseen, has made its way into the American domination of Spain", that "conferences were held and combinations formed in secret, among a race of men whom we shall distinguish by the appelation of Spanish Provincials. The example of North America is the great subject of discourse, and the great object of imitation."[4]

The example of American Independence, indeed, seemed to have affected the entire Spanish Domain. Immediately after its fulfillment there started to appear movements for the emancipation of the Spanish colonies, such as the conspiracy directed by the mysterious "don Juan", who in 1783 went to London in an attempt to obtain British aid; and two of a more local nature, one in Mexico in 1780, and Miranda's attempt to give Nueva Granada its independence. In Spain itself a constitution was drawn up by the Spanish Cortes in 1812 that was influenced to some degree by that of the United States. Foronda, a Spanish liberal, at that time *chargé d'affaires* of the Spanish Legation at Philadelphia, wrote a constitution that was revised by Jefferson himself and was sent to Spain to be used as a model for this occasion.[5]

Foronda's action is in keeping with the spirit of his times. It must be remembered that from 1776 to 1799, that is, from the beginning of the American War of Independence until the end of the French Revolution, republican ideologies enjoyed great popularity in Europe as well as in America. The majority of the Spanish and French functionaries during this period were liberals who looked upon the United States with favor, sometimes even with what seems a blind disregard for the interest of the Spanish colonial policies. As for instance, in 1770 when Pitt, fully conscious of the danger that these new republican ideas represented for all empires, proposed to France and Spain a treaty by which the three powers agreed to jointly defend their respective territories in America. Paris and Madrid did not accept the proposal, because they felt that the independence of the

[3] "(1810)—Proclama anónima a los habitantes de la Florida a quienes se exhorta contra el Gobierno Español para hacerse Ciudadanos de los Estados Unidos." Signed "El Amigo del Pueblo." Department of Archives and History, Jackson, Mississippi. This proclamation may have been a translation of an English propaganda sheet. The United States at the time encouraged trouble in that colony.

[4] James Penman to Miranda, London, August 26, 1783; in *Archivo del General Miranda*, V, 301 (sends copy of *Political Herald*). This article was probably paid for by Miranda during his trip of the previous year.

[5] Jefferson to Foronda, Monticello, Oct. 4, 1809; in P. L. Ford, *The Writings of Thomas Jefferson*, IX, 529.

English colonies would mean the end of the British in America and that its example constituted little, or no threat to the Spanish possessions.[6]

During the war for North American independence, France and Spain contributed generously toward the victory of the colonies. Spain with troops, coming from different parts of the Spanish empire, launched an attack upon the Floridas that cleared the English from the flanks of the American colonies, an action that was an important factor in bringing the war to an early close.

This participation created contacts between the two Americas that had never existed before. In some of the campaigns, as for example the attack on the Bahamas, Spanish American troops fought side by side with troops from the English colonies. Close friendships were established. It was as a result of the war that George Washington and General Cagigal wrote their interesting correspondence and that Francisco de Miranda visited the United States in 1783.

The most important act of the war, as far as Spain was concerned, was the campaign against Pensacola. Bernardo de Gálvez, the young governor of Louisiana, seized all the English ships within the delta of the Mississippi, captured Baton Rouge and laid siege to Pensacola, which was forced to capitulate. This brought all of West Florida under Spanish control, and thus cleared the English from the flanks of the revolutionists.

During the late eighteenth century, the part played by Spain in the war became a popular literary subject in both that country and Spanish America. There are two memoirs on this subject published in Madrid about this time. The first is a diary of the war, *Diario de las operaciones contra la plaza de Panzacola concluida por las armas de S.M.C. baxo las órdenes del Mariscal de Campo D. Bernardo de Gálvez,* which, according to the bibliographer Obadiah Rich was probably printed at Madrid about 1781.[7] The second is a memoir, *Memoria histórica de la última guerra con la Gran Bretaña desde el año 1774 hasta su conclusión.*[8] As the title indicates, it was originally intended to give an account covering the entire war. Unfortunately it appears that only the first volume of this work, with the subtitle "Estados

---

[6] B. Lewin, "El informe secreto de Aranda en 1783 sobre la independencia de las colonias españolas. El ambiente de la época y las dudas sobre su autenticidad," *La Nación,* Buenos Aires, 8 Oct., 1944. This decision was taken against the better judgment of Floridablanca, who foresaw the recklessness of such a policy. Gómez del Campillo tells that it was accepted "con la fuerte y decidida oposición del Conde de Floridablanca, que no acababa de decidirse nunca en esta cuestión, muy probablemente por evitar la guerra, que se temía, con Inglaterra, y a la que, al fin, fuimos arrastrados por Francia, que poco tenía que perder en aquellos países, mientras que España con su enorme imperio colonial, era vulnerable en tan numerosos y vastos territorios: y todo ello en defensa de un estado naciente, cuyo futuro desarrollo pocos políticos de entonces percibieron.. " *Relaciones diplomáticas entre España y los Estados Unidos,* I, x.

[7] Obadiah Rich, *Bibliotheca americana nova,* I, 300.

[8] Rich, *op. cit.,* I, 319, says that "the dedication of this work to Florida Blanca is signed D. Josef de Cobarrubias."

Unidos de América. Años 1774-1775", Madrid, 1783, was ever published. There is also a history of the war, *Historia de la última guerra entre la Inglaterra, los Estados Unidos de América, la Francia, España y Holanda: desde 1775, hasta 1783,* published in 1793 at Alcalá.[9] The diary,[10] the memoir and the history are by no means the only literary genres in which the war was discussed; there was also published in 1785 at Mexico City an epic poem, after the manner of Alonso de Ercilla y Zúñiga, with the title *Poema épico, la rendición de Panzacola y conquista de la Florida occidental por el conde de Gálvez. Componíalo el comisario de guerra D. Francisco de Rojas y Rocha,*[11] exalting the glorious deeds of the Governor of Louisiana during the siege of Pensacola.

The outcome of the war of 1776 was received with popular acclamation. Even in England there were many persons who felt that the independence of the colonies was another step along the way of human progress. Unfortunately this optimistic attitude did not last long. The excesses and anarchy of the French revolution had much to do with discrediting the liberal ideals of the day and precipitating Europe into one of the most reactionary periods of its history. After this, more than ever, Spanish America had to look toward the North for guidance an inspiration. Miranda tells his friend Gual to go to the United States because he has lost all hope of receiving any aid from England "due to the incalculable prejudice that the French anarchy had caused against liberty all over the world." He advises Gual that "they had two examples before their eyes: the American Revolution and the French," and adds: "let us imitate discreetly the former, trying to avoid with as much care as possible the disastrous effects of the latter."[12]

The example of the United States was not the only factor in determining the ideologies and attitude of the Spanish American writers of this epoch. As has been pointed out by critics, the independence of Spanish America came about through the example of the United States, the encouragement of England, and the ideas of France. During this period England favored the independence of Spanish America. If this were accomplished it would open all ports to British commerce and thus bring within the reach of England much of the wealth of these countries. Prior to the French Revolution, at least, England did not object if the governments of these new states were republican.

In the United States, on the other hand, feelings were of mixed nature. The masses of the people were sympathetic to the Spanish American cause,

---

[9] Maggs, *Bibliotheca Americana.*

[10] Miranda also wrote a Diary of the siege of Pensacola but it was not published until 1929: "Diario de Panzacola," *Archivo del General Miranda,* I, 141-191.

[11] Rich, *op. cit.,* I, 333.

[12] Francisco de Miranda, *Archivo del General Miranda,* XV, 404. The full force of this period of reaction is not felt until the fall of Napoleon, but as Miranda indicated it had its beginning with the French Revolution.

and many of them as individuals contributed in numerous ways toward the struggle for independence. The official attitude, however, seems to have been against it — at least at the beginning. It is true that as early as 1810 the United States had begun to send its agents to the Spanish colonies, and Henry Clay had already declared himself in favor of Spanish America in Congress, but according to Rippy, who has studied this question extensively, "there was no official propaganda worthy of mention, and the government seldom departed from the path of strict neutrality."[13]

England's encouragement of Spanish American independence is more evident. It has been traced back to 1741. Professor Lewin says that after the unsuccessful attempt against Cartagena, having considered the numerous difficulties that would be encountered if the conquest of the Spanish colonies were ever attempted again, Admiral Vernon expressed the opinion that it was to Britain's interest to encourage the Spanish colonies to secede from the mother country.[14] After the loss of their northern colonies the English became more persistent in this idea. In 1785 a stirring pamphlet was published in London entitled *La crise de l'Europe*, that proposed the emancipation of all European colonies in America by a league of nations composed of the leading powers, including the United States.

It is interesting to note that this plan had England's approval but not that of the United States. John Adams, at that time Minister to England, writes to John Jay with reference to this pamphlet that the object of the next war will be the liberty of commerce in South America, and the East Indies. "We should be puzzled to keep out of it," he explains, " but I think we ought if we can. England would gain the most in such a turn of affairs . . . and England, unfortunately, we can not trust."[15] Jefferson went even farther along these lines. He was of the opinion that it was against the interests of the United States for the Spanish Americans to obtain their independence. In a letter to Archibald Stewart, in 1786, he writes that "our Confederacy must be viewed as the nest from which all America, North and South, is to be peopled. We should take care, too, not to think it for the best interest of that great continent to press too soon on the Spaniards. Those countries cannot be in better hands. My fear is that they are too feeble to hold them till our population can be sufficiently advanced to gain it from them piece by piece."[16] As John Rydjord has said: "thus it would seem that the foreign policy of the United States in regard to Spanish America was to get possession of it piece by piece."[17]

---

[13] Rippy, *Historical evolution of Spanish America*, New York, 1943, p. 345.

[14] Lewin, "El informe secreto de Aranda . . .", *La Nación*, Buenos Aires, 8 Oct., 1944.

[15] Adams to John Jay, May 28, 1786; in *The diplomatic correspondence of the United States . . . 1783-1789*, V, 123-130.

[16] Jefferson to Archibald Steward, Paris, Jan. 25, 1786; in P. L. Ford, *Works of Thomas Jefferson*, V, 75.

[17] Rydjord, *Foreign interest in the Independence of New Spain*, Durham, N. C., 1935, p. 99.

Fear of English commercial hegemony in Spanish America and expansionistic views on the part of our leading statesmen prevented the United States from giving the Spanish colonies the aid they were so desperately crying for. Nevertheless, the hope of receiving such aid is one of the leading topics in the literature of the political essayists of that day. At first, when rumors of American help reached Venezuela, there were laudatory comments about the United States. The August issue, 1810, of the *Gazeta de Caracas,* one of the main organs of the rebels in this region, gives an account of the attitude of the people of the United States toward the independence of Spanish America that is similar to other editorials published about this time:

> The newspaper *The Evening Post* announces the arrival in Baltimore of our agents to the United States Don Juan Vicente Bolívar and Don Telesforo de Orea, and although we have not received any official statement, we have the satisfaction of announcing to the public that English America is very much in agreement with the sentiments of the Venezuelans. Our memorable resolution has filled the sons of Washington and Franklin with enthusiasm, and the subjects of Ferdinand the VIIth, in Caracas, have succeded in having an illustrious and liberal people pray to heaven for a fortunate conclusion to their patriotic efforts. Our Gazette is the object of admiration in the United States. Our statesmanship and our industry have the attention of those citizens, our manifestos, proclamations, and other public papers circulate in the original in that country and are the object of the most honorable comments.[18]

Without really substantial grounds for such hope, the Spanish Americans expected help from their northern neighbors. But seeing that this did not materialize, articles of a different nature, containing bitter reproaches and accusing the United States of cold-blooded and ambitious aims, started to appear. In the *Washington City Gazette* of April, 1818, there was published an address written to the president of the United States, by a Peruvian author, Vicente Pazos, accusing the administration of being unfriendly toward the Spanish American rebels. This address was given much publicity by a group of American liberals, and Henry Clay gave it his support in Congress.[19] Bolívar himself, looking back with misgivings upon the political affairs of the previous ten years, writes:

> In conclusion, we had hoped, and rightfully so, that all the cultured nations would hasten to our aid and help us obtain certain prerogatives, the advantages of which are reciprocal to both hemispheres. Nevertheless, how unfortunate were our expectations. Not only the Europeans, but our brothers from the north also have remained as simple spectators of this struggle.[20]

---

18 *Gazeta de Caracas,* 17 Aug., 1810.

19 Charles C. Griffin, *The United States and the disruption of the Spanish Empire,* 1810-1822, New York, 1928, p. 149. Pazos' Memorial grew out of the Amalia Island affair.

20 Quoted by O'Leary, *Bolívar y la emancipación de Sur América,* Madrid, 1915, p. 376.

After the French Revolution the attitude of the world toward the United States changed. This country continued to be a popular literary subject, except that from now on it was studied as a contagious sociological phenomenon to be avoided. The Duke of Richelieu, at one time French Minister, in a letter written to his colleague Hyde de Neuville in the United States, stated the problem quite clearly. He said that "if Europe wished to be tranquil, if she wished to improve, but not to destroy the institutions of her fathers, she would bring all the wisdom to bear to prevent the rise of a colossus in this hemisphere in direct opposition to her customs and habits. Thus it seems to us that under the double aspect of the peace of nations and of our special policy, we cannot desire that the two Americas tend too much to narrowly unite and to render themselves almost independent of the other continent. . ."[21] And as the reaction grew in Europe the idea that the United States constituted a threat to the established order became almost a phobia. After the Spanish American states won their independence in 1823, Canning feared that they might organize a republican league and overthrow the Brazilian monarchy and, "since the Emperor Iturbide had already fallen, there would be no monarchy left in America to cure the evils of universal democracy."[22]

Most Spanish Americans, however, did not share this conservative point of view. On the contrary, they now were closer than ever to their goal, their independence, and they continued to look upon the United States as a model until this end was accomplished. Bolívar, as well as a few other Spanish Americans of his day, was aware of the differences that existed between the two peoples, and pointed out that blind imitation of the institutions found in the United States would not be sufficient to solve the problems confronting Spanish America. Nevertheless, he believed that much could be learned from the example of this nation.

During this period the relations between the two Americas were closer than ever before. There are critics like Harry Bernstein and Arthur P. Whitaker[23] who claim that one has to go back to the first twenty years of our national life to find the true spirit of Pan-Americanism. Commercial intercourse was more frequent. Francisco de Miranda, who visited the United States in 1783, relates that large quantities of molasses were imported from the West Indies for the distilling of rum.[24] Whaling expeditions to the east coast of South America were a common thing,[25] and tropical fruits

---

[21] Richelieu to De Neuville, July 19, 1817; in Elizabeth Brett White, *American opinion of France*, New York, 1927, p. 51-52. French policy, however, was chiefly anti-English in this period and sought friendship with the United States.

[22] Rippy, *Historical evolution of Spanish America*, p. 369.

[23] Whitaker & Bernstein, *Latin America and the Enlightenment*, New York, 1942, p. 194.

[24] Miranda, *Diary*, p. 87.

[25] *Ibid.*, p. 96.

and sugar were as abundant here as in the islands of Cuba and Puerto Rico.[26] Spanish monopoly was less rigorous, but this in no manner diminished the volume of contraband between the two Americas. Spanish officials complained bitterly of "the scandalous contraband trade done from the United States."[27] Travellers and agents came to the United States or went to Spanish America. Books of a didactic nature giving geographical and historical information about the United States or the Spanish American countries became popular in both languages. American books on political subjects, such as Thomas Paine's *Rights of Man*, were translated into Spanish, and admiration for great American men such as Franklin, Washington, and Jefferson became general throughout Spanish America.

From this time on, we find that those Americans who were interested in Spanish America were also eager to learn the exact truth about the land and its civilization and to discard the errors then prevalent. Dr. Samuel Latham Mitchill, of Columbia College, and Benjamin Smith Barton, of the College of Philadelphia, are typical of that minority that had a real interest in things Spanish. There were likewise various historians such as John Pintard, Ebenezer Hazard, and Jeremy Belknap who carried on a personal correspondence with the various countries of Spanish America. Much was done by these men to help dissipate the "Black Legend", which they considered an obstacle to the relations between the two Americas. The *New York Medical Repository*, in reviewing Humboldt's *Political Essay on the Kingdom of New Spain* stated that "Nothing has been a more trite and erronous subject of vulgar remark than the ignorance of the Lazy Dons. This silly cant has been imitated in our country from the English. It has been so frequently repeated and so widely proclaimed that many of our honest patriots sincerely believe the Spaniards are by great difference their inferiors. This is a miserable and unworthy prejudice. A moderate inquiry will evidence that New Spain has produced a full proportion of respectable observers and of valuable writings. . . And as to public spirit and patronage it has been manifested in the endowments of learned institutions and in encouragements of scientific men to an extent of which no parallel exists in our state of liberality. . ."[28]

The literature of this period in Spanish America was a natural outgrowth of the military and ideological struggle that was taking place. The American continent was the frontier of the world. Nations were being created and there was little time to produce masterpieces of pure art. Literature had a practical function to perform. The peoples of America had to

---

26 *Ibid.,* p. 88.

27 Foronda to Cevallos, Philadelphia, August 4, 1807; No. 14 d. Legajo Estado 5633, Correspondence of the Spanish Legation in the United States, Diplomatic Section, Library of Congress Division of Manuscripts.

28 Quoted in Harry Bernstein, "Some Inter-American Aspects of the Enlightenment", *Latin America and the Enlightenment,* pp. 65-69.

be educated along republican lines, and those literary genres that lent themselves to social and political analysis flourished in abundance. These often took the form of journalism. During this period we have numerous gazettes published in every country: in México the *Gaceta de Literatura de México;* in Perú the *Mercurio;* in Argentina *La Gaceta de Buenos Aires;* in Chile *La Aurora de Chile,* and many others. They also took the form of oratory, the political essay, the diary, the memoir, the open letter. We have the thesis novel, the patriotic drama, the national hymn, the classical ode to be read in public. Even the traditional folklore took on a political significance, such as the *cielitos* of the region of the Río de la Plata, and romances or *corridos* that sang the lives of the caudillos from México to Argentina. The Spanish American men of letters were also, as a rule, men of political convictions. Many of them became agents, ambassadors, cabinet ministers and even presidents of the republics. They were often exiled from their native land, and as a result their outlook on life was generally cosmopolitan. In the literature of these men the United States, its institutions, its culture and its future is a topic of primary importance. The United States represented for them a number of ideals that were not the patrimony of any one nation, but of the entire human race. To them this country was the symbol of liberty and democracy—the great adventure of man. They seldom stop to think of the many difficulties involved in this republican form of government. Their outlook was essentially theoretical, and, with few exceptions, they did not touch upon any of the fundamental problems of government.

II. KNOWLEDGE OF THE UNITED STATES IN SPANISH AMERICA

1. North Americans In Spanish America

Knowledge about the United States came to Spanish America through various channels. It was brought by way of the merchant ships which were every day becoming more numerous, by travellers returning from the United States, and through the publication of books in which this country was discussed.

The few ships that came into Spanish American waters spread propaganda in favor of North American institutions. It was not merely coincidence that the two cities to initiate the independence movement were Caracas in Venezuela and Buenos Aires in Argentina. The former was nearest to the United States as the latter was to Europe, and both therefore were susceptible to influence from abroad.[1] At first, printed sheets with verses condemning the intolerable evils of despotism or exalting American principles and institutions were distributed at the places where merchandise

---

[1] Although Mexico is on the same continent it was more isolated than Venezuela or Argentina, because land travel at that time was slow and arduous, and that by water much more expeditious.

was sold. This propaganda, however, had little or no effect, for the verses were written in English, and there were very few people in Spanish America who were acquainted with this language.[2] About 1808 the verses were substituted by picture cards displaying republican or democratic mottoes. From 1808 to 1810 this form of propaganda became very common. Belaúnde says that "we have proof that it was effective in the decree of 1791, which ordered great vigilance in excluding from the country all medals or other articles which referred to the liberty of the Anglo-American colonies."[3] Collier and Cruz in their book *La primera misión de los Estados Unidos en Chile,* describe two cards of this period. The one is a picture of liberty which with one hand is breaking the chains that hold prisoner a dejected man—representing the people—while handing him with the other hand the scale of justice. The second card represents a king, his bloody crown about to fall; with one hand he holds his crown, while with the other he gives his favorite a sack of pounds sterling. At his feet there is a herd of sheep with human heads.[4]

Knowledge about the United States was also divulged by Americans who resided in these countries. The printing press that published the first national review in Chile, the *Aurora,* was owned by the American Vice-Consul, Hoevel, who although born in Europe was a naturalized citizen of the United States. And the first three typists of the *Aurora,* were also Americans; Garrison, Burbidge and Johnston.

There is a humorous anecdote told about these men. It seems that in 1812, a group of the most influential persons in Chile decided to celebrate the fourth of July as a tribute to the United States, which they all admired very much, and to honor Poinsett, then unofficial representative of the United States in Chile. The celebration took place at the home of Mr. Hoevel. It was an excellent affair, the most select of Chilean society being present. All went well, until Garrison, Burbidge and Johnston, who had drunk considerably, allowed themselves certain liberties with the ladies not in keeping with the decorum of so distinguished a company. They were requested to leave and they refused. An uproar followed in which even the army had to intervene. One of the printers was badly wounded, and the other two spent the night in jail. Johnston wrote a very interesting diary of his stay in Chile, which was published in Madrid in 1919 under the title *Diario de un tipógrafo yanqui en Chile y Perú durante la guerra de la independencia.* In it he mentions that on this occasion homage was paid to the United States, but makes no reference to the brawl that followed the celebration.

---

[2] Collier & Cruz, *La primera misión de los Estados Unidos de América en Chile,* Santiago de Chile, 1926, pp. 2-4.

[3] Belaúnde, *Bolivar and the political thought of the Spanish American Revolution,* p. 27.

[4] Collier & Cruz, *op. cit.,* p. 4.

In the decade from 1810 to 1820, the United States, with few exceptions, began to send its representatives to Spanish America not as official diplomats but rather as commercial agents.[5] The function of these men was to gather and bring back information of interest about the Spanish American countries. Many of them, however, were ardent republicans who, entirely on their own, became involved in the destiny of these countries. They played an important part in the drafting of the Spanish American constitutions, and often served as interpreters of the culture of the United States. At home they reversed their function. They published numerous books to make Spanish America known. As an example we have H. M. Brackenridge, American agent to Buenos Aires, who wrote two books entitled: *South America,* Washington, 1817, and *Voyage to South America,* 2 vols., London, 1820. Harry Bernstein claims that it was through the efforts of Brackenridge that Dr. Funes' history of Argentina was translated and printed in the United States. He also states that part of the duties of Jeremy Robinson, who was an agent to Argentina, Chile and Peru in 1818, was to invite correspondence between Dr. Samuel Latham Mitchill and noted Spanish Americans.[6]

Of all the American agents, perhaps the one who had the most influence was Joel R. Poinsett of North Carolina, a fanatical Jeffersonian democrat for whom Spanish America was a territory that was still living in the feudalism of the Middle Ages. This feudalism, as far as he was concerned, was more religious than political. Armed with these concepts Poinsett launched himself upon a Quixotic odyssey to save the continent. Of course, Spanish America being essentially conservative when it came to religious matters, it is not surprising that he should have encountered difficulties. He was first sent to Buenos Aires where the people of a homogeneous culture and European ideas received him with cordiality. Poinsett had a good knowledge of Spanish and became very active in the political affairs of that country.[7] He next went to Chile where he made for himself both

---

[5] In 1810 the United States appointed a few consuls, later retreated to the practice of appointing informal agents for commerce and seamen.

[6] Harry Bernstein, "Some Inter-American Aspects of the Enlightenment," *Latin America and the Enlightenment,* pp. 64-65.

[7] Lorenzo de Zavala, his friend and companion during his Mexican activities, describes him as follows: "Poinsett es un diplomático cuyas cualidades principales son un golpe de ojo seguro y certero para conocer a los hombres, medir sus talentos y pesar su valor; una franqueza reservada, por decirlo así, de manera que en sus conversaciones cualquiera se cree ver una especie de abandono por el modo natural y verdadero con que trata los asuntos, reservando únicamente lo que le parece, pero nunca mintiendo ni haciendo reservas mentales, Su amor a la libertad nace del convencimiento que tiene de no ser una cuestión abstracta ni una utopía puramente metafísica, habiendo visto sus ventajas prácticas en el dichoso pueblo de que es ciudadano y de consiguiente obra sienpre en el sentido más liberal. *Ensayo histórico de las revoluciones de México desde 1808 hasta 1830,* México, 1918, I, 340.

friends and enemies, the latter due to religious reasons. Finally being blamed as a meddler by the reactionaries, he returned to the United States, but did not lose interest in Spanish America, always continuing to advocate its separation from Spain.

Following Mexico's independence he was sent there as the first Minister from the United States, and here his difficulties were even greater than in Chile. Besides his religious ideas, which made him incompatible with Mexicans, the issues he supported were always in conflict with those of the English envoys, who as a rule were better informed and had more prestige than Poinsett, due to the fact that England had helped the revolutionists from the very beginning. Because of his ideological background, Poinsett was not a good choice at that time as a diplomatic representative. There, too, he was regarded as an intruder. There were demonstrations against him and finally he was forced to leave the country.[8] Remarkably enough, his treatment at the hands of the Spanish Americans never caused him to lose interest in these countries. Although he was not a diplomat, Poinsett was a keen, sympathetic observer of Spanish America. His diary[9] reflects his understanding and affection for the people of México, and for their fine taste and courtesy which he found to be inherent to their culture. In his diary he shows himself more benevolent than at other times, and tries to understand the beliefs and attitude of the Mexican people.[10]

Religion, indeed, seemed to have been the main obstacle to those who tried to spread republican ideologies in Spanish America. In 1810 a heated debate on religious tolerance took place in the columns of the *Gazeta de Caracas* which tended to cool enthusiasm for the United States. The motive for these discussions was a series of articles published therein by William Burke,[11] an Irishman who favored religious tolerance and advocated that the Spanish Americans follow the example of the United States. In reply to him there appeared immediately afterwards a number of articles by the leading clergymen of Venezuela which started as a discussion of religious tolerance and ended in a general attack against the United States.

The activities of North Americans in this continent are summarized, from a conservative point of view, by a Chilean of the period, Fray Melchor Martínez, in his book *Memoria histórica sobre la revolución de Chile, desde el cautiverio de Fernando VII, hasta 1814,* not published until 1848 in

---

8 In México Poinsett had friends as well as enemies. He was unfortunate in that his friends were defeated in Mexican politics.

9 Joel R. Poinsett, *Notes on Mexico,* 1825.

10 There is an excellent biography of Poinsett by J. Fred Rippy, *Joel R. Poinsett, Versatile American,* Durham, N. C., 1935.

11 William Burke also published two books that were intended for the purpose of obtaining British aid for Spanish American independence: *South American Independence or The Emancipation of South America, the glory and interest of England,* London, 1807; and *Additional Reasons for immediately emancipating Spanish America,* London, 1808. (There is an American edition of the latter.)

Valparaiso. Martínez reveals in this memoir an attitude of suspicion toward the United States that can be considered typical among certain elements in Spanish America. He says that:

> the Republic of Boston, isolated and surrounded by so many peoples desirous of imitating its ideas of liberty, recognizing and fearing the weakness of its existence, is making its greatest effort to enlarge its boundaries and to extend its system as the only method of providing for stability and permanence. To this end it puts into action all imaginable means, without hesitating at the most iniquitous and immoral, in order to attract the Spanish colonists to its depraved designs. Freedom of conscience and freedom of the press assist it in publishing and spreading subversive and seditious principles and maxims, which always find reception among the majority of men, ruled by ignorance and malice. The clandestine trade and permission to fish for whales introduces traders and adventurers from the United States into all the coast, islands, and other Spanish possessions, giving them opportunity to convince the Spanish colonists of the flourishing state and advantageous situation of their own country, decrying the Spanish colonial government and subjection to the mother country in Europe as ignominious slavery. They magnify the riches and extent of these provinces, proclaim the injustice and tyranny with which the wealth is carried off to enrich Europe, describe the state of obscurity, abandonment and civil nullity in which the colonists live; and offer with impudence all the aid of their great power to the people who may wish to shake off the yoke of a legitimate and just domination. Furthermore, they have adopted and put into execution the most powerful means to undermine and destroy the political and religious edifice of the Spanish colonies, sending clandestinely to all and each of these possessions subjects for the purpose of establishing themselves as residents with the design of perverting public opinion and destroying all alliances with mother Europe, and to accomplish these ends they find every possible means of marrying into principal families with influence upon the governments, without being embarrassed by the difference of religion, for they become nominally Catholics as a means to acquire freedom and security to insinuate themselves and take an active part in seducing the inhabitants.

2. Spanish Americans In The United States

Knowledge about the United States was also gained from the Spanish Americans who lived in this country. These were divided into two groups: Those who came with the approval of the Spanish government and therefore were able to return to their native countries, and those who came as refugees and remained here to carry on propaganda for the independence of Spanish America.

During the Revolutionary War and immediately afterwards the relations between the United States and Spain were friendly, and the Spanish government tolerated intercourse between the two Americas. It was during this period that Francisco de Miranda and José Felipe Flores came to the United States with the consent of the Spanish government.

Miranda, though a Spanish American, had come as a representative of liberal Spain. He came with a letter of introduction from Cagigal, Lieutenant-General of the Island of Cuba, to Washington. We must remember that a distinction exists between men who came as he did, and those who came as Spanish Americans in the real sense of the term. It was not until some time after he left Spanish territory that he declared his intentions of making Spanish America free from the mother country, and not until then did the Spanish government consider him an enemy.[12]

During his trip Miranda visited, among other cities, Charleston, Philadelphia, New York, Albany, Saratoga and Boston. He met most of the outstanding Americans of his day, including such men as Samuel Adams, Hamilton, Lafayette and Washington. Fortunately he left us a diary of his tour, extending from June, 1783, to December, 1784, in which he gives a detailed account of his impressions of the country and its people. The diary was first published in 1928 with introduction and notes by William S. Robertson; in 1929 it was published again in the first volume of the *Archivo del General Miranda*.

José Felipe Flores, a noted Spanish American scientist, was authorized in 1797 by the Spanish government to travel to perfect his studies, and came to the United States to meet the leading figures in the field of science. Here he became acquainted with the works of Benjamin Smith Barton and Samuel Latham Mitchill, who were responsible for the strong interest and respect felt at that time in the United States for Spanish American science. According to Bernstein,[13] in a letter of that same year, addressed to Father Goicoechea of Guatemala, Flores summarizes for the Guatemalan public the scientific achievements of this nation.

Interest in the United States for Spanish America was also shown in the election of Spanish Americans to North American scientific societies and in the publication and translation of books relative to Spanish American subjects.[14] Intellectuals such as Dean Gregorio Funes, of Cordoba, Argentina, Don Manuel Moreno, of Buenos Aires, Don José María Salazar, of Colombia, Manuel Lorenzo Vidaurre, of Lima, were honorary and corresponding members of the Massachusetts Historical Society. Some of these were also members of the American Philosophical Society.[15]

---

[12] See p. 52.

[13] Bernstein, "Some Inter-American Aspects of the Enlightenment.' *Latin America and the Enlightenment*, **p. 58.**

[14] See Whitaker, *The United States and the Independence of Latin America*, Baltimore, 1941; also Bernstein, "Some Inter-American Aspects of the Enlightenment", *Latin America and the Enlightenment*, pp. 65-69.

[15] "Honorary and Corresponding Members of the Massachusetts Historical Society, *The Jefferson Papers*, XVII.

Spanish American refugees started to arrive in the United States as early as the seventeen nineties, and many of them were to remain here until long after the Spanish American nations had won their independence. The main centers for their activities were New Orleans, Charleston, Baltimore and Philadelphia.

Most Mexicans and Central Americans entered the United States by way of New Orleans and then came up the Mississippi Valley. A good number of them, however, did not go beyond this city, and from here they continued to work for the independence of their countries. It was in New Orleans that José Antonio Rojas lived for some years. He was a Mexican Professor of Mathematics of the Colegio de Guanajuato who was sentenced to be imprisoned because of his ideas, and fled to New Orleans before he could be apprehended.[16] Alamán tells that from there he carried on correspondence with friends in Spanish America. He wrote a pamphlet about his life and sufferings at the hands of the Spanish authorities. "He concluded the narration by giving an account of the prosperity and happiness enjoyed by the inhabitants of the United States and by listing articles of the American constitution, which he hoped the Mexicans would imitate."[17] Of course, Rojas is not an impartial observer. His aim is to propagate the American institutions and therefore he speaks only of that which is favorable to the United States.[18]

In New Orleans, interest in Spanish America was not limited to those who spoke Spanish. The entire population, which at this time was represented by practically every country in Europe, followed closely the different developments in its struggle for independence. Many filibusters left from here to join the rebels. A good example of how popular the Spanish American cause was is the case of the famous pirate Lafitte, whose fleet flew the flag of Cartagena, one of the first centers to proclaim its independence. Lafitte claimed that he had documents from this republic auhorizing him to attack the Spaniards. On the island of Barataria, residence of most of the pirates near New Orleans, the only flag flown was that of the aforementioned republic.[19]

Another center for the activities of the Spanish American revolutionaries was the city of Charleston in South Carolina. Since the beginning of the Eighteenth Century, Charleston had a large population of Spanish Jews. The colony grew so numerous that according to James F. Shearer, by the Nineteenth Century, it was "the largest, most cultivated, and wealthiest

---

16 Alamán, *Historia de México,* I, 141.

17 *Ibid.,* I, 146.

18 A copy of this pamphlet as well as the correspondence of the Viceroy Brancaforte with regard to this incident is found, according to Alamán, in the *Secret Archives of the Viceroys,* México, *ibid.,* I, 146.

19 Arciniegas, *Caribbean: Sea of the New World,* p. 360.

Jewish community in America."[20] These Jews, like most Sephardim all over the world, continued to be concerned with the political and ideological development of the Spanish-speaking world, and took an active part in the struggle that was taking place between the liberals and the conservatives.

In Baltimore there were always Spanish Americans who came on political or diplomatic missions. Life here was more economical than in Washington, and at the same time not distant from it.

But by far the most important of the four centers was Philadelphia. There are several reasons for its popularity. It was centrally located. It was a publishing center where they could have their pamphlets printed economically. And not least in importance, it was the home of Manuel Torres, a Spanish liberal who served as liaison agent between the revolutionists and the United States.

The activities of the Spanish American refugees in this city consisted primarily in the spreading of propaganda. Their writings are generally known as pamphleteer literature, because they wrote small pamphlets. This was the most practical manner of disseminating their ideas. The propaganda was of two types: for consumption in Spanish America—which generally consisted of the glorification of the American way of life, so that it would be used as a model in these countries; and for consumption in the United States —which at first was designed to obtain the intervention of this country in favor of the revolutionists and later on, after the consummation of independence, to obtain the recognition of their governments by the United States.

The most successful of all the Spanish American agents was Manuel Torres, the nephew of a former viceroy of New Granada, who was forced to flee his country because of his political ideas. He came to the United States in 1797 and remained here until his death. He was well liked by everyone, and his home served as headquarters for the activities of the revolutionists. At one time or another, most Spanish American patriots who came to this country visited him. Rocafuerte, Mier, Toledo, and Salazar were among the many that could be named. Mier's letters were addressed in the following manner:

Dr. Mier at Mr. Torres
South Tenth St. No. 193
Philadelphia

Torres is the author of two books and many unsigned articles. The first of these, *An exposition of the commerce of Spanish America,* is a guide for American merchants wanting to do business in Spanish America. The

---

[20] James F. Shearer, "Agustín de Letamendi: A Spanish Expatriate in Charleston, S. C. (1825-1829)," *The South Carolina Historical and Genealogical Magazine,* XLIII, January, 1942, 19.

second, *An exposition of South America with some observations upon its importance in the United States,* was intended to arouse the interest of the citizens of he United States and to promote commerce between the two Americas.

Some Spanish American critics assert that Torres' works are generally regarded as having been written by Mier and Rocafuerte. This would be hard to verify. What is certain is that he had great influence upon these two men and that many of these works were written during the time they were living in his house. It is possible that he is the author of an anonymous pamphlet published in Phildelphia, 1812 entitled *Manual de un republicano para el uso de un pueblo libre.*[21] The ideas in this work are presented in the traditional form of a dialogue between a teacher and his pupil. It represents a defense of the American government in the form of an exposition of the ideas of Rousseau, and was intended to spread liberal political concepts throughout Spanish America.

Manuel Torres' circle of collaborators was not limited to Spanish Americans. He knew intimately most of the leading Americans of his day. Charles C. Griffin, who has studied Torres' activities as a propagandist, states that Torres "was intimate with Duane, the editor of the *Aurora,* and long before his official duties began had collaborated with him as a propagandist for the patriots, translating Spanish news and pamphlets for the latter and occasionally putting Duane's effusions into Spanish for the use of the patriot gazettes."[22] He was also acquainted with Baptis Irvine, editor of the Baltimore *Whig,* the *New York Columbian,* and the *City of Washington Gazette.*

Upon his death he was buried in St. Mary's cemetery in Philadelphia, the oldest Catholic cemetery in that city. Part of the original grounds were sold and eventually modern structures were built there. Fortunately, Manuel Torres' remains were in a small section of the cemetery that was never disturbed, and today one can read on a bronze plaque on the façade of St. Mary's church a statement to the effect that Manuel Torres, the first agent to represent the Republic of Colombia in the United States, lies buried there. This plaque honors a man who during a long life served Spanish American countries in various capacities. He was guide and counsel to practically every one of his countrymen who arrived in Philadelphia until they were able to overcome the innumerable difficulties that the United States presented to them.

---

[21] There are other anonymous works of this type published in Philadelphia about this t me. One of them is the *Historia concisa de los Estados Unidos desde el descubrimiento de América hasta el año de 1807,* Philadelphia, 1812.

[22] Charles C. Griffin, *The United States and the disruption of the Spanish Empire,* pp. 252-253.

3. North American Writings In Spanish America

The government of the United States had no intention of promoting a liberal revolution in Spanish America, and there is no evidence of official propaganda in these countries. On the contrary, some of the leading American statesmen seemed to resent the fact that the United States was being used as a model. This attitude can be sensed in Adams' remarks pertinent to a conversation with Abbe Correa, the Portuguese Minister, that went as follows:

> As to an American system, we have it, we constitute the whole of it; there is no community of interests or of principles between North and South America.[23]

And yet the influence of the political ideas of the United States was great. During this period some of the works of Franklin, Paine, Jefferson, and Madison were translated into Spanish, and news about the United States became a commonplace thing in the revolutionary gazettes.

It is possible that the Spanish Americans would have also translated works of a more literary nature, had any existed. There was, however, no real American literature at this time. In both Americas the little writing that was done was of a political nature.

Sympathy toward the United States and antipathy toward Europe was felt even by the dictators and *caudillos* who, in some cases, exemplified the exact opposite of the democratic principles of the United States. Belgrano, the *caudillo* organizer of Argentina, translated and carried with him on his campaigns George Washington's *Farewell Address*. He eventually published it with an introduction in which he comments on the "true ideas" of this "hero of true patriotism."[24] And Dr. Francia of Paraguay, the perfect type of dictator, was also a great admirer of North American democracy. Dr.

---

[23] John Adams, *Memoirs*, V, 176 - Adams' statement is not surprising when we consider that a few years earlier news of the French Revolution was received in a similar spirit. By 1798, a "Stop France" movement had attained considerable proportions, and there existed between the two countries a virtual state of undeclared war. "The American war faction," says Waldo R. Browne, "composed in large part of what James Parton has termed 'the silver-forked civilization of the country,' was politically organized in the Federalist Party, then holding power, and was led by Alexander Hamiton, whose ideal of government was the 'rule of gentlemen' and who believed that democracy could lead only to anarchy. The anti-war and pro-French elements, consisting in the main of small farmers and industrial workers, were led by Thomas Jefferson, champion of popular government and the common man, who thought that a revolution every twenty years might not be a bad thing for any country. In the presidential chair sat the former Vice-President, John Adams, protégé and partisan of the Federalists, a statesman considerably smaller physically and mentally than his illustrious predecessor in office, honest and conscientious but lacking in broad political judgment and obsessed by a dislike nearly as deep as Hamilton's for what he once spoke of as 'those democratical principles that have done so much mischief to this country'." Waldo R. Browne, "A Backward Glance in History," *The Nation*, September 13, 1947.

[24] Belgrano never exercised extra-legal power.

Francia gave the Argentine envoys who paid him a visit a portrait of Franklin, calling him "the first democrat of the world and our model for imitation". The dictator of Paraguay professed a rigid Americanism. He expelled all strangers and his ideal was that of a democracy governed by a Caesar.

Writings relative to the United States were prohibited in Spanish America, but in spite of the vigilance of the administration, seditious pamphlets containing information of a democratic nature circulated throughout the colonies. In 1810, Paine's *Rights of Man* was translated into Spanish by the Venezuelan J. G. Roscio; extracts from this translation were published in Caracas the following year.[25] Garcia de Sena wrote *La independencia de Costa Firme justificada por Thomas Paine treinta años ha,* containing the translation of the constitution of the United States and the declaration of independence.[26] During this same year, Miguel de Pombo gave a speech in which he stated that America "would avenge the blood of its Franklins and Washingtons." And Mariano Moreno published in the *Gaceta de Buenos Aires* Jefferson's defense of the future of America, written in his *Notes on Virginia.*

The following year, 1811, Pombo translated the *Constitution* of the United States, which he had published in Santa Fe de Bogota, (1811). Camilo Henríquez wrote his famous sermon on the anniversary of North America independence. And in Colombia, on the 14th of June, appeared the first number of Nariño's *La Bagatela,* a gazette dedicated to the divulgation of liberal ideas. It gave news of the United States and covered subjects such as the explanation of the constitution of this country.

In the libraries of the Spanish colonial officials books by American authors and books having the United States as their main subject became a common thing during the latter part of the eighteenth century. Irving A. Leonard[27] asserts that in the library of Don Manuel Gayoso de Lemos, Governor of Louisiana after 1797, there were a number of books about the United States in Spanish, French and English that can be considered representative of the type of literature that was read during this epoch. Among them were:

William Robertson, *The history of America,* London, 1777.
David Ramsay, *The history of American Revolution,* Philadelphia, 1789.
Jonathan Carver, *Three years travels through the interior part of North America,* London, 1778.

---

[25] J. R. Spell, *Hispanic Review,* IV, Jan. 1936, p. 85. Also, Chandler, *Inter-American acquaintances,* Sewanee, Tenn., 1915, p. 38.

[26] Belaúnde, *op. cit.,* p. 27. It should be made clear, that prohibition of United States writings held true for areas under Spanish authority only.

[27] Irving A. Leonard, "A Frontier Library", *The Hispanic American Historical Review,* Feb. 1943.

Thomas Jefferson, *Notes on Virginia,* Paris, 1784-1785.

Bell, *The American theater,* Philadelphia, 1792.

Histoire de Kentucke, nouvelle colonie a l'ouest de la Virginie, Paris, 1785.

Observation sur la Virginie, traduit de l'Anglais par André Moreller. Paris, 1876.

4. Books On The United States

As has been pointed out before, the relations of both the United States and Spanish America with Europe have always been more important than with each other. From 1776 to 1823, the two European nations exerting the greatest influence on Spanish America were Spain and France. Much of the knowledge South Americans had about the United States did not come from direct contacts, but indirectly through these two countries. It also happens that some European authors, owing to their unorthodox points of view, had a greater popularity in America than in their native countries. This is the case of Blanco White and the Abbe de Pradt, two writers, who although strongly criticized in Spain and France because of their liberal ideas, enjoyed a great reputation in the Western Hemisphere. Both were adopted, looked upon by Spanish America as their own, and their ideas had considerable influence upon the precursors of the independence.

It must also be remembered that during the eighteenth century, the Spanish leaders, in many cases, were not reactionaries but liberals who regarded the United States with friendliness despite certain conflicting viewpoints. Typical of this fact is the case of Juan Manuel de Cagigal, governor of Cuba, who in May 25, 1783, addressed a letter to George Washington, lauding him as the Fabius of his times and expressing the highest admiration for his North American neighbors. He likewise commended to him his envoy Francisco de Miranda, then about to leave for Philadelphia. Cagigal's letter reads as follows:

Most Excellent Sir:

The present circumstances have not permitted me, as the war is over and I am returning to Spain, to visit those famous countries and to have the honor of knowing the Fabius of these times as I had intended. Will your excellency allow me to do so by means of this letter, placing myself at your orders and at the same time commending to you my aide-de-camp, Lieutenant-Colonel Francisco de Miranda, who has just sailed for Philadelphia for that very purpose; his character, education and other qualities have particularly attracted me, and I hope that they will likewise gain for him your appreciation and esteem, for which I shall be extremely grateful.

I am a constant admirer of your Excellency's heroic virtues, and I shall, therefore, have a particular pleasure in serving you; pray command me at your will. May Our Lord guard your glorious deeds immortal.[28]

---

[28] Juan Manuel de Cagigal to George Washington, Habana, May 26, 1783; in *Archivo del General Miranda,* V, 243.

In determining the various contacts between the two Americas, it is very difficult at first to distinguish the Spaniards from the Spanish Americans, as many men might be considered as belonging to both, for example: Francisco de Miranda or Cagigal. The interest of the United States was also in things "Spanish" as a whole. They did not distinguish between the Spanish from Spain and the Spanish from America; to them they were all the same.

The part played by Spain in effecting the independence of the United States was also a point on which all Spaniards coincided. Those who helped came from various places; but the important thing is that they helped, and that they sympathized with the desire of the United States for separation from the mother country. This interest shows itself in Spanish literature by the appearance, immediately after the independence of the United States, of a number of books written about the British colonies and their historical and political progress.

Very little was known in the Spanish World of the United States prior to its independence. Books on this subject start to appear in large numbers shortly after the treaty of Versailles. Francisco Álvarez, a native of Asturias, published an encyclopedia about North America, *Noticia del establecimiento y población de las colonias inglesas en la América Septentrional; Religión. orden de gobierno. leyes y costumbres de sus naturales y habitantes; calidades de su clima, terreno, frutos, plantas y animales; y estado de su industria, artes, comercio, y navegación: sacada de varios autores* (Madrid, 1778). Other works of the same nature, comparing the British and Spanish colonies followed:

1. *The history of the New World* (London, 1779), written by the famous Spanish historian Juan Bautista Muñoz.

2. *Historia de la última guerra entre la Inglaterra, los Estados Unidos de América, la Francia, España y Holanda: desde 1775 hasta 1783* (Alcalá, 1793), written by Odet Julien Leboucher.

3. *Historia de la administración del Lord North, Primer Ministro de Inglaterra, y de la Guerra de la América Septentrional hasta la paz* (Madrid, 1806), first written in English then translated into French and then Spanish.

4. *Quadro comparativo de la extensión, comercio, y amonedación de los Estados Unidos del Norte, y de las Provincias Unidas de la Nueva Granada al tiempo de su transformación política, según los calculos de Brissot, Rochefoucauld, y Holmes* (Spain, circa 1806). "This paper gives some extremely interesting statistics on the newly emancipated United States, and the old dominion of New Granada, the data being supplied by Spanish economists, books in the possession of the Spanish American Viceroys, Rochefoucauld, Brissot, etc." (Maggs, No. 291).

5. *Quadro comparativo de la población de los Estados Unidos del Norte y de las Provincias Unidas de la Nueva Granada al tiempo de su transformación política*, Spain, circa 1812 (Maggs, No. 100).

6. *Historia concisa de los Estados Unidos desde el descubrimiento de América hasta el año de 1807,* Philadelphia, 1812 (Medina, Biblioteca Americana II, p. 423).

Information similar to that given in these books is also found in the dispatches of the Spanish officials in America, such as Francisco Rui,[29] Pedro Vial,[30] Jose Martínez[31] and Manuel Lanzos.[32] But by far the most important work of this type, from the point of view of its impartiality, exactitude, and truthfulness, is the *Diccionario geográfico-histórico de las Indias Occidentales ó América,* published in 1786-1789 by Antonio de Alcedo y Bexarano, which was destined to be for many years afterwards the best informed encyclopedia on Spanish American matters, and was also to have the distinction of being the first work ever written by a Spanish American where the newly born republic, the United States of America, was seriously studied. Besides geographic and sociological information, it gives a long account of how the British colonies came to establish themselves as an independent nation. It also includes in full a proclamation of 1774 to the inhabitants of Boston, exhorting them to take arms against the British, which is worth quoting:

> The severity of the British Parliament against Boston should make all the American provinces tremble; there now remains no other choice for them but imprisonment, fines, and the horrors of death; or the yoke of the law and servile obedience; the time for an important revolution has arrived, the fortunate or unfortunate outcome of which will perpetuate for all time the admiration of posterity. Liberty or slavery is the solution to the great problem that is to determine the fate of three million men and the happiness or misery of their innumerable descendants. Awaken then Americans, never before has the region you inhabit seen itself covered by such dark clouds. You are called rebels because you do not want to pay tribute; justify your pretensions with your valor, or seal the loss with all your blood.[33]

From the information he has selected it is evident that he is in sympathy with the United States.

In Spain Alcedo's work was destined to have very small circulation. The true and accurate information it contained made the Spanish authori-

---

[29] A description of the Illinois country by Francisco Rui, dated March 9, 1769, in *Wisconsin Historical Collections,* XVIII, 299-304.

[30] "Journal of his Voyage from Santa Fe to Saint Louis," Saint Louis, 1792, published in Houck, *Spanish Regime,* I, 329-333 (Trans.).

[31] "Report by Engineer Jose Martínez concerning the Americans and their explorations," New Orleans, Aug. 20, 1804, Missouri Historical Society.

[32] "Diario de que se ha llevado por el capitán del regimiento fijo Don Manuel Lanzos tocante a la sedición de los habitantes de este distrito al favor del comandante americano llamado Pope, y su comisario de limites Andres Elicot," Natchez, June 9-24, Department of Archives and History, Jackson, Miss.

[33] Antonio de Alcedo y Bexarano, *Diccionario geográfico-histórico de las Indias Occidentales o América,* Madrid, 1788-1789, II, 104-105.

ties look upon it with suspicion, and eventually the entire edition was suppressed. The copies which escaped were few. In 1815, G. A. Thompson, the editor of the English edition of the *Diccionario, The geographical and historical dictionary of America and the West Indies,* published in London, 1815, says: "I found after many inquiries, that a very small number, not supposed to exceed five or six, were existing in this Kingdom, and later endeavours to procure any from the continent have always been unsuccessful, even when attempted by official pursuit, and at ulimited expense."[34] In the Spanish American colonies, however, the *Diccionario* was to enjoy great popularity and exerted continued influence. For years after its publication Alcedo still received letters from all parts of Spanish America from persons who considered Alcedo's encyclopedia to be a patriotic work. The great Mexican patriot Mier saw the book during his exile in Spain and speaks of it with admiration in his memoirs.[35] Iturri, one of Alcedo's South American admirers, in one of his letters in the New York Public Library, tells of the favorable effect the book had on other fellow-Americans to whom he had spoken.

Not all books on the United States were of an economic or political nature. Great interest was also shown in the heroes of North American independence. Washington, Franklin, Jefferson, and later on Lincoln had qualities that made them popular literary subjects. In the Hispanic world Benjamin Franklin was better known than Washington. When Franklin arrived in France, as the first American Ambassador to that country, one of the first things he did was to hold a conference with the Conde de Aranda, the Spanish Ambassador to France, a liberal of great influence in the Spanish Court. Despite language difficulties, as Franklin knew only a little French, and Aranda spoke no English, he became convinced of the Spaniard's good faith. Aranda was no less impressed by the old man's personality.[36] Benjamin Franklin never did go to Spain as he had intended. Eventually John Jay went in his place. Nevertheless he became known in the Spanish world as the typical American. He was made the first corresponding member of the Spanish Academy from the United States and his biography was published in Spanish (Madrid, 1798) under the title *Vida del Dr. Benjamín Franklin sacada de documentos auténticos.*[37] In Spanish America he enjoyed a similar reputation. In México, José Antonio Alzate, the famous scientist, published in his *Gaceta de la literatura de*

---

34 G. A. Thompson, "Preface," in Alcedo, *The geographical and historical dictionary of America and the West Indies,* London 1815, V, viii.

35 S. T. de Mier quoted in Teixidor, *Viajeros mexicanos,* p. 27. Miranda also used the *Diccionario* as a source of information. See: *Archivo del General Miranda,* XV, 187-194, 404.

36 Germán Arciniegas, *op. cit,* p. 312.

37 Translated from the English by Pedro Garcés de Marcilla (1762-1816). Concerning the translators life see: Medina, *Biblioteca hispanoamericana,* V, 395.

México two articles devoted to Franklin. In the first he reproduces some of his letters and experiments. In the second, published shortly after his death, December, 1790, he praises Franklin as a great scientist. He maintained that the latter's discoveries "represent in practical physics, that physics that is useful to men, a memorable epoch. He was not one of those physicists who document their works with painful formulas, that alienate the common man from the sanctuary of science; experience, and observation of the examples of nature were the source of Franklin's discoveries, for this reason envy never triumphed over his merit." George Washington's biography was published in Spanish for the first time in Paris (1819) under the title *Jorge Wáshington: su vida, deducida de la que publicó M. David Ramsay,* and as the title indicates it is a tranlation of Ramsay's life of the first president. In the minds of the suppressed and persecuted people of Europe, the figures of Franklin and Washington became the symbols of our nation, romanticized and poetically conceived.

Ever since the times of the Greeks, and possibly even earlier, man has been preoccupied with the abstract notion of the ideal existance of man and with the perfection of mankind. When America was first discovered, exotic tales were told about it in Europe, and to the imagination of the average European, America became the promised land of plenty. But by the eighteenth century the European dreams of utopia were taking shape along definite social and political lines that were not based alone on the generosity of nature. The liberals of the world became republic conscious, and there were a few farsighted men who saw in the British colonies of North America qualities propitious to the eventual success of this new type of government.

One of these men was Raynal, a French historian and philosopher who had great influence in Spanish America. In his book *Histoire philosophique et politique des éstablissements et du commerce des Européens dans les deux Indes* (first published in 1770) Raynal expresses the opinion that if ever there took place a fortunate revolution on this Earth, it would be in America. Perhaps after the destruction of the Old World the New World would bloom in its turn, and it would serve as a haven for our peoples persecuted because of politics and wars. By this time the American savages will have been civilized, and the oppressed peoples of Europe will flock to its shores where they will once again become free.[38] Raynal's history became the bible of the revolutionists, and circulated throughout Spanish America in spite of the fact that it had been prohibited by the Inquisition. It was Monteagudo's favorite reading; and men like Rojas, Mariano Moreno, and Bolívar speak of it with admiration.

Just before the Declaration of Independence similar ideas were ex-

---

[38] Raynal, *Histoire*, VI, 179.

pressed by Fernando Galiani, the Italian philosopher and astute student of America. In a letter to Mme. d'Espinay of the 18th of May, 1776, the former, concerned with the terrible vices that were undermining civilization in Europe, tells his friend that "the time for the collapse of Europe and transmigration to America has arrived. Everything around us falls rotten: religion, law, arts, sciences; and everything will be reconstructed from its very foundations in America."[39] The future belongs to the New World.

Once independence was attained, the United States as the salvation of the human race became a commonplace idea. This was only the beginning. The republic was a means to an end rather than an end in itself. And its developments were closely followed by the Spanish economists and thinkers of that day. Soon, as success became more evident, many of them started to look upon the new state as a model. Rippy says that in 1798, the Spanish revolutionist Picornell was accused of printing the constitution of the United States for distribution in the Spanish colonies.[40] And many of the Spanish representatives who came to the United States and were able to study the country from first hand information, were won over to the new cause.

Even Martínez de Casa Irujo, a royalist who served Fernando VII during his era of absolutism, had something to learn from the new republic. This author, in 1792, had published a Spanish translation of Adam Smith's *Wealth of Nations*,[41] a book that has often been associated with the ideas of Hamilton and other leading American economists. Three years later Casa Irujo came to the United States in the capacity of Spanish Ambassador and remained here until 1807. During this time he married Sally McKean, the daughter of Governor McKean, of Pennsylvania. He was favorably impressed with the progress this nation showed, and though he left the country after having had serious difficulties with the American government, that declared him "persona non grata," once in Spain he suggested a policy of collaboration between the two nations. He also advised a series of changes in the Spanish policy toward her American provinces, inspired by what he had seen in the United States, that made him unpopular with conservative elements and the Spanish king. It was primarily for this reason that he was temporarily exiled from the court.

The fate of Valentín de Foronda, the Spanish Chargé d'Affaires in 1809, a noted philosopher and literary critic, was more adverse than Casa Irujo's. Before his coming to America, Foronda already had difficulties with the Spanish authorities because of his unorthodox ideas, but during his

---

[39] Galiani to Mme. d'Espinay, May 18, 1776; in Gerbi, *Viejas polémicas* p. 84.

[40] Rippy, *Historical Evolution of Hispanic America*, p. 345.

[41] Marqués de Condorcet, *Compendio de la obra inglesa intitulada Riqueza de las Naciones*. Traducido con varias adiciones del original por D. Carlos Martínez de Irujo, Madrid, 1792

stay in the United States he enjoyed to full advantage the freedom of the American press. It was during this period that he wrote some of his most forward-looking works. In an article published anonymously, *Sobre lo que debe de hacer un príncipe que tenga colonias a gran distancia,* Philadelpria, 1803, he went so far as to advocate the independence of Spanish America. Foronda lived in the United States for more than eight years. He was made honorary member of the American Philosophical Society, 1804, where he read many of his works and made a number of friendships that lasted long after he returned to Spain. Fortunately he left us a memoir of his impressions of this country, *Apuntes ligeros sobre Estados Unidos de la América Septentrional,*[42] 1804, in which he is constantly speaking of the economic prosperity of the nation, and the general well-being of its population. The main reason for this, he says, advising the Spaniards to imitate the United States in this respect, is that this country has a government dedicated to the good of the people, where everything had been simplified so as to facilitate the comfort of every citizen, in direct contrast to the European governments whose taxes, monopolies and red tape hold business at a standstill. His friendship with Jefferson influenced him considerably, and when he returned to Spain he tried to explain to the people the significance of republican ideals. He tried to help guide them through a period of political instability toward a more liberal form of government, but unfortunately the tide was against him. With the return of Fernando VII to the Spanish throne, the government, which up to then had had democratic inclinations, became reactionary. Foronda continued to write without reserve, until finally the inevitable happened: he was arrested in 1814 and sentenced to ten years of imprisonment.

Another economist influenced by this country was the Cuban Francisco de Arango y Parreño, who served as his country's representative to the Spanish Cortes of 1811. Arango was an expert on American economy, and had written a number of books on agriculture and commerce. During the discussions that took place that memorable year, Arango defended the interests of the Cuban slave owners against the abolitionists. His main argument was that if slavery had proven to be a prosperous and advisable measure for a liberal country like the United States, it should likewise be desirable for the Spanish provinces. Throughout his speeches he showed himself to be very well informed about the United States, and his attitude was one of respect and admiration. He advised the Cortes that changes were necessary and that the experiences the Anglo-Americans had undergone should be taken into consideration "not to be used as a fast rule, but rather as a guide".[43] The text of his speeches was published at Madrid in 1814

---

[42] Edited by J. de Onís, "Valentín de Foronda's Memoir on the United States of North America, 1804," *The Americas,* IV, 1948, 351-387.

[43] Francisco de Arango y Parreño "Representación de la ciudad de la Habana a las

along with other documents presented before the Spanish Cortes of Cádiz.[41] The proclamations of the Junta Central as well as those of the Cortes were published and circulated freely in Spanish America. According to García Calderón: "In these documents, independence, national sovereignty, the idea of the native country, and the function of the assemblies came over from the metropolis." Indeed, they were an important contribution to the development of revolutionary ideas.

There also seems to be some evidence to the effect that the example of the United States helped promote the abolition of the Inquisition. J. R. Spell maintains that Ruiz de Padrón, a Spanish priest who had lived in Philadelphia and at one time delivered there a sermon against the Inquisition, when the future fate of these bodies was being discussed at Cádiz in 1814, cited religious freedom in the United States as an argument in favor of the abolition of the Inquisition in the Spanish Empire.[45]

One notable exception to this group of Spanish liberals who advocated imitating the United States is José Félix Blanco, better known as Blanco White. Blanco at one time contemplated finding refuge in the United States,[46] but instead went to England where he spent most of his life in exile. From there he published several magazines for Spanish American consumption: *Las Variedades, El Semanario Patriótico,* and *El Español.* This last was the best known of the three. It was one of the main sources of information for the revolutionary review *La Gazeta de Caracas,* and is often quoted by the revolutionary leaders.[47] Bolívar said that "There were articles of great merit in the review *El Español",* and that "our history was very well treated there."[48] Blanco was a personal friend of the Mexican Mier, and the Venezuelan Roscío, with whom he had open discussions on Spanish American problems. In recognition of his support of the revolutionary cause, the government of the Venezuelan republic of 1810 made Blanco an honorary citizen.

In a statement he wrote in answer to a letter in which J. G. Roscío, Secretary of Foreign Affairs of the Caracas government, asked for his advice, Blanco tells the Spanish Americans not to use the United States as a

---

Cortes, el 20 de Julio de 1811, con motivo de las proposiciones hechas por D. José Miguel Guridi Alcocer y D. Agustín de Argüelles, sobre el tráfico y esclav tud de los negros: extendida por el Alféres Mayor de la ciudad, D. Francisco de Arango por encargo del Ayuntamiento, Consulado y Sociedad Patriótica de la Habana", *Obras del Excmo D. Francisco de Arango y Parreño,* Habana, 1888, pp. 175-179.

[44] *Documentos de que hasta ahora se compone el expediente que principiaron las Cortes extraordinarias sobre el tráfico y esclavitud de los negros,* Madrid, 1814.

[45] J. R. Spell "An Ilustr ous Spaniard in Philadelphia," *Hispanic Review,* IV, 1936, 136-140.

[46] Joseph Blanco White, *Life,* London, 1845, p. 105.

[47] *Gazeta de Caracas,* Aug. 31, 1810; Nov. 6, 1810; Nov. 23, 1810; Dec. 11, 1810.

[48] Simón Bolívar "Contestación de un Americano Mer dional a un Caballero da esta Isla;" in Blanco y Azpurúa, *Documentos,* V, 336.

model. He says that "the example of the United States was not adaptable to their circumstances. The United States was a mass almost without mixtures, for although it was made up of peoples that had very different origins, they all hated to depend on Europe; they all had abandoned it in search of liberty on the other side of the ocean." He then points out: "That this is not the case in Spanish America, populated by rich and powerful European land owners, full of office holders who depend upon their salaries, and who are expecting promotions and would be willing to put everything through blood and fire, rather than to hear the word Independence."[49] "The United States could count on the aid of France and Spain to defeat the power of England," but Spanish America, according to Blanco, could only count fo certain on the United States. "The United States, before the revolution. had a government that needed no changes to make itself independent." ". . .Spanish America was still going through her apprenticeship of liberty, and to want to do it all at once. . .was to run the risk of making a structure that was all appearance and that would collapse with the first wind." He says that Spanish America in time would obtain its independence, but should take things slowly because "Liberty is a delicate plant that weakens and dies if it is forced to bear fruit before its time."[50]

Fear as well as admiration for the United States was conveyed to the Spanish Americans by European books and authors. The idea that the United States constituted a threat to the Spanish colonies was expressed even before the independence of this country. In 1762, when Spain was about to cede the Floridas to England, Galiani was very much concerned with the fact that the English Empire in America constituted a solid block stretching from Canada to the gulf of Mexico. "This empire," he said, "is strong enough to dictate the law to the rest of sleeping America."[51] He was of the opinion that England was depopulating itself for the benefit of the American colonies, and that these represented a threat even to the metropolis itself.[52] And in 1771 he expressed the belief that "Within a century England would detach itself from Europe . . . and reunite with America, of which by this time she will possess the greater part and dominate the rest of it."[53]

Immediately after the War of Independence, Aranda, the Spanish Ambassador to France, predicted in a secret memorial addressed to Charles III, King of Spain, the independence of the Spanish colonies as a result of the example of the liberation of the English. He also warned

---

[49] Blanco White to Juan G. Roscio, London, July 11, 1811; in Blanco y Azpurúa, *Documentos*, I, 17.

[50] *Loc. cit.*

[51] Galiani to Tanucci, Dec. 8, 1762; in Gerbi, *op. cit.* pp. 56-57. The Floridas were ceded to England at the Treaty of Paris, 1763.

[52] *Dialogues*, 1770, VI, 218.

[53] Galiani to Mme. d'Epinay, April 27, 1771; in Gerbi, *op. cit.*, p. 83.

against the threat this new nation represented for the Spanish peoples to its south, regardless of whether they were part of the Spanish Empire or independent nations. The memorial went as follows:

> The independence of the English colonies has just been recognized, and this is food for thought and fear, in my opinion. This Federal Republic has been born a pigmy, so to speak, and has needed the aid of states as powerful as Spain and France to attain her independence. The time will come when she will be a giant, and even a colossus, much to be feared in those vast regions. Then she will forget the benefits that she received from both powers and will only think of aggrandizing herself. Her first steps will be to get possession of the Floridas in order to dominate the Gulf of Mexico. These fears are only too well founded and will be realized within a few years, if other more disastrous events do not previously occur in our Americas.[54]

To prevent the loss of the Spanish colonies, Aranda proposed that Spain withdraw from all except Cuba and Puerto Rico, and that out of the rest of the empire three kingdoms be created, all united under the King of Spain, who would take the title of Emperor.

Due to the fact that the original text of the Conde de Aranda's memorial was never found, there are a few historians who have doubted the authenticity of this document, namely, Antonio Ferrer del Río, Konetzke, Baumgarten, and Whitaker. Beleslao Lewin claims that of these four the only one who has actually studied the question is Ferrer del Río and that he presents no conclusive evidence to the effect that Aranda did not write the memoir. He also states that the memorial was in keeping with the spirit of the times and cites a number of instances before and after 1783 in which Aranda expressed the same or similar ideas to those found in the questioned document; all of which, according to Lewin, tends to make the authenticity of the memorial more than probable.[55]

During the first two decades of the nineteenth century warnings against future aggression on the part of the United States became more persistent. On December 27, 1807, Foronda writes to Cevallos of the increase in population and wealth of this nation: "... how this country does prosper! If no war occurs in forty years these areas will be thickly populated, and Spain must resent their strength because of the proximity of these republicans to the Kingdom of Mexico.[56] And in another letter written only two days later he tells of the fabulous wealth of the North American merchant marine: "Ten thousand vessels upon the seas — in

---

[54] "Informe secreto de Aranda" (Sept. 3, 1783); in Blanco y Azpurúa, *Documentos*, I, 186; also in Alamán, *Historia de México*, I, 146; English trans. in Chandler, *Inter-American acquaintances*, pp. 4-5.

[55] B. Lewin, "El informe secreto de Aranda en 1783", *La Nación*, Buenos Aires, Oct. 8, 1944.

[56] Foronda to Cevallos, Philadelphia, Dec. 27, 1807; No. 76 p, Legajo 5633, Archivo Histórico Nacional, Madrid.

truth, this is a wealth greater than the famous mountain of Potosi."[57] In 1811, in an address given before the Cortes of Cádiz, the Cuban Arango y Parreño, spoke of the future greatness of the United States, and pointed out the danger this meant to the Spanish possessions of America. He said that "in the North there was growing a colossus composed of all castes and languages that threatened to swallow, if not all of our America, at least the northern part of it." Arango also suggested as a defensive measure that Spain develop along the same lines as the United States. "The only escape," he says, "is to grow along with that giant, sharing with him his very breath of life."[53]

By 1809 the Spanish colonies, due to the example of North America, were ripe for independence, and the Junta Central sent Luis de Onís to the United States to try to prevent the dismemberment of the Spanish Empire. He remained here until 1819. During this time he wrote a number of pamphlets under the pseudonym of *Verus* that were intended to acquaint the North American public with the Spanish point of view. He also wrote, under his own name, a *Memoir upon the negotiations between Spain and the United States of America, which led to the treaty of 1819,* Madrid, 1820, in which he predicted the future conquest of Mexico and the North American domination of the Western Hemisphere. Onís also maintained an extensive correspondence with men in different parts of Spanish America, advising them of the activities and intentions of the United States.[59] This information was later used by England as a source of propaganda against the United States during their struggle for economic supremacy. Sir Henry Ward, the English Ambassador to Mexico, published an abridged edition of Onís' *Memoir* that was widely disseminated throughout Spanish America, and which was the center of a heated controversy that had its repercussions in Mexico, the United States, and Spain.[60] Onís' papers filed in the Mexican archives were also an

---

[57] Foronda to Cevallos, Philadelphia, Dec. 31, 1807; No. 80 p, Legajo 5633, Archivo Histórico Nacional, Madrid. Foronda's letters are also found in the Correspondence of the Spanish Legation in the United States; Diplomatic Section; Library of Congress Division of Manuscripts.

[58] Arango y Parreño, *Obras,* p. 209.

[59] A good example of the letters written by Luis de Onís is one from Philadelphia, Feb. 14, 1812; published in Blanco y Azpurúa, *Documentos* III, 608. Onís' letters were published at different times in: *Gaceta de Buenos Aires,* 1810-1821; *Mercurio Chileno.* 1811-1813; *El Argos,* 1821-1823. Fray Melchor Martínez published the "Avisos de Don Luis de Onís" in his *Revolución de Chile,* p. 42. Mier discusses these letters in *Memoria político-instructiva,* pp. 121-122.

[60] Onís' memoir first appeared in Spanish under the title *Memoria sobre las negociaciones entre España y los Estados Unidos de América, que dieron motivo al tratado de 1819. Con una noticia sobre la estadística del país. Acompaña un apéndice que contiene documentos importantes sobre el asunto,* Madrid, 1820. It was translated into English in Baltimore, 1821, *Memoir upon the Negotiations between Spain and the United States of America, which led to the treaty of 1819* By Luis de Onís. Translated with notes by Tobias Watkins. The following year the *Memoir* was refuted by H. S. Forsythe, Minister of the United States to Spain in a pamphlet entitled *Observaciones sobre la*

important factor in determining the Mexican point of view. They were used by Alamán in his condemnation of the United States.

Still another type of anti-American ideas came by way of France. France did not fear for the destruction of the Spanish Empire, in which she was not particularly interested. She was concerned with the salvation of the European way of life. "The great danger of the time," as Canning said, "a danger which the policy of the European system would have fostered, was the division of the world into European and American, Republican and Monarchical; a league of worn-out governments, on the one hand, and of youthful and stirring nations, with the United States at their head, on the other."[61] The author who did the most to prevent this condition from taking place was the Frenchman Dominique de Pradt.

Abbé de Pradt was an ecclesiastic who had been archbishop of Malines and Baron of the Empire under Napoleon. He was an expert on international affairs, and was at odds with the French government and the French press because of his many intrigues. He wrote more than forty books, many of which related to America. Due to his friendship with the liberals of Río de la Plata, particularly Bernardino Rivadavia, he was made honorary citizen by the government of Buenos Aires. De Pradt was convinced that a clash between the American Republican System and the European Monarchical System was inevitable. In this struggle that was to take place he regarded Spanish America as Europe's frontier in the New World, which, according to him, should be defended at all costs against the expanding influence of the United States. To prevent Spanish America from falling into the Republican system he favored the immediate recognition of the new governments by the European powers.[62]

Proof that this hostile criticism from abroad had a marked influence upon the attitude of the Spanish Americans is found in the number of Spanish and French authors that are quoted. For example, when the University of Caracas published an article against William Burke, with regard to the debate on religious tolerance that was taking place in Venezuela in 1810, they used entirely French sources: D'Auberleuil, La Rochefoucauld-Liancourt and Mably.[63]

Memoria del Señor Onís relativas a la negociación con los Estados Unidos. (Translated by Father Thomas Gough). In 1826 Ward published the *Memoria* in Mexico, and it was with the purpose of counteracting its effects that Poinsett wrote the *Exposición de la conducta política de los Estados Unidos,* México, 1827.

[61] Quoted in Temperly, "The Later American Policy of George Canning," *American Historical Review,* XI, 1906, 781-782.

[62] The ideas of de Pradt are expressed in *Du Congress de Vienne,* Paris, 1815, and in a series of articles that were published under the title *De la revolution actuelle de l'Espagne, et de ses suites,* Paris 1820. Concerning de Pradt's attitude toward the United States see: Whitaker, *The United States and the Independence of Latin America, 1800-1830,* Baltimore, 1941. pp. 102-109.

[63] "La intolerancia político-religiosa...", in Blanco y Azpurúa, *Documentos,* III, 96-98.

These two schools of thought—those who thought of America as the hope of the world, and those for whom it represented a threat to European civilization—liberal republicans on the one side and conservative monarchists on the other—came to a head in Spain with the Civil War of 1820. The liberals were finally defeated after the armed intervention of France with the "one hundred thousand sons of Saint Louis." In the United States, the principles at stake in this war were well understood. The contemporary papers are full of laudatory remarks about the Spanish liberals and bitter condemnation of Fernando VII, France, and the Holy Alliance. "It might not...be required that the American people should engage on the side of the Spanish nation; but her cause is virtually ours . . . since all the doctrines the allies attack we firmly hold."[64] And Henry Clay in a speech delivered in Philadelphia soon after the news arrived that the French armies were on the march says:

> And France comes to check her in her noble and patriotic career... She would restore the absolute sway of the monarch, and, I suppose, all the blessings of the Inquisition!.... One pleasing effect upon the people of this country, with regard to this war, will be that unlike the late wars of Europe, it will create no division of opinions among us. In spite of our partiality to France, in spite of all the grateful recollections with which her name is associated; in spite of our sincere desire to maintain with her specially the most amicable relations, there will be here but one feeling and one hope as to the issue of this wanton and unprovoked contest. We shall, in regard to it, be all federalists, all republicans, all Spanish: none, no, not one French.[65]

There can be no doubt that Spain served as an important vehicle for liberal ideas in Spanish America under Charles III and during the regency of the Spanish Cortes, but with the return of absolute power to Fernando VII, a new era of reaction was in store for the affairs of this nation and her crumbling empire. Even Blanco White during the latter years of his life, who was by this time under the influence of reactionary ideas, writes in his diary:

> Thursday, Jan. 14th, 1841
> In very low spirits. I am reading Abdy's Journal on the United States, a work that convinces me of the existence of national moral diseases. The antipathy to the negroes and their most distant descendants is a kind of madness. Much as I love liberty, I would not live within the Union, just because I love liberty. The United States are under the tyranny of ignorance and prejudice. I had sooner live under a Sultan. A mob is the worst of tyrants, because a mob has no individuality. A mob is a sort of monster, a "Tertium quid" resulting from passion mistaken for freedom.[66]

---

64 *National Gazette,* March 21, 1823; quoted in Elizabeth Brett White, *American opinion of France,* p. 75.

65 Quoted in *loc. cit.*

66 Joseph Blanco White, *Life,* III, 295-296.

III. IDEAS OF THE SPANISH AMERICAN WRITERS

The authors of the period of independence were men of action, who looked upon literature as a medium of propaganda and made history at the same time that they wrote about it. There are two main types into which Spanish American authors who write about the United States can be divided: those who had been to this country and whose ideas as a result were much clearer, if less idealistic, and certainly less commonplace; and those who knew of the United States from indirect sources, thus having a romantic and poetical notion of this nation, much closer to the Utopian ideal.

To the first type belong the travellers, who wrote journals and diaries of their experiences, and the political refugees, who produced the political memoirs having the United States as the main point of comparison with Spanish America. To this type also belong the writings of José María de Heredia, which represent the only pure literature written about the United States during this epoch. To the second type belong the essays and books by authors who depended for their information upon printed material, generally European. This includes also many Spanish Americans who arrived in this country with preconceived notions, and after a short stay left with their ideas unchanged.

1. Travellers

At the head of this first group stands FRANCISCO DE MIRANDA (1750-1816), a man who can truly be called the great precursor of Spanish American independence. He dedicated his entire life to this end, and although actual independence came some years after his death, it was he who created the bonds of interest between Spanish America and the outside world that eventually made its freedom possible.

Miranda was born in Caracas in 1750, and was educated at the Academy of Santa Rosa and at the University of Caracas.[1] In 1772 he was inducted into the Spanish Army, and in 1780, with the rank of Captain, he participated in the expedition that captured Pensacola. Once hostilities ended he visited the United States, and from here journeyed to Europe where he became one of the great personalities of his day. His numerous activities brought him in contact, in one form or another, with the leading nations of the world. In France he fought beside Dumouriez in the armies of the French Revolution. In Russia he became a protege of Catherine the Great. In England he obtained the approval of Pitt to lead a revolutionary expedition to liberate Venezuela. In the United States he was connected with an abortive scheme of a similar nature, involving such men as Hamilton and Washington. Miranda's fame grew to mythical proportions. In

---

[1] Concerning Miranda's life see: W. S. Robertson, *Life of Miranda,* Chapel Hill, N. C., 1929.

the opinion of some of his contemporaries his prestige and personality were worth more than entire armies.

It is not likely that Miranda had literary ambitions, yet many critics classify him as an outstanding author. Henríquez Ureña says that "the journal he kept during his trip through the United States gives him a unique position in the literature of Spanish America."[2] There are others that hold to the opinion that Miranda foresaw that some day his *Diary* would be published. William S. Robertson says that "the occasional use in the Spanish texts of the abbreviation "V.", meaning *Usted* suggests the possibility— which almost becomes a probability in light of the care taken by Miranda to preserve his journal and other manuscripts—that the egotistical and far-sighted Creole composed the *diario* with a future audience in mind."[3] If it was not published by the insurgents during the period of independence (1810-1823) it must have been due to the fact that the manuscript was not available to them. Its publication at that critical time would have fallen on Spanish America like a bombshell, and its influence indeed would have been great. Unfortunately the manuscript was to remain forgotten until the summer of 1922 when it was discovered in the town of Cirencester in Gloucestershire, England.

It is not clear when Miranda definitely decided to leave the service of Spain. Dissatisfaction with existing conditions, as well as personal difficulties, were the main reasons for his departure from Cuba. A letter written by Cagigal to Rendón, the Spanish Ambassador to the United States, gives us to understand that Miranda was at this time going through a period of transition, and that the plan, which was to be his future course of action, had not yet crystallized. Rendón treated him with great consideration and loaned him large quantities of money, which he certainly would not have done had he considered him an enemy of Spain.[4]

When Miranda first arrived in the United States in 1783 he came as a distinguished Spanish traveller, and enjoyed the advantages of being a Spanish citizen, at a time when the relations between the United States and Spain were unusually cordial. The Spanish American liberals who came at a later date, as insurgents and not as Spanish celebrities, found the going considerably more difficult. Their stay was generally limited to the radius of the city where they lived, and very often they lacked the bare necessities of life. Miranda on the contrary was feasted and entertained throughout the country, and was able to see and record at his leisure more of the United States than any other South American of his epoch.

---

[2] Pedro Henríquez Ureña, *Literary currents in Hispanic America*, p. 95.

[3] W. S. Robertson, *The diary of Francisco de Miranda*, New York, 1928, p. xxxi.

[4] Cagigal to Rendón, Habana, May 18, 1783; in Archivos del General Miranda V, 243. The charges presented against Miranda in Cuba were of a disciplinary nature, not political. See: "Cargos hechos a Miranda," *ibid.*, IV 421-422.

Gifted with a mind extraordinarily adept at critical analysis, Miranda gives a minute account of the places and people he saw and met. With uncanny ability he was able to catch the spirit of the people, to describe with bold strokes the psychology of the leading personalities who participated in the War of Independence, or to analyze the social, economic, and cultural conditions existing at that time throughout the land.

He had the good fortune of witnessing the birth of the American nation. He was in New Bern, North Carolina, when the news arrived that the war with England had ended. He describes the spirit of the people with enthusiasm: "About one o'clock there was a barbecue, and a barrel of rum. Everybody, bigwigs, country people, the dregs and the offscourings of the town were shaking hands and drinking out of the same glass. It would be impossible to conceive a more purely democratic assembly, and it bears out all that the Greek historians and poets tell us of similar gatherings among the free peoples of Greece. Toward the end some were drunk, there were a number of fights, one man was wounded, and when the night came everyone went to his bed, and with the burning of a few empty barrels as fireworks, the celebration came to an end." (*Diario,* p. 6).

On the 8th of December, 1783, Miranda was in Philadelphia as General Washington passed through the city on his way to present his resignation as Commander-in-Chief of the Army of Congress. Washington entered the city at 12 o'clock. Men, women and children lined the streets, cheering the arrival of the hero "as though the Saviour had entered Jerusalem." (p. 39). The following day Miranda went with Rendón, the Spanish Ambassador, to visit Washington. He presented him with a letter Cagigal had written on Miranda's behalf; as a result of this Miranda sat at his table as long as Washington remained in Philadelphia. He created quite an impression in American social circles. Overnight he became the fashion of the day. John Adams tells us "that Miranda was introduced to Washington and his aides, secretaries and all the gentlemen in his family, to the other general officers and their families, and to many of the colonels. He acquired the character of a classical scholar, a man of universal knowledge, of a great general, master of all military sciences, a person of great sagacity, an inquisitive mind, and insatiable curiosity. It was the general consensus that he knew more of the families, parties, and connections in the United States than any other man there; that he knew more of every campaign, battle, and skirmish that had occurred in the whole war, than any officer of our army or any statesman in our councils. His constant preoccupation was the independence of Spanish America."[5]

Miranda was more impressed by what he saw in the streets and by the behavior of the average American than he was by our great men. George

---

[5] *The life and works of John Adams,* X. 134-135.

Washington, for instance, does not seem to fulfill his ideal of greatness. He cannot understand why he alone in a country where there are so many men of distinction should enjoy the devotion of the populace. He describes Washington as being "reserved, melancholy and not very expressive; although his gentleness and moderation make his company tolerable. I never saw him lose these qualities, in spite of the fact that there was considerable drinking, good humor, and gayety. Whenever we drank certain toasts he would stand up and give his three cheers along with the rest of us." (p. 39-40). Lest it be considered presumptuous on his part, Miranda leaves the final judgment of the great American to posterity.

His description of Lafayette is even less generous. He finds him to be a man of mediocre character, "disguised by an aimless perpetual motion typical of the French." (p. 121). It is not surprising that these two men came to dislike each other intensely.

Samuel Adams was more to Miranda's taste. He found the republican propagandist to be a man of talent and of great knowledge. At the time of their first meeting they had a long discussion concerning the Constitution of the United States. Miranda saw two contradictions in the ideals set forth in this document. He could not understand how in the United States, a republic that should have "virtue" as its main foundation, no provision was made for it, whereas all the rights and powers of "property" are fully guaranteed. Again, Miranda sees a contradiction in the ideal of religious freedom co-existing with the exclusion of certain individuals from office because of their not being Christians. Miranda states that after a thorough discussion, Samuel Adams agreed with him that these two factors were inconsistent with the spirit of a truly democratic nation. During the visit Adams treated Miranda with familiarity, and supplied him with information concerning the origins of the independence of the United States that the Spanish American considered priceless. (p. 118). What Miranda means by "virtue" would be a risky thing to conjecture. As a Spanish liberal, the word for him would probably hold an entirely different meaning than for us.

Miranda admired the American institutions of government. In Charleston, South Carolina, he visited the court of justices and says that he "can't find words to describe the joy he derived from seeing in practice the admirable system of the English constitution." (p. 22-25). He also visited the general assembly of the legislature of the State of Massachusetts. He found the ignorance of some of the legislators appalling. He feared that the emphasis given to property in the Constitution and the ruthless methods practiced in commercial relations would finally lead to the loss of equality. (p. 120-121).

He admired the democratic spirit of the American people. He was in reality a democrat by belief, but an aristocrat by taste—an attitude typical of the majority of Spanish Americans of his day. In Springfield, Mass., he was shocked when the lad who had been driving the stage-coach sat at the table with the passengers.

> I should not forget to mention here that the spirit of republicanism is such in this country that the driver who conducted the carriage and the rest of us sat at the table together, and that it was very difficult for me to arrange that they feed my servant apart from us. (p. 82-83)

In New Haven, he was amazed to find that a captain in the cavalry of the Army prior to his induction into the service had been a miller and that one of the servants was an accomplished orator who knew Latin and Greek well. In Long Island he met two squires, Guilson and L'Hommedieu, both members of the New York State Senate who lived with great modesty —even scarcity, yet were men of decided virtue and understanding. In Providence he met David Howel, a member of Congress, who under the cover of almost vulgar simplicity was a man of worth who acted as Commissioner for the United States in the settlement of the North East boundary.

To illustrate the democratic spirit of the American people Miranda tells the anecdote of an American farmer, owner of a tract of land in Stony Point near West Point, New York, where the French Army was stationed after their retreat from Virginia in 1782. It seems that the farmer made a claim to the French Commanding Officer for payment for the use of the land. After being ignored for some time, the "clumsy farmer" one day appeared with the sheriff, with no other arms than the authority of the law, to arrest the French General, M. de Rochambeau, before his entire army. The story goes that the general was arrested and forced to pay the ten or fifteen dollars, which was the amount involved. "Is it any wonder that under similar auspices even the most arid and deserted countries should flourish? And that the most pusilanimous and insignificant man should become before long honest, just, industrious, wise and brave." (p. 62-63).

He approved of the high living standards found in this country, but is aware that differences existed between the different regions. For instance, in Charleston, S.C., he saw an aristocratic city where emphasis was given to social and rural life, the favorite entertainments being hunting, dancing and smoking. He said that the youth here was vain and ignorant but that the women had charm and knew how to dress with taste. The city was well situated for commerce. (p. 16-17).

In Philadelphia he found a different type of civilization. Of all the American cities it was the one that impressed him most. He describes it as free and enterprising and without doubt the most beautiful city on the entire continent. The streets were straight and laid out at right angles. The houses were comfortable, and built with good taste. The city hall was of mediocre quality. The churches were simple, without decoration. But there were two things that interested Miranda particularly in this city, the public lighting system (the streets of a city illuminated by hundreds of gas lamps, a spectacle which for the people of that day must have been something wonderful to behold), and the Philadelphia police force, with its regular uniforms and everything. One can sense a certain amount of American pride when he says "Philadelphia is one of the most pleasant and orderly cities of the world." (p. 29).

He does not say much about New York City although he was there for some time. He visited West Point, Albany, and Saratoga, and found that the people of these regions were poorer than the others he had seen before. Women often did not wear shoes. A good part of the population was black. To his surprise they all spoke Dutch and "it was as if it were a Dutch colony in the middle of the United States." (p. 70).

In New England he found that the land was poor, but that the industry of the people made up for the lack of fertility of the soil. "Such is the industry and spirit that liberty inspires among these people, that out of a small tract of land they are able to get enough to sustain a large family, pay taxes, and live comfortably a thousand times happier than the owners of rich mines, the fertile lands of Mexico, Peru, Buenos Aires, Caracas, and the entire American continent." (p. 129). He tells of the New England genius for invention, but was not impressed by its universities. He says that Mr. Manning, President of Rhode Island College (now Brown University), "was perfectly illiterate." (p. 113). The arts in general were in their infancy. (p. 29-30, 125). The libraries were very small, and there was no theater to speak of. The only entertainment available was going to church. (p. 17, 35, 86). In reality Miranda was an aristocrat who was more at home at the table of Catherine the Great than in New England seated with what he calls a "mechanic." What he really wanted was political, not social equality for all.

Miranda in his *Diary* gives more attention to women than to men. This might be due to the fact that he was only thirty-three at the time of his trip. Episodes of a romantic nature are not lacking. It is interesting to note that he found American women, all the way from South Carolina to Rhode Island, to be handsome. In Charleston he found that there were five women to each man, due to the many casualties suffered there during the War of Independence. (p. 16). In this city alone there were 1,200 widows. Strangely enough, he thought married women of South Carolina submissive and entirely devoted to their homes and husbands. The single ones on the other hand enjoyed considerable liberty. (p. 5). In Boston women had little culture. (p. 117). In Newport, R.I., the women were beautiful, gracious and dressed with good taste. (p. 107). The men in

general throughout the country he found backward and unpolished in dress
and in manner. Both men and women were extraordinarily healthy.

The prosperity of the nation he attributes to the industriousness of the
population. (p. 7, 58-59, 90, 129). Food was abundant and of high quality.
Grains and fruits of all kinds were plentiful. (p. 8). He describes the
general well-being of the population. (p. 3, 7, 107). The most common
disease was malaria, especially in the South. (p. 8, 23).

Miranda praises highly the freedom of faith as it existed at that time
in the United States—"each person is allowed to pray in the manner and
in the language he chooses" (p. 50) but he could not understand the attitude of the Protestants toward Sunday amusement. In Georgetown, S.C.,
he was asked to stop playing the flute, and in New Bern he was disgraced
when he absentmindedly started to play solitaire on Sunday. (p. 13-14).
In New Haven and Salem he inspected the archives of these cities where
he read the records concerning violations of the "blue laws." In company
of William Wetmore Esq. he visited "Gallows Hill" outside of Salem
where they used to hang the victims. (p. 128). Miranda says that religious
freedom had been in existence for the last twenty years but that there were
still many vestiges of the former fanaticism. In Long Island he witnessed
a scene where a young man was made to appear before the entire congrega-
tion and confess that he had had intimate relations with his wife before
they were married. "I have never been so embarrassed in my entire life."
(p. 95). In Newburyport he attended the Presbyterian church and heard
a preacher "start his sermon by praying to God for the extermination of
all Pagans, Mohammedans, anti-Christians, the Pope and all his followers,
all heretics . . . so that in one moment the entire universe, with the exception
of his small flock, was excluded from the Divine protection." (p. 136).

After Miranda there came other travellers but none left us as detailed
a description of the United States as he did. JOSE BERNARDO GUTIERREZ
DE LARA (1774-1841), from Mexico, and José Luis de Carrera, from
Chile, both wrote journals of their visit to this country which are of great
interest to us but which in no way attempt to evaluate our civilization.

Gutiérrez de Lara arrived at Natchitoches (Nov. 2, 1811) on the
Louisiana-Texas frontier and from there set out overland to Philadelphia
and Washington. During his trip he met many of the officials and men
of influence in the South, among them Governor Claiborn of Louisiana.
In Washington he visited President Madison and Secretary of State Monroe.
He discussed with them the possibility of Mexico receiving aid from the
United States, but Luis de Onís, reporting Lara's meeting with Monroe
to the Spanish Minister, states that Lara was dismayed when he realized
that they wanted to use him for their own plans and that American aid

might prove to be more dangerous than Spain itself.[6] Nevertheless, Lara came to the United States in the best of faith and the picture he gives of this country in his diary is warm and appreciative. He did not know English, and very often he lacks the correct geographical information, but he sees clearly what are the real values of North American culture. He looked with admiration on the general prosperity of the country, its industrial life, the growth of its cities, its social advancements, and the health and elegance of its inhabitants. He visited prisons, hospitals and other public institutions. In one of these visits he met a Mallorcan, who had the reputation of being a philosopher. He had been sentenced to ten years' imprisonment because he gave false testimony. "But in him I observed sound judgment, and that as a good philosopher he had made a rigorous examination as to whether this American government was just and wise in its procedure; and satisfied that he had solved this problem, he expressed himself in these words: 'Friend', he said to me, 'in the lands through which I have travelied, I have not seen a government which is wiser than this one and which contributes more to the general happiness. Most of the prisoners who live here are guilty of crimes which in Spain would be capital offenses; but this government in its mercy sentences no man to death; what it does is to sentence prisoners to remain in this prison more or less in proportion to their crimes. Here they put us to work at tasks which we know and are able to do; they pay us a wage of 30 pence a month, 15 for food and 15 for washing and other things we need; they give us ready made clothing, good clean beds, and very good food; so that when any one of us has completed his term a debit and credit account is rendered us. There is a man who drew as much as three hundred pesos clear for his maintenance (after leaving prison). Each individual is credited according to whether he has worked more or less during his term of prison. The result is that men are highly benefited by the fact of being punished, because they go out with money, with a trade, and what is more, reformed and grateful.' 'Blessed and happy is the country that has a wise government."[7]

JOSE LUIS CARRERA (1785-1821), the first president of Chile and the author of numerous political studies, came to the United States trying to obtain help against the royalist forces that had reconquered his native land. To my knowledge, the diary he kept during his trip has never been published. His early biographers, Diego Barros Arana,[8] Benjamín Vicuña Mackenna,[9] and Amunátegui[10] do not seem to be acquainted with it.

---

6 Blanco and Azpurúa, *Documentos*, III, 608. Also see: Pereyra, *El mito de Monroe*, Madrid, 1914, p. 269.

7 Gutiérrez de Lara, "Diary," *American Historical Review*, XXXIV, 1928, 55-76, 281-294.

8 *Historia general de Chile*, XI.

9 "El ostracismo de los Carrera," *Obras completas de Vicuña Mackenna*, cap. V, pp. 56-65.

10 *Dictadura de O'Higgins.*

As a source of information concerning this epoch in Carrera's life they usually quote the abundant correspondence he had with his wife and with his brother Juan José. Varas Velásquez, in his book *Don José Miguel Carrera en los Estados Unidos,* 1912, uses the diary as a source for the first time. Other critics, like Guillermo Feliú Cruz, when speaking of it refer to Velásquez's work.[11] From the information given by these different authors there does not seem to be much difference between the correspondence and the manuscript. In both he is concerned with the same problem, one being in most cases a repetition of the other.

Collier and Feliú, summarizing the work done by their predecessors, tell us that when Carrera arrived in Baltimore in 1816, he was primarily interested in surveying the attitude that the United States had at that time toward the independence of Spanish America. Carrera immediately set out to collect and evaluate information along these lines. From the very beginning he believed that he had made an advantageous discovery. The United States was emerging from a long war with Great Britain, and as a result of its recent victories, the spirits of its citizens were in accord with militaristic ideals and eager for heroic adventures. Understanding this frame of mind of the American people, Carrera thought that he had a propitious situation for his undertaking. He did not fail to notice, nevertheless, certain negative conditions. He had observed that many of the American people had neither interest nor orientation concerning their South American fellows. For one thing, the South American countries were far distant from the Northern Republic. For another, the constant rivalry among the leaders of this country, beclouded the fact that the break with Spain was a vital, final separation. And lastly, the facts of the six years struggle were obscured by inadequate and non-representative news coverage and by fatuous information concerning it.[12]

Carrera soon found that under the tutelage of the ardent orator, Henry Clay, a feeling of sympathetic understanding of the struggle for independence had grown among the American younger generation. This group recognized among the Spanish Americans motives similar to those which had impelled them to separate themselves from England. As a result of the respect which they had for human life they rejoiced in the triumphs of the patriotic forces over the royalists. Moreover, even if the aspirations of the South Americans were unknown to the majority of the people, the business firms, the shipyards, and the dealers in military supplies were willing to enter into pacts with the patriots and to aid them in their war preparations.[13]

To Carrera's disappointment, the American government still continued

---

11 Collier and Feliú, *La primera misión de los Estados Unidos de América en Chile,* pp. 186-214.

12 Collier and Feliú, *ibid.,* pp. 193-196; Vicuña Mackenna, *op. cit.,* pp. 47-49.

13 Collier and Feliú. *ibid.,* p. 195.

to follow a conservative policy with regard to Spanish American affairs. Since 1810, the American government had made it its business to inform itself of what was going on in those countries, and by 1816 the final outcome of the war had not yet been determined. The president of the United States was Madison, and the Secretary of State Monroe. The latter's friendship for the cause of the insurgents was well known, but even he had to consider American interests first.[14]

Carrera was aware that the United States found itself in a difficult situation as a nation maintaining friendly relations with Spain. Notwithstanding many disturbing incidents, the United States was obliged not to permit the Spanish colonial subjects to make American ports bases of propaganda or springboards to launch their expeditions against the mother country; at least not until the revolutionists had acquired the international status of belligerents. In reality the United States was the country that had worked more than any other nation to formulate and secure the recognition of the doctrine of neutrality with its corollary of non-intervention. In spite of this, Carrera found that there existed a constant struggle between the sympathy that a great many Americans felt for those fighting for the liberty of Spanish America, and the policy that necessarily obliged the government to do nothing that would signify a violation of the principles of international law.[15]

There were other obstacles in Carrera's way. The negotiations which had been in progress between the United States and Spain for the purchase of the Floridas had been delayed by conditions in Spanish America. Luis de Onís, who was the Spanish representative directing the transaction in Washington never missed the opportunity to break down organized assistance to the revolutionists. He would send angry notes protesting the complacency of the government, and on several occasions interrupted the negotiations altogether. As a consequence of this, President Madison on September 15, 1815, directed a proclamation to the citizens of the United States prohibiting the sale of arms and all attempts to aid the Spanish American countries in the war against Spain. In order to make the prohibition effective he solicited special legislation from congress to prevent future abuses. Thus Onís was assured of the neutrality of the federal government.[16]

Carrera met President Madison. In a letter to his brother Luis, dated March 12th, 1816,[17] we find a brief reference to this event, but it fails to reveal the real impression his conversation with Madison left on him. Carrera must have been convinced after this interview of the impossibility of

---

14 *Ibid.,* p. 196.
15 *Ibid.,* pp. 197-200.
16 *Loc. cit.*
17 Quoted in Vicuña Mackenna, *op. cit.,* cap. V.

obtaining official support for his cause. After this we find him working with American private interests and meeting with considerable success.

2. Political Writers

Among Miranda's friends there was the Peruvian PABLO DE OLAVIDE (1725-1804), a scholar and an author of considerable prestige, who according to his critics "came to embody the spirit of innovation of the period of Charles III."[18] Miranda tried several times to obtain Olavide's support in his conspiracies to free Spanish America, but the standards of values of the two men did not coincide. Olavide belonged to the previous generation. It is true that he was a liberal and a disciple of Rousseau, but first and last he was a Spaniard. For him to plot the disruption of the Spanish Empire in common agreement with the traditional enemies of Spain was outright treason. Olavide had dedicated his entire life to the enlightenment of Spain and Spanish America. He was one of the main exponents of liberal reform in the Spanish colonial policy. But he believed that the way to do it was through education and evolution from within. Miranda on the other hand was a man whose sense of values was above nationality and racial patriotism. He often said that "his country was humanity." These characteristics often gave the mistaken impression that he was an opportunistic adventurer or an impractical idealist.

> ... who and what is Miranda? He is either an Achilles, hurt by some personal injury, real or imaginary, by having been deprived of his girl, as likely as anything else that we know, who has adopted the maxim of so many other heroes, "Jura negat sibi lata, nihil non arrogat armis"; or he is a knight-errant, as delirious as his immortal countryman, the ancient hero of La Mancha.[19]

However unfair this interpretation of Miranda might be, it was one shared by most of those Americans who belonged to the Jefferson-Adams school of thought; which included also such Frenchmen as Lafayette.

Olavide would have been a worthy associate for Miranda. He would have added stability and scholarly prestige to Miranda's already numerous and extraordinary abilities. He knew the United States well. He was one of that small group of Spanish liberals who had advised Charles III to support the thirteen colonies in their struggle against the mother country. He had met personally some of the great men of America. In the company of John Adams he had often attended festive convivial dinners given by the Duke of Rochefoucauld, and other French celebrities. Adams knew his

---

18 Pedro Henríquez Ureña, *Literary currents in Hispanic America*, p. 88. His most famous work, however, is *El Evangelio en Triunfo*, Valencia, 1778, in which he revoked many of his liberal ideas.

19 *The life and works of John Adams*, X, 142.

history, and had great respect for his character and knowledge. "One of the highest frolics I ever engaged in was with this Olavide, at a dinner with the highest characters in France, ecclesiastical and civil, in which the question was discussed between Olavide and me of an alliance, offensive and defensive, between North and South America. The history of it would be as diverting as the feast of Plato."[20] Unfortunately there is to our knowledge no record giving the details of the discussion that took place that night, and therefore it would be practically impossible to conjecture what the ideas on inter-American solidarity expressed by Olavide and Adams were. It would be difficult to bring together two men, at that time or any other, better fitted for such a discussion than these two. An exposition of the ideas presented might throw considerable light on the origins of the Monroe Doctrine and other fundamental problems of inter-American relations. For Olavide was a man of infinite resource and originality. He was one of the first to put into effect the idea of controlled immigration that later on in the century was to play such an important part in the development of the United States, and which the Argentinian Sarmiento and the Chilean Rosales copied from this country. Paradoxically enough, these measures were at this time applied by Olavide, a native of America, not to Spanish America but to Spain. The experiment had to do with the populating of Sierra Morena, an area of empty lands where bandits and criminals took refuge, by Flemish and German settlers of Catholic faith, a measure that proved very effective.

Olavide, like Casa Irujo, Aranda, Foronda, Campomanes, Covarrubias and many other Spaniards who had been interested in the United States, was eventually persecuted by the Inquisition. Under an assumed name he fled to France, where his merits as a man of great learning were recognized by the French and the residing Americans alike. He later became reconciled with the Spanish authorities and was allowed to return to Spain.

Also closely related to the work of Miranda is that of the Peruvian Jesuit JUAN PABLO VIZCARDO Y GUZMAN, known by the pseudonym of Rossi. Born in Arequipa, 1747, he entered the Company of Jesus in Cuzco where he remained until the expulsion of this order in 1767. After this he spent several years in Italy. From there he went to France and later to England, where according to Parra Pérez he received a pension from the British government of three hundred pounds. It seems that Vizcardo and Miranda did not visit each other. Prior to Vizcardo's death Miranda seldom mentions him in his correspondence. Afterwards, however, Vizcardo willed his papers to Rufus King, the American Ambassador, who later gave them to Miranda. Among them there was a Manifesto entitled "Las Verdades Eternas" challenging the legitimacy of Spain to rule over Spanish America. His main thesis

---

20 *Ibid.*, p. 144.

was that the conquest was accomplished by the Spaniards and not by Spain itself, therefore, Spanish America was under no obligation to the Spanish crown. He also advised his fellow countrymen to follow the example of the English colonies and to throw off the yoke of the mother country.

> The valor with which the English colonies of North America have fought for their liberty, which they gloriously enjoy, covers our indolence with shame, we have yielded to them the palm with which they have been first to crown the New World by their soverign independence.[21]

Miranda had this proclamation translated into French and published in Philadelphia, on the 10th of June, 1799, under the title *Lettre aux Espagnols-Américains*. It proved to be very effective propaganda. The fact that it was written in French placed it within the comprehension of many Americans, Englishmen, and Frenchmen, as well as South Americans, French being at the time a more universal language than Spanish. Later on, it was translated back again into Spanish for the benefit of those who could not read French. Chandler in his book, *Inter-American acquaintances*, tells of an anonymous proclamation, which was circulated in Buenos Aires about 1809, that might well have been Guzmán's *Letter*. A section of this proclamation published in Chandler's book coincides precisely with Guzmán's French version.[22]

While Miranda and his companions were doing their part on behalf of liberty and independence in the capitals of Europe, ANTONIO NARIÑO (1765-1823) was trying to educate the creoles within Spanish America itself.

Like the majority of his countrymen who became interested in foreign cultures and in new forms of government, he was an aristocrat of wealth. Picón-Salas describes him as a man of leisure, who devoted most of his time to horseback riding over his large hacienda in Bogotá and to reading books in his private library.[23] He had more than six thousand volumes. His collection of publications prohibited by the Inquisition had the reputation of being the finest in the land. Chandler claims that among Nariño's books were found: a summary of the Revolution of the United States in French; a compilation of the fundamental laws of that country, also in French, and dedicated to Benjamin Franklin; *The Freeholders Monitor;* and a Spanish-English dictionary in two volumes.[24] His favorite pastime was to lock himself in his study with friends to discuss the different ideas he came across in his books from day to day. In his study there was a large portrait of Benjamin Franklin, whom he imitated. Like the latter, he performed chemistry experiments.[25] Nariño's activities, however, were not

---

21. "Lettre aux Espagnols-Américains," in *Archivo del General Miranda*, XV, 321-342.
22. Chandler, *Inter-American acquaintances,* p. 33.
23 Picón-Salas, *De la Conquista a la Independencia,* Mexico, 1944, pp. 216-217.
24 Chandler, *op. cit.* p. 16.
25 Eduardo Posada, "Prefacio," *Biblioteca de historia nacional,* II, xv.

limited to conversation. He acquired a printing press, and was in the habit of translating and printing sections of books he found interesting. He distributed copies among his friends in Popayán, Quito, Cartagena, and Caracas.[26] It was in this manner that he came to translate and print parts of *The Declaration of the Rights of Man*,[27] which was eventually to cause him so many hardships. Through this publication Nariño's activities were discovered. His property was confiscated and he was sent as a prisoner to Spain. Perhaps without realizing it, he had touched upon the most explosive document of the period of independence. The civil authorities tried to supress it by every means within their power. They threatened with grave punishment anyone who was found with a copy in his possession, and the Catholic church put up posters announcing that the offenders would be excommunicated. All this was in vain, for the Spanish authorities did not have to contend only with the printed copies which Nariño had distributed. These in turn were copied and circulated in manuscript form.

During the proceedings of his trial, Nariño gave indications of being well acquainted with the United States. He defended himself upon the grounds that the social experiment which had taken place in this country had proven to be of advantage to humanity. This being so, how then could it be evil or even unlawful to write about something which by common consensus was considered good? At one moment during the defense, in an exalted and dramatic manner, he calls the new republic "the sanctuary of reason, liberty, and tolerance." And then he continues, "Oh, country of the Franklins, of the Washingtons, of the Hancocks and of the Adamses, who is not glad that they lived both for themselves and for us?" He goes on from here to speak of the United States as the "most fortunate country."[28] He concludes his defense with an argument of a practical nature, which had already been expressed by Aranda and other Spanish students of foreign affairs: that the independence of Spanish America, due to the example of the United States, was inevitable; and that nothing that he or any one else might do, or have done, could alter this course.

> And who can doubt but that, when our colonies shall have grown in population and industry, they, too, will want to be independent sovereign states, following the example of their Northern Neighbors? And if they so plan or attempt, who will be strong enough to prevent it?[29]

Arrest, trial, imprisonment and loss of property in no way discouraged Nariño. By 1811 he was once again in the midst of the fray. This time as the editor of *La Bagatela,* a gazette devoted to spreading liberal ideas. It

---

26 Picón-Salas, *op. cit.,* p. 217.

27 Translated from the French.

28 Nariño, "Derechos del hombre," *Biblioteca de historia nacional,* II, 80; also in Blanco y Azpurúa, *Documentos,* I, 235.

29 Nariño *op. cit.,* II, 81.

gave news about the United States, and covered topics such as: "Sketch of William Penn," and "Explanation of the Constitution of the United States."

It would be a mistake, however, to think that by 1811 Nariño's friendly attitude was prevalent in Spanish America. When on the 19th of February, 1811, William Burke published in the *Gazeta de Caracas*[30] his article on religious tolerance, in which he presented the United States as the model that the Spanish Americans should follow, there appeared immediately after this three publications that can be considered typical of the attitude that existed toward the United States among the more conservative elements.

The first of these, *Apología de la intolerancia religiosa,* directed by the Archbishop of the Convent of St. Francis of Valencia, published the 2nd. of March, 1811, attacks religious tolerance but does not mention the United States.[31]

The second, *Ensayo político contra las reflecciones del señor William Burke, sobre el Tolerantismo en la Gazeta de 19 de Febrero último,* published at Caracas, same date as the first, by Don Antonio Gómez,[32] attacks religious tolerance but admits that the United States enjoys certain advantages. These, according to Dr. Gómez, however, were not derived from religious tolerance as Burke had indicated. He points out that a national religion had the advantage of giving unity to the country. "Furthermore, the Federal Constitution of North America was still in its infancy if compared with governments of other states; there can yet come a day when this flowering country, shaken by internal differences of opinion, and aroused beyond control at the time of its representative elections, might confirm the ominous forecasts made by some students of political science with regard to its future destiny."[33] Gómez believes that a national religion might prove indispensable in holding the nation together in a moment of crisis. He claims that it was with this possibility in mind that Washington, at the time of his generous abdication in 1796, said with great feeling to Congress: "Religion and moral fitness are the backbone of a nation."

In the third, *La intolerancia político-religiosa, vindicada, o refutación del discurso que en favor de la tolerancia religiosa, publicó don Guillermo Burke, en la Gazeta de Caracas, del martes 19 de Febrero de 1811. No. 20 por la R. y P. Universidad de Caracas,* June 6, 1811, the Catholics of Vene-

---

30 William Burke, "Los derechos de la América del Sur y México," *Gazeta de Caracas;* Friday, Nov. 23, 1810; Friday, Dec. 7, 1810; Friday, Dec. 21, 1810; Tuesday, Feb. 19, 1811.

31 "Apologia de la intolerancia religiosa," in Blanco y Azpurúa, *Documentos,* III, 37-46.

32 *Ibid.,* pp. 46-61.

33 Gómez probably gets this idea from the French author Mably. His book attacking the United States was well known in Spanish America.

zuela start by criticizing religious tolerance and end up by making a general attack upon the United States.[34]

They explain that in the United States each man is responsible to no one except God. This belief, in their opinion, is heresy. "The detestable source of all 'sectas', an authorized pretext to commit all sort of crimes and wickedness. The origin of impious skepticism, a chaos more horrible than the very night of the world's creation."[35]

As for religious tolerance, the article suposes that if any exists in the United States it must have developed after the War of Independence, because before this time the intolerance of the colonies was notorious. It then gives a long list of abuses committed during colonial times against Catholics, Quakers, and followers of other sects. It also cites a number of blue laws that were never revoked and which it considers incompatible with religious liberty.[36]

It also accuses the United States of discrimination. In Massachussets, New Hampshire, and South Carolina, distinctions were made between Protestants and Catholics. The article mentions a number of cases, in these and in other states, where the fact of belonging or not belonging to a given religion eliminated a person from certain rights or privileges.[37] "Where is that equality of rights, that general protection given to all regardless of religion or creed, that true tolerance? We just can't see it." "The United States are indifferent, not tolerant, when it comes to religious matters."[38] In conclusion it says that "the Anglo-American system, concerning religion, cannot serve as a model for any nation."[39]

Still more critical of the United States is an editorial published in the *Gazeta de Caracas* of the 18th of October, 1815, in which it says: "And to think that there have been fools capable of thinking that some day there could be a 'Republic of Muchuckies and Timotes': two small Indian towns that are not even important in the province of Maracaibo to which they belong. We have to agree with the learned Vitet that the 'spirit of independence' is a malady that belongs to the genus 'mania.' Vitet gives a detailed description of its symptoms; constructs an exact case history of its development; and after following its tribulations in North America, France and Holland comes to the conclusion that there is but one cure, to apply the law with all its rigor to those who are contaminated by so deadly

---

[34] "La intolerancia político-religiosa, . . .," Caracas, June 6, 1811; in Blanco y Azpurúa, *Documentos*, III, 61-102.

[35] *Ibid.*, p. 95.

[36] *Ibid.*, p. 97.

[37] The sources for this information are French: D'Aubertauil, La Rochefoucauld-Liancourt, Mably.

[38] Blanco y Azpurúa, *op. cit.*, IV, 97.

[39] *Ibid.*, p. 98.

a disease . . . it is beyond doubt a contagious malady, and its symptoms are uniform in all those who have been affected."[40]

By 1816 Spanish America was receiving the full force of the reaction that had set in in Europe after the French Revolution. Yet owing to its state of isolation, it was not until now that the liberal ideas of the late eighteenth century were actually reaching the people. We have an accumulation, or simultaneous superposition of epochs — a phenomenon common to Spanish American in all centuries. It was now that the work of the precursors was starting to be felt. The fight was far from won, and if it was Miranda who had laid the ground work for the liberation, it took a younger man, a compatriot of his, to complete it.

SIMON BOLIVAR (1783-1830), the principal figure in the independence of Spanish America, was a Venezuelan of aristocratic family, who had many contacts with Spain and other European countries, where he obtained most of his ideas of independence. At the age of 23 he visited the United States, arriving in Boston from Hamburg in 1806. He visited Lexington, New York, Philadelphia, Washington and Charleston, trying everywhere to find help for his cause, but succeeding only to a minor degree. He returned to La Guayra about the middle of September, 1807.[41] As for his writings he was more of a politician than an author, and his Constitution and other publications, although written in a clear and vivid language, are not of strictly literary interest.

His ideas on the United States are of a mixed nature, for although he was a liberal he was at the same time quite conservative. He did not approve of a federal representative popular government such as that of the United States, because this system would require political talents and virtues superior to those possessed by the South Americans. For the same reason he disapproved of a monarchy, a mixture of aristocracy and democracy, such as England possessed. He wanted for South America something in between the governments of these two nations.[42] He had hoped to create a Federation of States composed of Bolivia, Perú and Colombia, more united than that of the United States and governed by a president, a vice-president and the Constitution of Bolivia.[43] His foreign policy was to consist of five main points:

1. A large army for defensive purposes.
2. Diplomacy with Europe as a safeguard against the first attacks.
3. Intimate alliance with England.
4. A similiar intimate alliance with the United States.

---

[40] *Gazeta de Caracas*, Wednesday, October 18, 1815, V, 324.
[41] Mancini, *Bolívar et l'emancipation des colonies espagnoles*, Paris, 1912, p. 158.
[42] Quoted in O'Leary, *Bolívar y la emancipación de Sur América*, I, 386.
[43] *Ibid.*, II, 584.

5. A congress of the governments of the American Republics at the Isthmus.[44]

Bolívar looked upon the United States as "the great adventure of man" that was to serve as the model for the old world. Within his relative liberalism he thought that "all of Europe would come to be free upon seeing the principles of America and upon seeing the effects that liberty will have upon the prosperity of the nations; and that the entire civilized world within one hundred years would be governed by philosophers, and there will exist no kings."[45]

Yet in spite of his great admiration for those institutions initiated in the United States Bolívar was determined that the new Spanish American states should have governments designed to suit their own needs. "If we want to consult monuments and models of legislature," he said, "Great Britain, France and North America have excellent ones"[46] but "our people are not those of Europe, nor those of North America."[47] "As long as our compatriots do not acquire the talents and virtues that distinguish our brothers of the North, entirely popular systems, far from being favorable for us, I fear will be our ruination."[48] And in a letter to O'Leary of September 1827, he says: "I believe that it would be better for America to adopt the Koran than the government of the United States although it is the best in the world."[49] Bolívar believed that Spanish America should consult the *Esprit des Lois* by Montesquieu rather than "that of Washington."[50] "Not the best way but the most accesible."[51] The truth of the matter is that Bolívar was surprised by the fact that the Federal Republican Government succeeded at all in North America. "It is amazing", he said, "that this model in North America should subsist so prosperously and should not become entangled at the appearance of the first obstacle or danger — although that nation is a rare model in political virtues and in moral examples — and granting the fact that liberty was its cradle, and that it was reared and nourished on freedom — I will say it all, although this nation is unique in the history of mankind — it is prodigious, I repeat, that a system so weak and complicated could have governed it through circumstances so difficult and delicate as the past ones."[52]

---

44 Quoted in Blanco Fombona, *Cartas de Bolívar 1823, 1824, 1825.* p. 297.

45 Quoted in Monsalve, *Ideal político del libertador Simón Bolívar*, Madrid, 1916, p. 495.

46 O'Leary, *op. cit.*, p. 610.

47 *Ibid.*, p. 598.

48 Simón Bolívar, "Contestación de un Americano meridional a un caballero de esta Isla." Blanco y Azpurúa, *Documentos*, V, 338.

49 Bolívar to O'Leary - Guayaquil, Sept. 13, 1829; in O'Leary, *Ultimos años de la vida pública de Bolívar*, pp. 576-577; also in Monsalve, *El ideal político del libertador Simón Bolívar*, p. 25.

50 Quoted in O'Leary, *Bolívar y la Emancipación de Sur América*, p. 595; also in Monsalve, *op. cit.*, p. 381.

51 Blanco y Azpurúa, *op. cit.* V, 339.

52 Quoted in O'Leary, *op.cit.*, p. 595.

Bolívar, like most of his contemporaries, had utopian dreams. His most famous, which has been somewhat distorted by Pan-Americanist historians, was that all Hispanic nations would unite in a confederation of states having for the location of its capital the Isthmus of Panama. He realized, however, that this would never take place, that the Spanish-speaking peoples would divide into many nations and that each one of these would suffer a different fate. In Kingston, Sept. 6, 1815 under the pseudonym of "A South American," Bolívar wrote an open letter, *Contestación de un americano meridional a un caballero de esta Isla,* in which he predicted the destiny of the different Spanish American nations that were to be. At the end of this prophecy he wrote his famous utopian discourse, which if read in its totality is quite clear and has no need for profound interpretations. It goes as follows:

> It is a grandiose idea to pretend to create of the entire New World one sole nation with one lone (organ) to unite all of its parts among themselves and to the whole. Since it has one origin, one language, one tradition and one religion, it should have therefore one sole government that would confederate the various states that might be formed. Yet this is not possible due to different climates, and the dissimilar characteristics that divide America. How beautiful it would be if the Isthmus of Panama were for us what that of Corinth was for the Greeks. Would that some day we might have the good fortune of installing a congress of representatives from the various republics, kingdoms and empires to deal with and discuss the high interests of peace and war with the nations of the other three parts of the world.[53]

According to O'Leary it was at Bolívar's suggestion that the first Pan-American Congress was held in Panama in 1826.[54] It was called for the purpose of obtaining security for the New States. If there were any ideological motives behind this move, it was a simple desire for Spanish American solidarity. (When Bolívar uses the pronoun "us" he invariably means Spanish America.) The United States was invited to send representatives, against what seemed to be the wishes of some of the Spanish American Republics, and Bolívar himself seemed to have some reservations.[55] He objected to having the assembly take place in Mexico, because it would be too much under the influence of this power "and that of the United States."[56] He was also concerned lest England should disapprove of the participation of the United States in this conference. There is no evidence to indicate that Bolívar thought of the United States as a member of the proposed league of nations. All facts tend to indicate that it was to

---

[53] Bolívar, "Contestación de un Americano..." *op. cit.,* V, 340.

[54] O'Leary, *op. cit.,* II, 621.

[55] Bolívar to General Tomás Hases, in Blanco Fombona, *Cartas de Bolívar 1823, 1824, 1825,* p. 335.

[56] O'Leary, *op. cit.,* II, 643.

[57] See letter quoted in Blanco Fombona, *op. cit.,* p. 301.

be a Spanish American unit, friendly toward the United States and under the patronage of England.[57]

This does not mean that Simón Bolívar, who, according to Henríquez Ureña, was the most brilliant and original of the liberators, was not fully aware of the significance of the United States. His generous and disinterested admiration for George Washington, with whom he often compared himself, is proof to the contrary. During the later years of his public life, when his republican compatriots were fearful that he would establish himself as a dictator, Bolívar reminds them of the political record of the first president of the United States. "In vain the example of Washington wants to defend men."[58] In a conversation with an Amerian naval officer concerning this same accusation he presented the question in the following manner: "They say that I want to establish an absolute government, placing myself at its head; but it is all false, and they do me great injustice. If my heart does not deceive me, it is more probable that I will follow the steps of Washington. I prefer to have a death like his than to be monarch of the entire world."[59] Another detail which reveals Bolívar's attitude toward our first great citizen, was the esteem with which he regarded the Washington medallion, containing a lock of his hair and bearing on its face a miniature portrait by Stuart. On the reverse side of the medallion there is engraved an inscription in Latin that says: "This portrait of the author of liberty in North America was donated by his adopted son to him who achieved equal glory in South America." The medallion appears in a number of Bolívar's portraits, and there are some Pan-Americanists who claim that "from the day that Bolívar received the medallion until his death he wore it constantly around his neck." That he regarded the jewel with great esteem is beyond doubt. In a letter to Lafayette, who was commissioned by George Washington Parke Custis to make the gift for the Washington family, Bolívar wrote: "By the public press I have learned with inexplicable joy that you have had the goodness to honor me with a treasure from Mount Vernon — the portrait of Washington, some of his venerable relics, and one of the monuments of his glory, which are to be presented to me at your hands in the name of the brothers of the Great citizen, the First-Born Son of the New World. No words can set forth all the value that this gift and its embodying considerations. so glorious for me, hold in my heart. The family of Washington honors me beyond my hopes, even the most imaginative: for Washington presented by Lafayette is the crown of all human recompense. He was the noble protector of social reforms, and you were the citizen hero, the athlete of liberty, who with one hand served America and with the other, the old continent. Ah, what mortal would be worthy of

---

[58] Letter, Caracas, Feb. 6, 1827; in O'Leary, *Ultimos años de la vida pública de Bolívar*, p. 164.

[59] Quoted in Monsalve, *op. cit.*, p. **494**.

the honors which you and Mount Vernon have seen fit to heap upon me."[60]

Bolívar was severely criticized because of his conservative ideas by most of the contemporary North Americans who knew him. It should be said in his behalf that these men were often prejudiced and not always fully acquainted with existing conditions in Spanish America. Martin Van Buren, more objective and understanding than some of the others, wrote near the end of 1829:

> Public opinion will not require from the Liberator. . .more than the actual conditions of his country will allow. It is well known that circumstances, which are the result of centuries, cannot be overcome in an hour. The world will, therefore, give him full credit for advising. . .the establishment of institutions as liberal as existing circumstances will permit.[61]

SIMON RODRIGUEZ, the teacher of Simón Bolívar,—from whom the "Libertador" got most of his ideas—in his essay "El Libertador del Mediodía" explained the relativity of the parallel that existed between Bolívar and Washington. Unlike most of his compatriots, Rodríguez does not give much importance to the form or type of government in itself. He saw the United States not only as a country with a Republican form of government, but also as a democratic civilization, a philosophy of life, so to speak. "The ground in the United States is softened with ideas of freedom." He finds that what is really important is not so much the institution itself as the psychology of the people. He feared that Spanish American publicists were wasting their time with their propaganda in favor of this nation, because what they were importing was the form and not the spirit, which was more important.

In the United States the President was not an exception, "he was the common product of the land," and he was called by his name and not by his title.[62]

In his opinion Washington, too, was a product of his medium in the same manner that Bonaparte was of France and Bolívar of Spanish America. A comparison between these three men would have been impossible because they do not meet on a common ground. The scene of their actions was entirely different, and they as individuals were as far apart as were the civilizations of the nations they represented. What he was certain of was that any one of these three men could have been outstanding had he found himself in the circumstances of the other.[63]

This judicious analysis did not stop contemporaries from making com-

---

[60] Quoted in *Memorias del General O'Leary: Cartas del Libertador*, XXX, 187-188.

[61] Quoted by Rippy, "Bolívar as viewed by contemporary diplomats of the United States," *The Hispanic American Historical Review*, XV, 1935, 287-297.

[62]. Simón Rodríguez, "El Libertador del Mediodía," in Lozano y Lozano, *El maestro del libertador*, Paris, n.d., pp. 262-266.

[63] *Ibid.*, pp. 133-134.

parisons between the two men. The subject has been a favorite topic of Spanish American writers ever since, and today the banner has been picked up once again with unparalleled fervor by our fellow Pan-Americanists.

Typical of the times was a meeting celebrated by the patriots of Caracas on January 2, 1814, during which Domingo Alzuru said referring to Bolívar: "We are more fortunate than that other Republic, Rome, because we have a hero, whose name shall be engraved in all the nations of the Universe along with that of Washington..."[64]

In the meantime, those Spanish Americans who had taken refuge in the United States had the rare privilege of observing the great republic go through one of the most important periods of its formation. Fortunately for us, what they saw and thought is recorded in numerous pamphlets that found their way into the remotest corners of Spanish America.

Of all these men, VICENTE ROCAFUERTE (1783-1847), one-time President of Ecuador, was perhaps the most persistent admirer of the United States. He was born in Guayaquil, and educated in Europe. Upon coming to the United States in 1820 he was impressed with its political system, and decided to spread the knowledge of American ideas throughout Spanish America. Like many others sharing this point of view, he lived and wrote in Philadelphia. He made translations of various political writings among which can be mentioned: Thomas Paine's Common Sense,[65] a dissertation on the primary principle of government,[66] a sketch of the constitution of the United States,[67] a speech of Thomas Jefferson,[68] "Washington's Farewell Address,"[69] a speech of John Quincy Adams,[70] and "The articles of the confederation and constitution of the United States."[71] He is also the author of numerous original pamphlets on political subjects. His primary aim was to attain clearness and give emphasis to his ideas. These are not numerous and he repeats them over and over again.

His opportunity as a man of state came late. In 1835, long after the vogue enjoyed by the United States was over, Rocafuerte was elected president of Ecuador. He immediately set to work with incredible energy. He promoted a new system of public education; reorganized the administration

64 "Acta popular celebrada en Caracas el día 2 de Enero de 1814," in Blanco y Azpurúa, Documentos, V, 51.

65 "El sentido común," in Rocafuerte, Ideas necesarias a todo pueblo americano que quiera ser libre, pp. 23-51; also in Ensayo político, pp. 39-57.

66 Thomas Paine, "Disertación sobre los principos del gobierno," in Rocafuerte, Ideas necesarias a todo pueblo ..., pp. 52-92; also in Ensayo político, pp. 57-82.

67 "Bosquejos de la Constitución," Ensayo político, pp. 82-133.

68 "Discurso del Presidente Thomas Jefferson", Ensayo político, pp. 189-197.

69 "Discurso de despedida de Washington," Ensayo político, pp. 202-222.

70 "Discurso" [Pronunciado en el capitolio de Washington el día 4 de julio de 1821, en conmemoración de la primera declaración de la augusta independencia americana,

71 "Artículos de Confederación de los Estados Unidos." in Ibid., pp. 139-194.

Philadelphia 4 de julio, 1776] Rocafuerte, Ideas necesarias a todo pueblo ... pp. 93-138.

of the nation; fomented industry and commerce; protected the Indians from exploitation by the upper classes; and guaranteed religious liberty. His liberal aims were misinterpreted by the average citizen of his country. He was accused of wanting to introduce Protestantism, and in 1839 was replaced by his rival, the conservative Flores, who in a short time destroyed most of Rocafuerte's progressive reforms.

His views are unusual considering his European educational background. In the introduction to his pamphlet, *Ideas necesarias a todo pueblo que quiera ser libre,* he explains the purpose of this work, which by the way would hold true for all his other publications as well.

> I shall have accomplished my purpose, if this small work, which has no value as a literary production, contributes to acquaint us with the spirit of liberty and tolerance which are the result of the enlightened opinions of the heroes and great men of North America. Let us follow their tracks, and soon we shall have established among us peace, abundance, industry, the sciences and arts.[72]

Indeed, the idea of the United States as a model is present in every one of his pamphlets. In the *Ensayo político* he tells us of "The disadvantages of the monarchies, and of the great utility of the popular representative system as it exists in the city of Washington."[73] But he warns against the weakness of the Federal System. "The United States, that land of liberty..., education..., and the rights of man was exposed to great danger during the last war with the English, not because they lacked resources, nor love of country, nor bravery, but because this system produces natural weakness in the action of the government."[74] The Spanish American countries should work for greater unity within their governments. Decentralization, in Rocafuerte's opinion, is the only weakness of the American system, otherwise possessing utopian perfection.[75] "The American constitution is superior to the English."[76] "The only hope for the suppressed people." And it should be imitated by all America. "If we succeed in putting it into execution, with internal peace and enjoying prestige in foreign countries, having opened the channels of industry and commerce, and propagated public education, perhaps we might after some years imitate more closely our brothers from the North by establishing the Federal System, which up to now has offered many difficulties."[77] The model to be followed according to Rocafuerte was "the sublime institutions left us by Franklin, Hancock, Hamilton and those other great men, whose wisdom is admired and will

---

[72] *Ibid.,* p. 20.
[73] Rocafuerte, *Ensayo político,* p. 7.
[74] *Ibid.,* p. 181.
[75] *Ibid.,* p. 172.
[76] *Ibid.,* p. 37.
[77] *Loc. cit.*

continue to be admired always by the entire world."[78] Rocafuerte advises Spanish Americans to control their passions, to overcome their mania for government employment, to put the interest of the nation before their own, to foment education as a means of overcoming despotism, servility, and superstition. If these aims were accomplished, then there would bloom on Spanish American soil "the delicate plant of liberty, which is only found by the shade of the laurels and cypress trees that cover the tomb of the immortal Washington."[79]

Rocafuerte is the first conscious exponent of the idea of continental solidarity. The heroes of America should be common to the entire new world. "How lively will beat the heart of every generous American upon seeing the sublime association of the name of Bolívar with that of Columbus and Washington."[80] The true creed to be followed is to be found in the works of Paine, in Jefferson's *Inaugural Address,* in the speech of Bolívar on taking the oath under the constitution of Cúcuta, and in Washington's *Farewell Address.* European models such as Rousseau, Montesquieu, Benjamin Constant and de Pradt, which were at that time very popular among some Spanish Americans, were to be discarded.[81] "Let us dismiss the sinister system of Machiavelli, and follow only the maxim of the great Franklin—honesty is the best policy."[82] Rocafuerte is particularly bitter against those European authors who had anti-American inclinations. Of Mably he said:

> When I see that famous Mably, that illustrious defender of liberty, write recommending aristocracy and salon politics: false prophet that he is — prognosticating the short duration of the new-born government of the United States; I cannot help but feel sorry for the weakness of human nature, the very error of talent itself, and the enthusiasm with which men of genius look upon antiquity with all its defects. I am not surprised then that many respectable Americans of merit and virtue should be in favor of the absurd system of the monarchies, and should be followers of the Bourbons in good faith. Far from pursuing and tormenting them, it is necessary, as Jefferson says, to protect them, it is necessary, to bring them closer. and to allow them to live peacefully among us, so that they may serve as irrefutable proof.[83]

George Washington is, in his opinion, the very epitome of human perfection. The name is to him "synonymous of great virtue and patriotism." He speaks of Washington as being "the glory of the human race, the hero of all centuries, the true great hero of impartial history: he was as prudent

---

[78] Rocafuerte, *Ideas necesarias a todo pueblo que quiera ser libre,* p. 10.
[79] *Loc. cit.*
[80] *Ensayo político,* p. 7
[81] *Ibid.,* p. 37.
[82] *Ibid.,* p. 35.
[83] *Ibid.,* pp. 34-35.

as Fabius, as active as Marcellus, as unselfish as Cincinnatus, more sublime than Caesar,..."[84]

Rocafuerte was very favorably impressed with the American cities. He calls Philadelphia "the city of liberty," "asylum for the oppressed."[85] Yet he found New York more important and modern. In one of his letters, written upon his arrival in the city, he gives us an excellent description of what he saw:

New York, 31 of June 1821.

Beloved Friend: I arrived happily to this city, although somewhat tired from the trip and from the rough going of the stage coach.

New York is up to now the best city that I have seen in the United States, I like it better than Philadelphia or Baltimore, it has an air of opulence, a certain elegance, luxury and life of a metropolis which pleases me very much, it gives me the impression of being in one of those beautiful sections of London.

I have seen the famous government house known as City Hall. As a work of architecture it has a great reputation here, but as such I do not find it to have any merit at all. What I have found to be original and worthy of our attention, is that they have represented the statue of justice, which is placed at the very top of the dome, with the scales on the right hand, the sword on the left, and without a blindfold, while in Europe all the statues of justice are blindfolded. This is a very subtle allegory. In America, justice has beautiful eyes, and it is guided by the light of heaven, it does not need any other aid than that which comes from liberty and reason, but since in Europe justice is blind, despotism and superstition, are her guides. They guide her at their will, and the edge of her sword falls upon the innocent, on him who tries to remove the bandage to cure her of her blindness.

Tomorrow I shall go to Saratoga Springs and I shall talk extensively with Chaves.

With my friend Thomas, an enthusiastic young man, I am sending you the best pair of suspenders that I was able to find in the city.

Give my regards to Dr. Manuel Torres, also to Carlota and her sister, and you don't forget your affectionate friend q. l. M : B

(Signed)
Victe Rocafuerte[86]

He sees the United States as the frontier of the world. Here everything is new and better than in the mother countries. The natural sciences and the industrial revolution which, according to him, in Europe had caused confusion and darkness, upon crossing the Atlantic were purified and "have

---

84 *Ibid.*, p. 201.

85 *Ideas necesarias a todo pueblo que quiera ser libre*, p. 3.

86 Rocafuerte to Mier, New York, July 31, 1821; Ms. in the García Archives, University of Texas.

given to America as a result, that pure, clear and brilliant spirit of philosophy, which the Europeans will never be able to obtain as long as the Holy
Alliance continues to exist." He wants the Spanish Americans to become
Protestants. He attributes the greatness of the United States to its religious
principles. He quotes John Quincy Adams to the effect: "that it (the adop-
tion of Protestantism) is the greatest step forward that man ever took in
the history of civilization." "Even greater than the discovery of the printing
press."[87] His passion for being modern is not limited to the spiritual and
ideological. He also wants to change conventional things of a much more
material nature. He says that a legislator bent on improving the costumes
of his country should prohibit the use of the traditional shawl and skirt,
and oblige all women to walk in the streets with their faces uncovered,
dressed with the decorum, decency, and modesty which characterizes the
fair sex in the United States.[88] Due to his ideas on religion it is not surprising that Rocafuerte did not last long as the President of Ecuador, as
Spanish Americans were then, and still are, very attached to their traditional
habits and stout defenders of their religion.

For Rocafuerte the Protestant religion and being modern went hand in
hand. In his *Ensayo sobre la tolerancia religiosa* he says that with Protestantism there will come the reform of social manners, the abolition of beg-
gary, the establishment of foreign colonies, the development of agriculture
and commerce, the progress of industry, and the general increase of the
population.[89] As we shall see in the next chapter, Rocafuerte's ideas, although not accepted by the majority of the South American people, had a
marked influence on a small group of progressives, especially in Mexico.
His pamphlet was condemned by the church and by some of the leading
literary men of the day, including the historian and statesman Alamán. An
account of the polemic which took place after its publication is given in
the second edition of this pamphlet under the section called "Defensa."[90]

Modernization and Americanization are likewise synonymous to Rocafuerte, and Spanish America had to be modernized. He knew, as did Sarmiento later on, that education had an important part to play in this process.
Texts were needed for the simple instruction of reading and writing and
what could be better than the Bible for such a task? With this purpose in
mind, and having the Scriptures as the main foundation for its text, he
published in New York, in 1823, *Lecciones para las escuelas de primeras
letras*. In its introduction he tells us that he hopes that this text will "give
birth to new virtues unknown among the slaves, such as love of country,
love of liberty, love of justice, and love of laws. These are the true prin-

---

87 *Ensayo político*, pp. 30-31.
88 *Ibid.*, p. 10
89 Rocafuerte *Ensayo sobre la tolerancia religiosa* (second ed., Mexico, 1831), p. 85.
90 "Defensa," *Ibid.*, p. 109.

ciples which must be engraved on the tender souls of the children who are forming our new generation."[91]

The most practical and realistic of all the arguments he presents in the defense of the United States is that in which he justifies the republican form of government from the point of view of economics. Here he compares the expenses necessary to run a monarchy with those of a republic, and comes to the conclusion that the economy of the American government is infinitely superior.

Besides the works already mentioned Rocafuerte wrote: *El sistema colombiano es el que más conviene a la América Independiente* (New York, 1823), and *Breve relación de las Indias* (n.d., n.p.). In these works he repeats the ideas already mentioned, at times verbatim, and includes translations such as that of Paine's *Common Sense* which appears in his other publications.

Rocafuerte's associate, JOSE SERVANDO TERESA DE MIER (1765-1827), a bigger and better known man, shares many of his companion's points of view. So much so, in fact, that at times it is difficult to determine the authorship of their respective writings. This is the case with the *Memoria político-instructiva* (Philadelphia, 1821), and with *La revolución de México* (Philadelphia, 1822). The first of these, generally listed in our libraries under Rocafuerte, according to the critics Bustamante and Lockey, who have studied its authorship, really belongs to Mier.[92]

The Mexican friar, Mier, is more representative of the views and ideas existing in Spanish America during the period of Independence. He was a Dominican who was exiled to Spain in 1794 because of a sermon he had delivered on the day of the Virgin of Guadalupe. He remained there for seven years, escaped and went to Paris where he met Simón Rodríguez, the teacher of Bolívar. From there he went to Rome (1802) where he translated *Atala*. In 1809, he returned to Spain to fight against Napoleon. We later find him in London, where he published his *Cartas de un americano* (1812-1813). In 1816 he came to the United States and participated in Mina's expedition, of which he was one of the leaders. In Mexico he was taken prisoner by the Spaniards in 1820. Upon his escape in 1821, he again came to the United States and remained in Philadelphia, until Mexico was declared independent. Julio Cejador y Frauca describes him as the most aggressive, rebellious, and restless Creole of his epoch, who was in no way handicapped by his religious cloak.[93]

---

[91] Rocafuerte, "A la juventud americana," *Lecciones para las escuelas de primeras letras, sacadas de las Sagradas Escrituras, siguiendo el texto literal de la traducción del Padre Scio, sin notas ni comentarios,* p. ii:.

[92] Bustamante, *Historia del Emperador Iturbide,* p. 201; also in Lockey, *Pan-Americanism: Its Beginnings,* New York, 1920.

[93] Julio Cejador y Frauca, *Historia de la lengua y literatura castellana,* VI 363. Concerning Mier's life see: *The Hispanic American Historical Review,* XII, 359-361.

Primarily a writer and propagandist—his books although autobiographical read like fiction—he is better known because of the part he played in Mina's expedition. During his stay in London, at that time a center for the activities of the Spanish American rebels as important as Philadelphia, Mier surrounded himself with Spanish Americans and individuals of other origins with whom he had a common interest. Among these was Francisco Mina, over whom Mier had considerable influence. It was Mier who induced him to lead the expedition to liberate Mexico. Together they sailed for the United States. They arrived in Baltimore and immediately set to work, but things there proved to be more complex than they had anticipated. American official aid was not to be had, and private citizens were not ready to support an expedition that, as it proved later on, was to be a failure. American adventurers who were willing to join the expedition and suffer with it a common fate were numerous enough, but capital was much more elusive and difficult to obtain. Mier was finally able to secure a hundred and twenty thousand dollars from Daniel Smith, which was to pay the costs of the expedition. They spent that winter on the island of Galveston and the following Spring continued to Mexico. They were defeated, and Mier was taken prisoner and placed in the custody of the Inquisition. After this he changed plans. The failure of the expedition proved to him that the independence of Spanish America would have to be won from inside, that a small punitive force could never hope to succeed unless the minds of the people of those countries were ripe for the political movement. Spanish America had to be educated along ideological lines. Propaganda was needed in which the United States would serve as a model and it was with this purpose in mind that he started to compose his *Memorias.* In 1821 he was ordered to Spain. When he arrived at Havana he escaped and made his way to Philadelphia where his friends were waiting for him. He had known Manuel Torres since his first trip in 1816. There was also Rocafuerte and soon they were to be joined by others: Alvarez de Toledo, Chaves, Vicente Pazos, Salazar, Palacio Fajardo, and Vidaurre. Many of these men were experienced pamphleteers. Torres had been doing it for years. Immediately after his arrival he started to write his *Memoria político-instructiva* which he published in Philadelphia, 1821. He also wrote "Puede ser libre la Nueva España,"[94] arguing for the cooperation of the United States in securing the independence of Spanish America.

The ideas expressed in Mier's works, with the exception of those referring to religion, are the same as Rocafuerte's, but Mier is not satisfied with using the United States as a model. He goes further. He sees the danger that a monarchical country within the hemisphere would represent to the other nations. With reference to Mexico, at that time a monarchy under

---

[94] "Puede ser libre la Nueva España," autograph draft F 117, The Mier Archives, University of Texas.

the Emperor Iturbide, he warns his countrymen that if the ruler of Mexico should become more powerful, influenced by his European ties he would try to defeat the Republic of the United States. "Europe, jealous of its great growth and being a natural enemy of all republics, would offer her cooperation." "I can assure you that the Anglo-Americans would have in their favor our South America, all of which is republican. No, the latter also would not allow us to have monarchy and they would fall upon us to prevent their own danger." The only solution is "to complete in both Americas a general system of republics ... This is the only way that will permit us all to prosper in peace and with the rapidity of the United States."[95]

Mier even plays with the idea of annexation. He claims that Spain, wanting to stop the Anglo-Americans, had contemplated giving the Californias to Russia. "As if it were a lesser evil for us to be given to the barbarous slaves of a despot than to our compatriots of the United States who only make confederations adding another star to the flag of liberty, allowing each new state to be independent and sovereign and to govern itself according to its religion and to its own laws."[96] In the "Carta de un patriota sobre la cesión de las Floridas"[97] he congratulates this region for its good fortune. Mier says that in this manner "the Floridas have obtained their liberty; today they are part of the United States, and although sold, they are released from the humiliating servitude in which they have been held by the mother country. But what will be the fate of our other regions that might be bought by nations of a different nature? Theirs will differ from that of the Floridas in the same manner that the fate of a slave who is bought by a friend in order to be set free differs from that of another who is bought by an enemy to be served by him retaining his condition of slave."[98]

Among the men of letters who participated in Mina's expedition we should also mention JOSE ALVAREZ DE TOLEDO, an old fried of Manuel Torres' and Mier's who at one time had represented Santo Domingo at the Spanish Cortes. Believing, as did many other Spanish liberals of that day, that the independence of Spanish America was inevitable, he had left Spain and arrived in the United States in 1811. Here he at once started to work, at first, for the independence of Cuba and later for that of Mexico. In Philadelphia, 1812, he published a pamphlet, *Manifiesto o satisfacción pundorosa a todos los buenos Españoles de Europa y a todos los pueblos de América, por un diputado de las Cortes reunidas en Cádiz*, addressed to the liberals of Spanish America as well as those of Spain, advising them to embrace the principles of liberty and democracy represented by this

---

95 Mier, *Memoria político-instructiva*, p. 45.

96 *Ibid.*, pp. 104-110.

97 There are at least two editions of *Memoria político-instructiva*, both published in Philadelphia, one in 1821 and the other in 1822. In the first ed. the "Carta" is on p. 119; in the second on p. 144.

98 *Loc. cit.*

country.[99] A complex personality not to be judged hastily, he eventually became an agent in the service of Luis de Onís and the Spanish government.

As we have already stated, the Spanish American insurgents working from Philadelphia were also concerned with public opinion in the United States. There were those who wrote propaganda in both languages, Spanish and English, some of them possessing considerable talent, as for instance VICENTE PAZOS (1780-1851?), an Indian of Aymara race, native of La Paz, Bolivia, who had taken an important part in the revolution of his country and in Buenos Aires.[100] His life reads like a novel of adventure. He collaborated on the *Gaceta de Buenos Aires* during the time of Mariano Moreno, and after the latter's death, on *El Censor*. Due to his ideas, he was forced to flee to England in 1812. He returned in 1816 with a printing press, and published two liberal reviews: *La Crónica Argentina*, edited by himself, and the *Observador Americano* edited by Juan Antonio Castro.[101] He was exiled by Pueyrredón, and came to the United States. During his stay here he wrote articles for the newspapers and two manifestos addressed to the Congress of the United States protesting against the hostile attitude displayed by the American government toward the insurgents.[102] He visited Portugal and Spain, and much to his surprise—prior to this he had been rabidly anti-Spanish—he enjoyed this latter country very much. In Paris he published his history of the United States, *Compendio de la historia de los Estados Unidos de América: puestos en castellano por un Indio de la Ciudad de la Paz*. He lived in England from 1825 to 1850, where he published the *Memorias histórico-políticas de don Vicente Pazos* (London, 1834). He finally returned to Buenos Aires and founded the review *Diario de Avisos* in 1851.

As to the future of America, he cannot conjecture what the political situation of these great countries will be, as every day they present a different aspect. "But the history of the United States teaches the consoling truth, that civil and religious liberty has transformed her trackless forests, which were once the habitation of savages and wild beasts into the garden of the world, where cities have sprung up; manufacturing, art, sciences, and commerce flourish; and where a system of legislation has been established,

---

[99] It is probable that Alvarez de Toledo is the author of a number of other pamphlets. James F. Shearer says that he published one in Charleston, 1812 entitled *Objeciones satisfactorias del mundo imparcial al folleto dado a luz por el Marte filósofo de Delaware, Don José Alvarez de Toledo*. "French and Spanish works printed in Charleston, South Carolina," *Papers of the Bibliographical Society of America*, XXXIV, 1940, 162.

[100] Griffin, *The United States and the disruption of the Spanish Empire*, p. 123.

[101] Otero, "Prólogo," *Mercurio Histórico Político*.

[102] Vicente Pazos, *Letters on the United provinces of South America, Addressed to the Hon. Henry Clay . . .* (New York, 1819). Translated by P. H. Crosby; *The exposition, remonstrance and protest of Don Vicente Pazos, Commissioner on behalf of the republican agents established at Amelia island, in Florida under the authority of the independent States of South America; with an appendix*. Presented to the executive of the United States on the 19th of February 1818. Trans. from the Spanish . . . Philadelphia 1818.

which Solon and Lycurgus never imagined,..." According to Pazos, the same will happen to Spanish Americans when they follow the enlightened institutions of their brethren from the North.[103]

He is of the opinion that "the practical lesson afforded by the United States leaves no doubt that religious liberty and rivalry of different sects is the best means of maintaining in their purity the morals of the people."[104] The United States is better prepared than Spanish America for liberty, because here education is brought within the reach of all classes. Newspapers are widely diffused and the people are easily and universally instructed in the political sciences; while in Spanish America the process of public education is slow and tedious.[105]

Pazos praises the natural, unaffected manner of the American people. He says that the citizens of this country were accustomed to seeing their supreme chief treated as an ordinary gentleman, without any particular marks of distinction or ceremony. This behavior was in direct contrast to the honors which were paid to the presidents of some of the Spanish American "juntas" such as Posadas and Pueyrredón.[106] Mariano Moreno lost the favor of the "Junta de Buenos Aires" for expressing these same ideas.

He wants the two Americas to cooperate. "It is here in the Americas that the people, strong in their principles and rich in resources, and displaying humanity and justice, constancy and courage, should erect a formidable barrier against the encroachment of the European tyranny."[107].

MANUEL PALACIO FAJARDO (1784-1819) is also one of those who wrote in English. A Venezuelan, he took part in the revolution of 1810, and when the liberals were defeated he was forced to flee his native land. In 1812 he arrived in Washington, where he sought but did not obtain recognition for his country. He was received by President Madison, who is reported to have preserved a glacial reserve during the interview. In order to create interest in the Spanish American cause, he wrote *An Outline of the Revolution in Spanish America,* an almost personal account of the revolution, full of color and interesting details. The book was intended for the North American public, at the same time Palacio expressed in it opinions concerning the United States that would be of greater interest to a Spanish American. He speaks of the liberality of Congress and shows the effects of the example of this nation on the Venezuela of 1810. He points out that when the plan of the constitution was formed by F. X. Ustariz, he and many others of the greatest respectability had intimated from the first the opinion that, in case of a final separation from Spain, the best

---

103 *Ibid.,* pp. 123-124.
104 *Ibid.,* p. 84.
105 *Ibid.,* p. 121.
106 *Loc. cit.*
107 *Ibid.,* p. 242.

form of government to be established in Venezuela was a federal one, of which the United States offered an excellent example. The idea that the United States should be used as a model for the Spanish American governments appears repeatedly throughout the book.

Surprisingly enough the majority of the men who belonged to this small group of persons interested in the United States came from countries north of the equator: Mexico, Colombia, Venezuela, and the Caribbean region. Argentina and Perú seem to have maintained closer associations with Europe. Chile, in a way, was an exception, and this was due to a great degree to Poinsett's influence in that country.

Perú was the most conservative of the Spanish colonies and the one least likely to be inspired by the independence of the United States, but even there its influence was felt. In 1810 MANUEL LORENZO DE VIDAURRE (1773-1841) pointed out the grave defects of the Spanish colonial system, and offered a plan of reform without leaving the monarchical structure. Twelve years later this same man visited the United States and came under the influence of Rocafuerte. Belaúnde says that he became as enthusiastic as the latter in his admiration for American institutions. "In his *Cartas Americanas* he criticizes the English government. In his speeches in Trujillo, 1824, he repeated the comparison of the English and American governments, conceding the superiority to the American because of the organization of the executive and judicial powers."[108]

In the region of the Río de la Plata, the authors often manifest an attitude of friendliness toward this country, but it never goes beyond that. They seldom express ideas. MANUEL BELGRANO (1770-1820), the famous Argentine general of the Independence, in the introduction to his translation of Washington's *Farewell Address*, speaks of Washington as "that hero worthy of the admiration of our times and of future generations, example of moderation and loyal patriotism." He wishes that his countrymen would read the address and capture some of its spirit. "Let us imitate the great men," he said, "and in this manner we shall finally obtain our objective of being a free and independent nation."[109] JOSE ARTIGAS, the warrior of Uruguay, carried on an extensive correspondence with President Monroe[110] and pointed out to his compatriots the example of the United States.[111] José de San Martín, the liberator of Argentina, praised this nation but warned against the Federal system.[112] Mariano Moreno in the *Gaceta*

---

108 Belaúnde, *Bolívar and the political thought of the Spanish American revolution,* p. 30.

109 Manuel Belgrano, "Introducción", *Despedida de Washington al pueblo de los Estados Unidos* (1813).

110 Artigas to Monroe, Purificación, Sept. 1, 1817; in Chandler, *Inter-American acquaintances,* p. 67.

111 Eduardo Acevedo, *José Artigas, su obra cívica,* Montevideo, 1909, p. 15.

112 San Martín to Godoy Cruz, first part of 1816; Acevedo, *op. cit,* p. 91.

de Buenos Aires wrote concerning Jefferson's *Notes on Virginia*,[113] and in his *Doctrina democrática* expressed ideas parallel to those current in the United States.[114]

These writers could be classified as moderate liberals. The tone of the *Gaceta de Buenos Aires* was relatively conservative. Even while Moreno was the editor, articles condemning the excesses of the French Revolution or showing distrust of North American institutions were often published. It is interesting to note that John Quincy Adams, speaking to one of the envoys from Argentina, expressed the opinion that Artigas seemed to him the only republican in those parts.[115] Too much weight should not be attached to this statement. Adams was fair, but in most cases—as far as Spanish America is concerned—a stern critic. We should be nearer the truth if we said that there were republicans, but that they were of the European rather than the American type. During the later years of his life Rivadavia saw this very clearly. Bartolomé Mitre, who knew the great liberal statesman intimately, says that in 1823, when Rivadavia was in exile in Paris, he read Tocqueville's *Democracy in America*. For the first time he was able to conceive a system of government suitable for free people. Rivadavia told his companions, with his accustomed modesty, "we have to confess that we were completely ignorant when we attempted the republican form of government in our country." Rivadavia made a Spanish translation of Tocqueville's book, which still exists in manuscript form.[116]

Representative of the conservative point of view in Argentina is PEDRO VICENTE CAÑETE, Assessor of Potosí, with whom Vicente Pazos had heated discussions on political matters.[117] He believed that Spanish America was incapable of creating an original form of government, "as projected by the followers of Philadelphia," and predicted civil wars that would bleed the land white. He feared that, weakened by internal strife, these countries would fall an easy prey to Europe or to North America. "Either one or the other would easily take possession of their governments and their numerous properties."[118]

In Chile, on the other hand, contacts had been of a much closer nature. In 1811 there arrived in that country Joel Roberts Poinsett, our first agent there. Before long he had become a close friend of José Miguel Carrera, Manuel de Salas, Camilo Henríquez and the other leading liberals. He

---

[113] M. Moreno, "Jefferson, Notes on Virginia", *Biblioteca Argentina*, I, 276.

[114] "Doctrina democrática", *Biblioteca Argentina*, I, 231-237.

[115] John W. White, "Uruguay, Bulwark of Pan Americanism," *The Inter-American Monthly*, Nov. 13, 1942.

[116] Bartolomé Mitre, *Oración*, La Plata, 1945, p. 34.

[117] Gustavo Adolfo Otero, "Prólogo," Vicente Pazos, *Memorias histórico-políticas*, London, 1834, p. xiii.

[118] Dr. D. Pedro Vicente Cañete, *Gaceta Extraordinaria de Buenos Aires*, martes 3 de julio de 1810, pp. 4-5.

collaborated with them in preparing the constitution of Chile, 1812. With this purpose in mind he wrote the "Código Constitucional de las Provincias Unidas de Chile," which was one of the documents used by the Chileans as a model upon this occasion. It was at Poinsett's suggestion that Carrera came to the United States trying to obtain aid for his country. Poinsett was followed in 1818 by Mr. William Worthington, Special Agent from the United States. During the time of O'Higgins, Worthington wrote the "Constitution of the State of Chile" which, as in the case of the one written by his predecessor, was consulted when they wrote Chile's constitution of 1823. Also in 1818, Jeremias Robinson came to this country. Through him the scholarly Salas became acquainted with the leading scientists of the United States and was elected to several North American honorary societies.

Of the three Chileans mentioned above, the most eloquent apologist of the United States was CAMILO HENRIQUEZ (1769-1845), often known by the pen-name of Horacio Cayo. A friar—eager for new ideas and an idealistic admirer of this nation—he directed the policies of the three leading revolutionary newspapers: *Aurora de Chile, Semanario Republicano,* and *Monitor Araucano.*[119] On the anniversary of the independence of the United States, 1812, he published an editorial in *La Aurora* that was received with great enthusiasm by the liberals throughout the continent. This eulogistic discourse, entitled *Ejemplo Memorable,* started by telling about the War of Independence between the United States and England, quoted at length from Thomas Paine's *Common Sense,* and concluded by presenting this nation to the Spanish Americans as the model they should follow in the future.[120] Henríquez translated the national anthem (*Hail Great Republic of the World*) and several speeches given by eminent North Americans. He also wrote poems expressing the great Pan-American ideal of liberty and fraternity. Palomeque attributes to him the following verse:

> Toward the strong south the illustrous fatherland of Washington extends its arms. The entire New World unites in an eternal confederation.[121]

His ideas about the United States are not based upon first hand information, yet he knew this country better than any other man in his section of the continent. His numerous translations and articles are documented with innumerable details. Like many of his contemporaries, he looked upon the United States as the model to be followed, but feared the weakness of the federal government.[122] He believed that the freedom of the press was

---

119 Concerning Camilo Henríquez's life see: Amunátegui, *Camilo Henríquez,* Santiago, 1911.

120 "Ejemplo memorable," *Aurora de Chile,* no. 17, June 4, 1812; also in Collier and Cruz, *La primera misión de los Estados Unidos de América en Chile,* pp. 66-69.

121 Palomeque, *Orígenes de la diplomacia Argentina,* Buenos Aires, 1905, pp. 74-75.

122 Horacio Cayo, "Semanario Republicano," no. 3, Nov. 13, 1813, *Colección de historiadores y documentos relativos a la independencia de Chile,* XXIV, 137.

the basis for all the other liberties. "The newspapers in the United States have published bitter statements against James Madison, the President of those United States." "But the fact is ... that there is hardly a favorable measure adopted by the government that was not first suggested by some writer."[123] His ideal man was George Washington.

3. Literary Men

Of all the Spanish American authors who wrote about the United States during this period, JOSÉ MARIA DE HEREDIA (1803-1839) is the one who comes closest to being a purely literary figure. Born in Cuba, he spent part of his childhood in Santo Domingo and Venezuela. In 1820 he went to study law at the University of Mexico, where he wrote some of his best poems including the Odas. He returned to Cuba and completed his studies of law at the University of Havana in 1821. Shortly after this he was accused of plotting against the Spanish Government and was forced to flee to the United States. During his stay here, first in Boston and later in New York (1823-1825), he eked out a miserable existence by writing and by giving private lessons in Spanish. Heredia's experience was most unhappy. He could not get used to the cold weather and the English language sounded harsh and barbaric to him. "I do not understand how so great a people has come to use so execrable a jargon."[124] While in the United States he composed the well-known poem Oda al Niágara, one of the finest in Spanish American literature. On the whole, he liked the United States and showed an appreciation of the significance of the little things as typifying differences in civilization and culture. For example his explanation as to why in the United States they use blunt-pointed knives: "Here one may kill a man with his fists without fear of punishment; but they hang without fail one who attacks another with a pointed knife. Thus it is that here table knives have round ends so as to avoid trouble."[125] Heredia knew that to understand a people and its civilization much depends upon the details which, although seemingly unimportant, have a definite moral basis. His letters on the United States, Cartas sobre los Estados Unidos, were first published in 1826 in the Cuban review El Iris, and later in La

---

123 The Aurora de Chile (reprinted, Santiago, 1903) devoted much space to translations of Washington, Jefferson and Madison. The Monitor Araucano (no. 45, July 20, 1813, reprinted in Colección de historiadores y documentos relativos a la independencia de Chile, XXIV, 300-309) gave news about the present war between the United States and Great Britain. It also published a selection taken from a speech given by James Madison. The Semanario Republicano (no. 1, Oct. 30, 1813, in Ibid. XXIV, 113-115) printed numerous articles concerning the United States, including a claim made by the State of Massachusetts against Congress and a translation of a speech given before the Senate, on June 15, 1814, by Timoteo Bigelow.

124 Quoted in E. C. Hills, The Odes of Bello, Olmedo, and Heredia, New York, 1920, p. 14.

125 Quoted in loc. cit.

Moda y Recreo Semanal in 1829. In 1825 he had already published his *Poesías* in New York. From this date on he spent most of his life in Mexico. There he held several positions of importance—congressman, professor, judge.

Heredia is one of the first romantic poets in the Spanish language. His poem *Oda al Niágara*, written when he was only 21 years old, is characterized by a profound and sensitive awareness of the American landscape, intimate melancholy, and an almost mystical introspectiveness typical of many of the Romantics. Heredia himself tells us that early in the morning of the 15th of June, 1824, he arrived at Manchester. Stopping at the Eagle Inn, and without losing a moment, he rushed to the falls eager to satisfy his curiosity. Attracted by the dramatic grandeur of nature, he abandoned himself to his melancholy reflection. "It seems to me that I see in that torrent the image of my own passions..." And right there and then, inspired by the imposing spectacle, he wrote the famous Ode, which as he himself says "was but a pale reflection of his feelings."[126] Heredia sings to the majesty of the falls, unparalleled in the beauty of its terror by the storm or the hurricane. He feels alone before a nature that is eternal, and almost broken with nostalgia, the unhappy exile longs for Cuba's palms and sun. Yet almost symbolically he tells us that the rugged pine is a more fitting background for this nation than the graceful palm.

> But no, Niagara,—thy forest pines are fitter coronal for thee.
> The palm, the effeminate myrtle, and frail rose may grow in gardens,
> And give out their fragrance there, unmanning him who breathes it.
> Thine it is to do a nobler office. Generous minds behold thee, and
> Are moved, and learn to rise above earth's frivolous pleasures;
> They partake thy grandeur, at the utterance of thy name.[127]

It would be a mistake to give Heredia's poem political significance, yet the proportions and the quality of the nature which he is describing are essentially American. One cannot fail to feel a continental consciousness on his part, which in itself is very close to being a political concept. His attitude is not unlike Rocafuerte's when he says that everything in America is better and bigger than in the mother countries, just as the rivers and lakes are larger here than those of Europe.

Before Heredia, there had been other writers who told us of the beauty of Niagara Falls. The most famous one was Peter Kalm who visited the falls in September, 1750. During the nineteenth century, people came from all over the world to pay tribute to this great shrine of nature; yet for the peoples of the Spanish-speaking world, it was Heredia who immortalized this scene. In their minds it has become one of the characteristic features of this nation, just as much as its democratic institutions or its great men.

---

[126] See Hills, *The Odes of Bello, Olmedo and Heredia*, p. 120.

[127] "Ode to Niagara," Thomas Walsh, *Hispanic Anthology*, New York, 1920, pp. 405-411 (Translation attributed to William Cullen Bryant).

Heredia is also one of the initiators of literary relations between the United States and Spanish America. While in New York he met William Cullen Bryant, who, according to Van Wyck Brooks, was the first American poet to become interested in the literature of Spanish America. Bryant translated Heredia's poem "The Hurricane." He is also believed to have collaborated in the translation of Heredia's "Ode to Niagara" which first appeared in the *United States Review and Literary Gazette,* of which Bryant was the editor. It was as a result of this friendship that Bryant visited Mexico and Cuba and that for many years afterwards he discussed relations with Spanish America in the *Evening Post,* which he also edited. In Van Wyck Brook's own words "thus began in North America an interest in Latin American culture that was to grow in time, though slowly indeed. For neither of the continents was culturally independent enough to be deeply concerned about the other: both still looked toward Europe in literary matters in a way that scarcely conduced to a mutual respect."[128]

Besides Heredia there were other essentially literary men who wrote about the United States, but these, like their compatriots, the pamphleteers and the writers of travel memoirs, were primarily concerned with political ideas rather than esthetic values. As an example of this attitude we have the Colombian poet and statesman JOSE MARIA DE SALAZAR (1785-1828), who writes praising the United States, though at the same time warning against the dangers of the Federal system. "If we were to practice it, as it is done in the United States, I would be in favor of it," but due to existing conditions in Spanish America he believes the system to be inadequate for their purposes.[129]

Indeed, Heredia's poem is an exception to the kind of literature written by the Spanish Americans about the United States at this time.

4. *Conclusion*

During the period of Independence the traditional prejudices and differences that had existed between the two peoples during colonial times continued to play an important part in determining the opinion of the masses of the people. As exemplified in Fray Melchor Martínez, distrust of our political motives and abhorrence of our religious beliefs seem to have been the predominant characteristics of a good part of the conservative population.

From the very beginning there were authors like Miranda, Nariño, Arango y Parreño, and José Alvarez de Toledo who predicted that the example of the independence of the United States would eventually cause the

---

[128] Van Wyck Brooks, *The World of Washington Irving,* New York, 1944, p. 242

[129] José María Salazar to Rocafuerte, June 26, 1823: in Rocafuerte, *Ensayo político.* p. 175.

liberation of Spanish America. The above-mentioned authors looked forward with hope to this day, but to the clergy and other conservative elements it was a source of fear and regret.

Both liberals and conservatives expressed concern over the great growth and general prosperity of the United States. Some of them, like Arango y Parreño, feared that some day the young republic would dominate the entire continent, North and South. Already at this early date they speak of North America as the "Colossus of the North."

The majority of the writers of this era looked upon the United States as a utopia. Its political perfection was used as a model. Travellers like Flores, Miranda, Gutiérrez de Lara and Carrera express admiration for the prosperity and well-being of the population. They see definite advantages to this type of civilization. The pamphleteer writers like Mier, Rocafuerte, Vicente Pazos, etc., recommended imitating the American constitutions and other political institutions. The United States becomes "the hope of the human race," "the great adventure of man." One of their favorite topics is the advantages and disadvantages of the Federal System.

Continental conciousness and solidarity is evident in the interest shown for North American political writings, the admiration felt for North American heroes such as Franklin, Washington, Jefferson and Adams, and in the publication of news and translations about this country. The motto of the times becomes: "The future belongs to the New World."

Most of the writers advocated freedom of religion. Rocafuerte went so far as to express preference for the Protestant Church. These ideas were strongly combatted by the conservatives, who in this respect represented the majority of the population. They describe the United States as being indifferent when it came to religious matters and not liberal. Both liberals and conservatives accuse us of religious discrimination.

Mier sees advantages for some of the Spanish American states in being anexed to the United States.

Bitter resentment is expressed by most liberals against the non-intervention policy adopted by this nation.

Bolívar, Simón Rodríguez and others were aware of the many differences that existed bewteen the United States and Spanish America and pointed out that a simple imitation of institutions would not be sufficient to solve their many problems.

Many of these ideas were not the result of direct contact between the two Americans. The influence of Spanish and French authors was at all times considerable.

III

SECOND PERIOD: THE FORMATION OF
THE SPANISH AMERICAN NATIONS
1823-1890

1. GENERAL CHARACTER OF THE PERIOD

During the years from 1822 until 1890, those Spanish American republics that had won their independence from Spain were primarily concerned with domestic problems, that is to say, the writing of their constitutions and the development of their social and economic structures. Inter-American relations during this period were few. Intercourse was limited even among the Spanish American republics themselves. Whatever contacts Spanish America had were with Europe — especially with France and England. It is during this time that the term "Latin America" became prevalent. France obtained intellectual hegemony in these countries in a manner similar to England, which achieved an economic and political monopoly.

Cuba, Santo Domingo and Puerto Rico, at this time still part of the Spanish Empire, continued to be vitally interested in the United States, and contacts between these islands and this nation were more frequent than with the rest of the Spanish world. Travellers and political refugees arrived yearly from them to our coastal cities. Many of them, like Varela and Trelles, took up residence in this country. From here they published reviews and organized secret societies intended to promote the independence of their native countries. Several attempts to emancipate the Caribbean islands, as for example, López's expedition to Cuba, were promoted in the United States and financed with funds, a good part of which were supplied by private American citizens.

In North America the United States was also going through a period of isolation. The conquest of the West, the Civil War and the many internal difficulties that had to be overcome consumed most of its energies. Here also interest was felt for Europe and not for Spanish America. The Mexican war was considered by the average American as a domestic problem. The lands involved were almost depopulated and taking them over was seen as part of the natural growth of the nation.[1]

---

[1] Speaking of the future expansion of the United States, de Tocqueville said in 1835 that Mexico represented the only barrier to the natural development of this country. "Thus, the Spaniards and the Anglo-Americans are, properly speaking, the two races which divide the possessions of the New World. The limits of separation between them have been settled by treaty, but although the conditions are favorable to the Anglo-Americans, I do not doubt that they will shortly infringe it. Vast provinces, extending beyond

It is difficult to generalize upon the history of Spanish America during this formative period, due to the great variety of conditions existing in the different countries. Independence did not bring the long expected happiness. Most of the countries found their wealth destroyed and their population decimated by the long, bloody struggle. Reactionary elements in most cases took the lead, resulting in the setting up of dictatorships and the use of force. The attitude of admiration for the United States, so generally felt by Spanish Americans of the previous generation, was retained by only a few men such as Rocafuerte and Sarmiento.

Prior to the independence ideas on government were of a theoretical nature, but along with freedom came realistic problems that had to be solved. In each country, owing to variations of geography, race and climate, the problems were different and the solution had to be adapted to the circumstances.

The interpretation of the United States during the period of independence had been idealistic rather than ideological, and, as a consequence, had little lasting influence upon the new republics. We find that many admirers of the United States, in spite of their professed republicanism, upon inheriting the responsibilities of directing the governments of their respective nations, established political systems that were in spirit the very opposite of that of the United States. This is the case with Dr. Francia of Paraguay.[2]

In the United States the policy of neutrality and non-intervention in Spanish American matters followed up to 1823 was now replaced by the Monroe Doctrine. It is interesting to note that these two policies were formulated by the same group of men, and that, although on the surface they seem to be in contradiction, a more detailed examination shows that in reality such is not the case. Both were intended to protect American interests. The circumstances changed, once the Spanish American colonies had won the right to be recognized as belligerents. After this, a new system was

---

the frontier of the Union towards Mexico, are still destitute of inhabitants. The natives of the United States will people these solitary regions before their rightful occupants. They will take possession of the soil, and establish social institutions, so that, when the legal owner at length arrives, he will find the wilderness under cultivation, and strangers quietly settled in the midst of his inheritance." "It cannot be denied that the British race has acquired an amazing preponderance over all other European races in the New World; and it is very superior to them in civilization, industry, and power. As long as it is surrounded only by desert or thinly-peopled countries, as long as it encounters no dense population upon its route, through which it cannot work its way, it will assuredly continue to spread. The lines marked out by treaties will not stop it; but it will everywhere overlap these imaginary barriers." (*Democracy in America,* Vol. I, pp. 554-555.)

2 Chandler in his book *Inter American acquaintances,* p. 44, relates how when Belgrano and Echevarría bade goodby to Dr. Francia, the famous dictator of Paraguay, on October 12, 1811, he offered them a steel engraving of Franklin that hung in his study, and how he remarked that Franklin was the first democrat in the world, a model that they should imitate. During their conversation they also took notice that he was acquainted with the main facts leading up to the independence of the United States.

necessary, and thus a theory that had been popularly discussed for some time by the authors of America and Europe, the two continents theory, was put into effect.

It was initiated after Canning suggested to Rush that a policy of this nature, sponsored by the United States and England, would be of benefit to all concerned. Monroe's doctrine, however, differs from Canning's proposal in several important respects. It was not a joint declaration as the Englishman had intended it to be. It contained no self-denying clause. Adams, who was mainly responsible for this doctrine, was unwilling to bind the United States never to acquire Spanish American territory. Finally, in direct opposition to British interests it forbade European colonization as well as European political interference in the Western Hemisphere. We might add that it seems that the United States (and it is probable that this still holds true today) was interested in the independence and security of Spanish America only in so far as it affected its own security. There is no indication that the rights of the sovereign Spanish American nations ever played a primary role in the minds of Adams and his colleagues. As we have seen previously in this study. Adams' attitude toward Spanish America was notoriously unfriendly.

Adams was not alone in this attitude. There were other Americans who believed that the United States should follow a practical, realistic course in its relations with the Spanish American countries. Appeals based on the community of the American name, or the partnership of our continent they considered fallacious.[3] Some even implied that talk about continental solidarity was a convenient cloak for a Yankee imperialism, similar to other imperialisms of European and Asiatic nations.[4] Edward Everett, editor of the *North American Review* wrote in the April issue of 1821:

> We have no concern with South America; we have no sympathy with them. We are sprung from different stocks, we speak different languages, we have been brought up in different social and moral schools, we have been governed by different codes of law, we profess radically different codes of religion. Should we espouse their cause. they would borrow our money and grant commissions to our privateers, and possibly extend some privileges to our trade, if the fear of the English, which bringeth a snare, did not prevent this. But they would not act in our spirit, they would not follow our advice, they could not imitate our example. Not all the treaties we could make, nor the commissioners we could send out, nor the money we could lend them, would transform their Pueyrredons and their Artigases, into Adamses or Franklins, or their Bolivars into Washingtons.[5]

---

[3] Edward Everett, "South America", *North American Review,* no. XXXI (Vol. III, no. 1, New Series, 1821), pp. 432-443.

[4] "The President's Message", *National Gazette,* Nov. 24, 1820.

[5] Edward Everett, *op. cit.,* pp. 433-435; also in Whitaker, *The United States and the Independence of Latin America,* Baltimore, 1941, p. 336.

Adams shared Everett's misgivings concerning the political and social virtues of the Spanish American people. Arthur Preston Whitaker says of him that he "was impartially prejudiced against Spaniards and Spanish Americans alike, for he had swallowed whole the "Black Legend" of the inveterate cruelty, faithlessness and fanaticism of the Spanish people, and he still regarded the Spanish Americans as Spaniards even after they began their struggle for independence against Spain."[6] The Spanish Americans had for some time been acquainted with this kind of attitude, and they were starting to feel that the United States was indeed interested in Spanish America and the material wealth these nations represented but that they were totally indifferent when it came to the future of the Spanish Americans themselves.[7]

Unfortunately, there is no general study of the attitude of North Americans toward the new Spanish American Republics. There is an excellent article by Rippy on Bolívar as viewed by the contemporary North American diplomats, that throws considerable light on the subject. His conclusion, in this particular case, is that prejudice on the part of the Americans placed Bolívar in an unfavorable position, which he did not deserve. We can be certain that lack of understanding for Spanish American traditional values and temperament was not limited to the case of the Liberator for, after all, he represented the best and most typical that these countries had to offer. It is of course dangerous to generalize when it comes to attitudes. Clay and Webster, for instance, were ardent defenders of the Spanish American cause and often attacked in their speeches the materialistic indifference of their compatriots.[8]

It is not surprising then that Monroe's declaration should have been received in most Spanish American countries with qualified enthusiasm. In a sense, the interpretation which the United States gave the new doctrine was a disappointment to most of them. According to Rippy, Henry Clay informed the government of the United Provinces of La Plata that the Congress of the United States alone could decide whether the Monroe Doctrine would be enforced and that the Doctrine did not constitute a pledge which foreign nations might call upon the United States to fulfill.[9] The Caribbean was the section to be most vitally affected by this doctrine, but even there it caused little comment. "It is a surprising fact, but true," says Trelles in his *Estudio de la bibliografía cubana sobre la doctrina de Monroe*, "that none

---

[6] Whitaker, *The United States and the Independence of Latin America*, pp. 147-148.

[7] "Siempre ha valido más para la América del Norte, como para todos los pueblos de la raza sajona, cualquier roca estéril que las olas del mar batieran cerca de sus playas, que la suerte de extrañas naciones o la justicia y el honor de pueblos de origen diferente." Benjamin Vicuña Mackenna, *Obras completas*, IX, 48-49.

[8] Rippy, "Bolívar as viewed by contemporary diplomats of the United States", *The Hispanic American Historical Review*, XV, 1935, 287.

[9] Rippy, *Historical Evolution of Hispanic America*, p. 385.

of the eminent Cubans of this epoch, such as D. Francisco Arango y Parreño, Padre Varela, and D. José Antonio Saco, refer to or even mention the said doctrine. Padre Varela did state in 1824 and 1826 that he wanted to see Cuba as isolated politically from other countries, as it was by nature." To Trelles' knowledge "the first son of the 'Antillas' who studied the Monroe Doctrine was Porfirio Valentín, in the book *Reformes dans les îles de Cuba et Porto Rico* (Paris 1869), in which he devotes ten pages to the origins and development of the aforementioned doctrine." The Cuban who has studied it most extensively is José M. Céspedes. His work *La doctrina Monroe* published in Havana in 1893, says Trelles, "is the most extensive and important that has been published in our country on this matter."[10]

The incident of the Falkland Islands in 1833 gave the Spanish Americans further grounds to doubt the sincerity of our motives. Those islands, two hundred and fifty miles off the southern coast of Argentina, were first settled by the French in 1764. They were acquired by the Spanish in 1767 and retained by them, with the exception of one brief interlude of British control, until the independence of Argentina was recognized. At this time the islands passed under the sovereignty of the new republic. Troubled by domestic problems, Argentina neglected their care and like many other islands during the beginning of the nineteenth century, they became headquarters for smugglers and pirates. In 1831 a detachment of United States Marines ousted the pirates and the island was eventually turned over to England in 1833.[11] This action on the part of the United States was interpreted by the Argentinians as a violation of the national sovereign rights. More important was the attitude assumed by other Spanish Americans who felt that the Monroe Doctrine had been purposely forgotten and it would continue to be so whenever American interests warranted it.

As concerns England, Monroe's declaration meant open political and commercial competition. The struggle between these two nations was most violently fought in Mexico. Here as everywhere else, with the exception of the Caribbean, the influence of the United States was on the wane. Iturbide and the other Mexican leaders who followed him had reasons to suspect future aggressions on the part of the United States. Luis de Onís' accounts of the purposes and ambition of the North Americans had left a deep impression upon the Mexicans. And the attitude of our administration respecting the question of limits between the two countries also tended to increase their suspicions. The Minister of the United States to Mexico, Joel R. Poinsett, tried to combat anti-American feeling. He

---

10 M. C. Trelles, *Estudio de la bibliografía cubana sobre la doctrina de Monroe.* Habana, 1922.
11 Wilgus and d'Eça, *Outline history of Latin America,* p. 265; Rippy, *Historical Evolution of Hispanic America,* p. 386.

reminded them of the friendly interest with which the people of the United States had viewed their struggle for independence and the many affinities that existed between the two countries. His arguments had little effect, and realizing hat his efforts would be fruitless unless there was a change in the administration of the country, he associated himself with the party of the opposation. He had hoped that in this manner he would be able to influence the Mexican Congress and eventually, if there was a change in the administration, the Mexican Executive himself. Poinsett was instrumental in creating the Lodge of York Rite Masons, which came to constitute the chief organ of the opposition party. Its platform, to put it bluntly, was—America for the Americans, and it was intended to exclude Europeans, especially the British and the Spaniards, from participating in the national life of the country.

Poinsett's activities were combated by Henry George Ward, the British Chargé d'Affaires, who in turn associated himself with the party in power. Upon his arrival, Alamán, the Mexican Minister of State, ostentatiously acclaimed him as the representative of England, the nation which, as he said, had done more than any other to secure and maintain the independence of the Mexican nation. Ward launched a full-fledged propaganda campaign against the United States which was very effective. It was with this purpose in mind that he reprinted Onís' memoir predicting the conquest of Mexican territory.

In general, Great Britain was victorious both politically and commercially. Canning obtained commercial treaties with Argentina, Colombia and Mexico, which gave Britain a privileged position in these countries. By 1883 the Spanish Americans had become accustomed to looking to Britain for economic and political assistance[12] and to France and Spain for spiritual and cultural values. Forbes, American representative to Argentina, reported bitterly to Adams that England derived from that country all the advantages of a colonial dependency without the responsibility or expense of a military administration.[13]

In Spanish America the literature of this period is essentially Romantic, but there is a group of writers who continue to write political essays. Some of these authors saw in the United States the value of certain ideas that would be acceptable to their type of culture and environment. José Vitorino Lastarria of Chile and Juan Bautista Alberdi of Argentina are good examples of men characterized by this attitude. The two main topics of discussion in these political essays were: the Federal System, and the question of religious freedom. The first of these two varied from country to country. As concerns the second, Spanish America was always essentially

---

12 Rippy, *Historical evolution of Hispanic America*, p. 385.
13 Forbes to Adams, November 11, 1824; quoted in E. J. Pratt, "Anglo-American commercial and political relations," *The Hispanic American Historical Review*, XI, 317.

Catholic, and in spite of the fact that there have been many excellent essays written for and against religious freedom, Catholicism is still considered in most Spanish American republics as the national religion.

Domingo Faustino Sarmiento's interpretation of the United States represents an attitude different from the rest of his contemporaries both in depth and originality. It is for this reason that he will be studied in a separate chapter

II. CONTACTS BETWEEN THE TWO AMERICAS

When we speak of contacts between the United States and Spanish America during the nineteenth century, we do not mean exactly the 100-year span between 1800 - 1900, but rather that between 1820 and 1890. During this time various points of coincidence are seen in the more or less parallel development of the two Americas. Both were in a formative period and occupied with their internal problems, which tended to draw them into greater isolation, and both looked upon each other with an attitude of relative indifference. There were, nevertheless, many Spanish American travellers who came to the United States for various reasons. Of these, many were interested in cultural problems. During this century numerous memoirs of scientific expeditions to this country were published. Interest was shown in American hospitals, penal institutions, the progress and growth of large cities such as New York, Chicago and San Francisco, and the famous landmarks such as Niagara Falls and Yellowstone Park. No one came to America without visiting the model jail in Philadelphia. There are several works on this subject alone. But most travellers came simply to know the United States. This nation was considered one of the great curiosities of the century, and was part of a grand tour which generally consisted of a visit to the United States, Europe, and the Holy Land.

The ideas expressed by these travellers were in most cases conceived prior to their landing upon the American shores, and often came from reading some memoir written by a previous traveller, Tocqueville's *De la démocratie en Amérique* being one of the most widely known.[1] The greater part of the authors did not attempt to evaluate American culture. They limited themselves to repeating certain commonplace ideas and to relating personal anecdotes in which the writer almost invariably played the part of the hero. Visitors to the United States became so numerous during this epoch that a special travellers' guide in Spanish, giving a detailed description of the different cities encountered en route from Mexico to New York, was

---

[1] Paris, 1836; transl. into English by Henry Reeve, London, 1836; into Spanish by A. Sánchez de Bustamente, Paris, 1836-1837. Other editions in Spanish, Madrid, 1854, and Madrid, 1911.

published by the Mexican publicist S. Adalberto de Cardona, that enjoyed considerable circulation in both hemispheres.[2]

Another point of contact between the two Americas was the number of boys and young men who came to study in this country. As early as 1815, two Chilean brothers, Luis and Mateo Blanco, enrolled as students in the Yorktown School. These same boys, at President Madison's recommendation, were later taken into the United States Military Academy at West Point. Among the other young men who received instruction in this country we find Pedro Valdés y Carrera, nephew of the first president of Chile, José Miguel Carrera; and Fernando Bolívar, nephew of the Liberator, Simón Bolívar.[3] In 1848, Domingo Faustino Sarmiento found several young men from Chile studying at the Saint James College, a Jesuit institution in New York.[4] As we advance into the nineteenth century the number of Spanish American students diminishes. More and more we find them going to France and to other European countries for their education.

The most lasting bond between the two cultures, however, was the refugees who came from the region of the Caribbean and settled in our coastal cities. These men, endowed with an excellent intellectual background —among them we find some of the leading Spanish American writers: José Antonio Miralla, Félix Varela, Carlos Manuel Trelles, Eugenio María de Hostos and José Martí—came to understand the United States, in some cases even better than the Americans themselves. They were gifted with the rare quality of possessing perspective and synthesis, as outsiders often have, and at the same time they had an intimate knowledge of the problems of this country, acquired from having lived here the greater part of their lives. They played the important role of being the interpreters and propagators of both cultures. As Englekirk has so ably stated in his book *Edgar Allan Poe in Hispanic Literature,* these refugees not only disseminated a knowledge of North American literature in Spanish America through their numerous translations and excellent critical studies, but were to a degree responsible for the vogue enjoyed by our literature in some of the European countries such as Spain and France during the latter part of the nineteenth century.

The publication of books on political subjects, initiated by Rocafuerte and Mier during the previous era, were now followed by others intended to be used as texts in elementary schools. The important publishing house of Appleton and Company of New York specialized in editing educational and scientific texts in Spanish, which, according to James F. Shearer, con-

    2 S. Adalberto de Cardona, *De México a Nueva York. Guía para el viajero en que se describen las principales ciudades de México y los Estados Unidos del Norte. Con profusión de grabados,* San Francisco, 1890.

    3 M. P. González, "Las relaciones intelectuales entre los Estados Unidos e Hispanoamérica". *Universidad de la Habana,* año VIII, nos. 24-25, pp. 84-110.

    4 Domingo Faustino Sarmiento, *Obras,* V, 427.

stituted in itself a small but interesting chapter in inter-American cultural relations.[5] Domingo Faustino Sarmiento, Eugenio María de Hostos and José Martí were among the many distinguished Spanish American writers who became associated with that firm during this period.

Among the books published in New York during the earlier part of this period there were two in particular that enjoyed considerable circulation. One was a translation of the Bible intended to teach children how to read and write. It had a preface by Rocafuerte himself, and went by the title *Lecciones para las escuelas de primeras letras* (New York, 1823). This book became particularly popular among pro-American elements in Mexico and Colombia with Protestant inclinations. The second of these two works was the *New Pronouncing Dictionary of the Spanish and English Languages* by Mariano Velázquez de la Cadena, Professor of Spanish at Columbia College, which was for many years a stand-by for all those who were learning either Spanish or English.

Important Hispanic influence on our literature and thought, which indirectly were to have a marked effect on the attitude of the South American writers toward the United States, have come not directly from Spanish America but indirectly through the mother country. There was in the United States at this time a large and important group of students of American history who were interested in reconstructing the origins of our civilization, namely, to study the society that had produced the discovery, the process of the discovery itself, and the early phases of the colonial era. These men, as we have said, were primarily interested in America, in the broadest sense of the word, but they believed that the key to this study was to be found not in this continent but in the old archives of Spain itself. Such figures as Obadiah Rich, Washington Irving, Prescott, Ticknor, Everett, Longfellow, Motley, Bryant and Lowell, to mention only some of the more important, became profound students of Spanish matters.[6]

The American Ambassador to Madrid at the time was Alexander Everett of Boston. Everett was a cultured gentleman, and a historian who

---

[5] James F. Shearer, "Pioneer publishers of textbooks for Hispanic America: The house of Appleton," *Hispania*, February 1944.

[6] Sarmiento, *North and South America:* a Discourse delivered before the Rhode-Island Historical Society, December 27, 1865 (Providence, 1866): "Who has read an American book? asked the English historian Macauley. Washington Irving replies by writing the *Life and voyages of Christopher Columbus,* and England and the world read a book of North American birth but of South American and Spanish descent. Ferdinand and Isabella, monarchs of Aragon and Castile, Columbus and the discovery of Hispaniola are the first page of the history of North America, and every time the North American mind has to recur to its origin, it must return to the Spain of Charles V, Philip II, and there meet the historian of another language, of another nation, and of other colonies. Washington Irving, in following Columbus, pointed the way to Spanish and South American chroniclers and historians, and to the dusty documents hoarded in the archives of Simancas, for the guidance of the whole school of North American Spanish historians who followed in his footsteps."

had shown a sincere friendship for the South Americans during their struggle for independence. An important part of the Grand Tour, which every
young Bostonian of means felt himself under the obligation to make and
which consisted of a year's residence abroad in the several cultural centers
of Europe, was a visit to Everett in Madrid.

Closely associated with the American Ambassador was Obadiah Rich,
the bibliographer. Rich is one of those unfortunate individuals whom history has forgotten. There is no biography of him, and little is known of
his personality and character, although he is a forerunner of Sabin, Maggs,
Brown, and the other great bibliographers on America. He was born in
Massachusetts of an excellent family. At home he had already attained a
reputation as a local bibliographer, but it was not until he went to Valencia
that his lifetime vocation was definitely determined. Rich was moved by a
consuming passion for books and manuscripts pertaining to the early history of America. When he was sent to Madrid as consul and later as secretary to the legation, he spent most of his free time scouring the bookshops
and finding many of the books and manuscripts that later on were to make
up the "Rich Collection of Manuscripts on America," one of the finest of
its kind in the world.[7] Visitors describe his house as being more like a museum than a home, and no one writing on early American history came to
Madrid without visiting his collection.

It was Rich who turned Irving to the writing of Spanish books. Irving
had been interested from his youth in Spanish America. One of his earliest
literary accomplishments was his translation of Depons' voyage to the northern part of South America.[8] Everett was acquainted with Irving's fondness
for Spanish history and when don Martín Fernández de Navarrete published
the first volume of his *Collection of Spanish Voyages* taken from contemporary official documents, Everett immediately recognized the importance
and interest that this publication would have for the American public. He
invited his friend and compatriot Irving, who was then in France, to come
back and study Navarrete's work, and, if he found the book worthwhile, to
make a translation of it as he had done in the case of Depons' work.[9] When
Irving came to Spain he went to live in Obadiah Rich's house, and it was

---

[7] Part of this collection is at present in the New York Public Library.

[8] Depons, Francois Raymond Joseph (1751-1812), *A voyage to the eastern part of
Terra Firma, or the Spanish Main in South America during the years 1801, 1802,
1803 and 1804*. Containing a description of the territory under the jurisdiction of the
Captain General of Caracas, composed of the provinces of Venezuela, Maracaibo, Varinas,
Spanish Guiana, Cumana, and the Island of Margaretta; and embracing everything relative
to the discovery, conquest, topography, legislation, commerce, finance, inhabitants and
productions of the provinces, together with a view of the manners and customs of the
Spainards, and the savage as well as civilized Indians, by F. Depons ... Tr. by an American gentleman. New York, I. Riley and Co., 1806.

[9] Domingo del Monte y Aponte, *Revista de Ciencias, Literatura y Arte,* Sevilla, 1856,
II, 754-773; quoted by Ferguson, *American literature in Spain,* pp. 151-154

while browsing through Rich's manuscripts, among which were works like Alcedo's *Biblioteca americana*, that he made up his mind to write the life of Columbus. Navarrete's collection of voyages, along with Rich's books and papers, would serve as a source book for this task, but he would have no part of a translation.

While he pursued his studies, he became fascinated by the moving drama of the Christian conquest of Granada, and with the by-products of the research done on his first work, he wove the fabric of his chronicle of Fray Antonio de Agapida known as the *Conquest of Granada*. In this work he almost identified himself with a Spanish friar, a contemporary of Cisneros. Aside from these two works, Irving wrote others purely peninsular in inspiration, such as the *Tales of the Alhambra*, but we are particularly interested in these first two because of their bearing on American history. The *Conquest of Granada* represents the prelude to the conquest, and the *Life of Columbus* the discovery of America.

The other American historian to complete this cycle in American history was William Prescott of Boston. As a boy Prescott passed several years in the Canary Islands with an uncle who was the United States Consul at Tenerife. Here at the front entrance to America he acquired an understanding of the Spanish past that was to be very valuable in days to come, and although he never saw Spain or Spanish America because of his later blindness, he was so steeped in the literature and history of those countries that we feel, when reading his history of the Catholic sovereigns, that he knew them "palmo a palmo." Prescott, "with less luxuriance of imagination"[10] than Irving, but with greater historical penetration, sought to describe in his works the whole genesis of America. He was first tempted to initiate his career as a historian by writing the history of the downfall of the Roman Empire. Instead he wrote the history of Ferdinand and Isabella. The contemporary Cuban, Domingo del Monte y Aponte, said of him, ". . . this painstaking writer, besides raising a beautiful monument to the intellectual glory of his country, has done a great service to historical studies in the United States."[11] After this first work Prescott wrote the *Conquest of México* and later the *Conquest of Perú*, thus filling in a gap which was noticeable in English literature and completed his great trilogy of the discovery of the New World.

George Ticknor, Prescott's biographer and friend who occupied the chair of foreign literature at Harvard, taught countless pupils to understand and appreciate Spanish civilization. During his lifetime he collected many valuable books, a good part of which dealt with Spanish America. The famous Ticknor Library, which he willed to the city of Boston, constituted then, and still does, an important source of knowledge of the Spanish

---

10 Del Monte y Aponte, *ibid.*, p. 151.
11 *Loc. cit.*

world. [12] His history of Spanish literature is considered by many critics as the best written outside the Spanish-speaking countries up to his day and is still ranked among the most distinguished. Ticknor was aided also by Obadiah Rich in making his famous collection. In one of his letters he writes to him:

> I wish to give you "carte blanche," and feel sure that with my letter of January 27, and this list of my books, you cannot mistake my wants; which you know, have always been confined to Spanish belles lettres, and whatever is necessary to understand the history of Spanish elegant literature.[13]

Much the same can be said about Longfellow. During his lifetime he also taught hundreds of young men to understand those cultural elements —language, literature, hitorical background, moral values, — that are the common heritage of the Spanish speaking peoples all over the world. As in the case of the period of independence, these North Americans made no distinction between the Spaniards of Spain and those of America; for them they were all one. Longfellow, for instance, spent some of the happiest periods of his life in Spain. While there, he learned Spanish from the pretty daughter of his innkeeper. He occasionally went on jaunts into the country-side and gained first-hand knowledge of its people. He even learned to dance the *jota* —a Spanish national dance. It was as a result of this intimate understanding of Spain that his translations of Spanish works, especially the famous *Coplas* of Jorge Manrique, are worthy of comparison with the original. And it was also as a result of this understanding that the Spanish Americans who visited the United States and had the opportunity of meeting him, found him to be a warm and sympathetic individual.[14]

A product of this same environment was William Wheelwright, the great American engineer, who contributed more than any other of his compatriots to the development of Spanish America. In fact, it could be said that he did more than most great South Americans, for as Alberdi remarked, "a foreigner, even if he is not a citizen, may do more to promote its welfare than the most distinguished patriot."[15] He was responsible for the construction of some of the most important railway systems in the southern continent, including the first railroad to cross the Andes between Argentina

---

[12] There were other important collections of books on Spain and Spanish America. Sarmiento wr:tes in a letter of 1865, "I came to visit the Vice-President of the Rhode-Island Historical Society, to take care of a few matters of interest to Argentina, and to visit the Amer:can Library of Mr. Brown, the finest of its kind in the world." Sarmiento to Mrs. Mann, New York, Nov. 25, 1865; "Cartas de Sarmiento," *Boletín de la Academia Argentina de Letras*, 1936, IV, 351.

[13] *Life, letters, and journals of George Ticknor,* London, 1876, II, 249.

[14] Eusebio Guiteras, "Una visita a Longfellow," *Liceo Matanzas,* October, 1866.

[15] Alberdi, *Life and industrial labors of William Wheelwright in South America,* transl. by Caleb Cushing, Boston, 1877, p. 13.

and Chile. He also constructed ports and charted steamship routes that are still in existence today.

His contemporary J. B. Alberdi, the famous Argentinian author, describes him as a typical product of the New England of his day. "To such society Wheelwright owed his birth, his early education, and his superior capability for great enterprises. This society, whose sound and robust character takes the place of noble family and classic education, gave a double diploma to him whose fortune it was to have been nurtured therein. The fact of coming into existence under such conditions is equivalent to being born of a race wholly distinct, if, as Franklin says, 'Nobility consists in virtue'."[16] Alberdi continues by asserting that New England was the cradle of the United States both by virtue of the fundamental ideas of its social order and the multitude of great men Wheelwright numbered among his compatriots. "Such were the philosopher Franklin, the statesman Webster, the abolitionist Sumner, the philanthropist Peabody, the poet Longfellow— all of them from Massachusetts, whose capital, Boston, called the modern Athens, has eclipsed the ancient city in its love of liberty."[17]

As in the case of his countrymen, Wheelwright, too, was interested in early American history. He became an expert in sixteenth and seventeenth century cartography. This knowledge he used to great advantage in charting steamship routes. "A countryman of Prescott, Irving and Motley, Wheelwright was careful not to imitate the Spanish Americans in their contempt for every Spanish source of information simply because it was Spanish."[18]

As a tribute to his many accomplishments Alberdi called him a hero of peace. "Bolívar and San Martín well earned their titles of 'heroes of the Andes' by scaling those lofty summits with their cannon; but shall we deny the same title to Wheelwright and Meiggs, his countryman, who have crossed them with iron locomotives?"[19]

Yet not all contacts between the two Americas were as fortunate as those already mentioned. There was for instance the Walker incident in Honduras.

Since the purchase of Louisiana in 1803 the United States had been slowly creeping westward until it engulfed a great part of what was originally Mexico. This immigration, toward the land of the setting sun, was stimulated in 1848 by the discovery of gold in California. Overnight hundreds of covered wagon trains galloped over the Western plains, racing to be the first to get there. It was a strenuous journey and not all those who started out arrived. Every possible route was being tried, and there

---

16 *Loc. cit.*
17 *Ibid.*, p. 14.
18 *Ibid.*, p. 40.
19 *Ibid.*, pp. 6-7.

were those who did not fail to realize that the quickest way to get to California was by steamship to Central America, cross the Isthmus and then once again over sea to their destination. With this purpose in mind, Commodore Vanderbilt had built a shuttle system across Lake Nicaragua, which proved to be tremendously successful. A good part of the westward migration went in this manner, and there were some Americans who believed that this strip of land, serving as a connecting link between the eastern and western parts of the United States, should be under the American flag.

William Walker was one of those who shared this point of view. Born in New Orleans, his unquestioned beliefs included the two following premises: "That slavery was the natural destiny of the Negro," and "that it was the 'manifest destiny' of the United States to swallow up the lands of the Caribbean."[20]

Walker came to León with fifty-six settlers. Soon after his arrival he dominated the political scene of this small country. He became head of the army, and before the local population could take notice of what was happening he had made himself dictator of Nicaragua. The rest of the Central American countries opposed him, but he was able to retain control of Honduras and, since this was during the presidency of Franklin Pierce,[21] his government had no difficulty in being recognized by the United States. He surrounded himself with North Americans who eventually came to hold all the offices of the nation. One market day he had Salazar, his main political opponent, hanged in the market square where the spectacle could be seen by everyone. Everything seemed to be going well for Walker, but he made one mistake, he confiscated Commodore Vanderbilt's holdings. A revolution followed. Walker was defeated and sent back to the United States, where he was received as a hero. After this he made two unsuccessful attempts to return to Honduras. He was finally captured by the English and handed over to the authorities of Honduras who had him shot.

Incidents such as the above-mentioned were not uncommon during the era of "Manifest Destiny." But more important for us than these individual cases is what was happening in the Mexican territories taken over by the United States.

In California the impetus of the immigration was so great that soon there was very little left of the original Spanish civilization. Before long all that remained were Spanish place names and a legendary, romantic Spanish past that Californians sentimentally still cling to. Nevertheless, an important contact that should not be overlooked was the many adventurers who came to California from Chile, Peru and the rest of South America once the mad rush for gold was started, and who returned to their respective countries to tell of their North American experiences. It took months before

---

20 Arciniegas, *Caribbean,* p. 370.
21 Vicuña Mackenna, *Obras completas,* I, 252.

the overland journey across the continent could be accomplished, but the overseas route from the western coast of South America was only a matter of weeks. Many Spanish Americans took advantage of this opportunity and were among the first to arrive in California. Among them was the novelist Martín Palma and the essayist Pérez Rosales, who wrote a memoir of his experiences, *Recuerdos del pasado,* which is without doubt one of the finest and most interesting written during this period.

Quest for gold produced bitter rivalries between the South Americans and the Yankees which cost many lives on both sides. Vicuña Mackenna, who visited California in 1852, tells us that one afternoon when he was wandering about six miles from the city he came upon a cemetery by the side of a hill not far from San Francisco. The turbulent history of California could have been written from the epitaphs of the gravestones: murder, shipwreck, starvation and pestilence had been the cause of the death of most of those who were buried there. He also took notice that many of the names were Spanish.[22] Pérez Rosales, who had visited California in 1848, had stated that there was not a single family in Chile that did not count at least one member in the new state, but by 1852 most of them had returned to their original countries. Sarmiento, discussing the problems of immigration in the United States, wrote about this same time: "California, in itself a disorderly conglomeration of men that hardly constitute a society, is starting to expel the thousands of inhabitants that it cannot assimilate; today it is the Chileans and the other Americans (Spanish) who are starting to return to their homes, and tomorrow it will be the Europeans who will be looking for other places to migrate and build their industries."[23]

In the other territories the impact of the two civilizations produced different results. In New Mexico and Colorado, for instance, a land populated by a kindly people descended from the early Spanish peasants who colonized the valley of the Río Grande in 1598, the impact was less formidable than in California. This was due primarily to the absence of gold in this region. Here for a long time after the coming of the Americans the majority of the population continued to have a typically Spanish culture. What effect would the introduction of new dynamic forces have upon this society? Would these people be absorbed to their benefit by this new overwhelming civilization that was threatening to engulf all of North America? This was the question that many Spanish Americans were asking themselves.

Historians who have studied such problems tell us that when a new and vigorous civilization comes in contact with an older one — the so-called process of opening a country to modern methods of agriculture and in-

---

22 Benjamín Vicuña Mackenna, *Páginas de mi diario,* p. 2.
23 Sarmiento, "Emigración alemana al Río de la Plata," 1851, *Obras,* XXIII, 201-202.

dustry—[24] the results of this contact may or may not be of beneficial influence on the welfare of the native population. The anthropologist, Raoul Allier, believes that societies should be allowed to develop within their own cultural stream, that if the difference is too great between the two civilizations "at first there comes an inevitable retrogression because the so called guardian, making a clean slate of the past which *a priori* he regards as evil or else does not give himself time to know, effaces it as it stands without troubling himself to make the necessary transition. It is during this transition crisis that there occurs, in the protected peoples, a general moral and physical decline which is sometimes irremediable."[25]

As far as New Mexico is concerned, this theory would hold true in part. The Hispanos were not a primitive people at the time of the occupation, and their society was not marked then, nor is it today marked by the social or moral disintegration that often characterizes people of a less stable culture under similar conditions. We must admit however that the lot of these people has not improved during the last hundred years.

When General Kearny took Santa Fe in 1846, the Hispanos of New Mexico were seventeenth century peasants who had been isolated from the world for 200 years. Their ways were similar to those still in existence in some primitive sections of old Castile. The villages were ringed by irrigated farms, watered from a community ditch. All stock ran together on the "ejido", a tax-free pasture which took up the greater part of the territory. New Mexicans say that it was a good life while it lasted. Then, with the Treaty of Guadalupe Hidalgo, they were taken into the Union. They were given a constitution and the right to vote, which would have been excellent had they known how to use it. The government applied modern methods that were incompatible with their medieval system. They taxed the common lands, and as a result of this the villages lost them. Land grabbers and frontier lawyers added their share to the chaos. Our modern progress hurt the Hispanos. With the railroads came stockmen who got control of the range, and pastured thousands of head of cattle where hundreds had been before. As a result, the thin protecting layer of sod was destroyed and thus started the erosion and floods which are now the scourge of the land.

We should like to point out here that these lands had been out of contact for centuries with the rest of the Spanish world. Rather than a frontier of the Spanish Empire, they could be described as its last outposts. When they were populated in the seventeenth century they represented the outermost fringe of a medieval society that was already giving signs of decadence, and they were the first to be left stranded once the energies of

---

24 Toynbee calls this process "putting new wine in old bottles."
25 Raoul Allier, *La psychologie de la conversion chez les peuples non-civilisés* ... Paris, 1925, p. 190.

the mother country were exhausted and the process of expansion was inverted into a process of retrogression. In a way these territories became the frontier of the Spaniards when they were menaced by the United States for the first time in 1819. After this they hold the interest of South America until the end of the century.

More prominent in the annals of Spanish American literature was the conquest to Texas. Here the event of its occupation had been anticipated even before the independence of Mexico,[26] and by the time the act had been consummated considerable writing had been done on the subject. The problem was clearly presented by Tocqueville ten years before this territory seceded from Mexico:

> The State of Texas is a part of Mexico, and is upon the frontier between that country and the United States. In the course of the last few years, the Anglo-Americans have penetrated this province, which is still thinly peopled; they purchase land, they produce the commodities of the country, and supplant the original population. It may easily be foreseen, that, if Mexico takes no steps to check this change, the province of Texas will very shortly cease to belong to that government.[27]

The Texas occupation was, and still continues to be, an important obstacle in inter-American relations. Here more than in any of the other territories the incompatibility of the two cultures became evident, for unlike the New Mexicans, who were almost pure white, the majority of the people of Texas were Indians or mestizos and therefore subject to the color prejudice so deeply rooted in the tradition of the new population.[28] The Spanish Texans (I say Spanish because they had been Europeanized) were looked upon by the Anglo-Saxons as an inferior race and very often were denied even the fundamental prerogatives of equal justice before the law. Loss of prestige, within their own native land, made many of them claim to be Mexicans rather than Texans. The treatment received by the Spanish-speaking people of Texas was condemned by Spanish American writers in general. Even the most ardent admirers of the United States found it difficult to justify a case of open discrimination against the people of

---

26 In the National Historical Archives of Madrid there are several reports of Irujo relative to the designs of the United States on Texas and the Floridas (1804-1806); there is the correspondence of various Spanish officials concerning encounters between Spanish and American troops on the Texas frontier (1806); there are also numerous papers referring to the revolutionary movements in Texas, and the encroachment of the United States on that province (1813). In the Mier Archives, Garcia Library, University of Texas, there is an interesting letter from Juan Bernardo de Mier to José S. T. de Mier, June 21, 1822, giving greetings to the family and asking for military protection for his district. He discussed the rapid increase of Americans and its danger to the province (Autograph draft F 472).

27 Tocqueville, *Democracy in America*, II, 448.

28 This problem has been studied by Pauline R. Kibbes in her book, *Latin Americans in Texas*, Albuquerque, 1946; another excellent study is Carlos E. Castañeda, "Some Facts on Our Racial Minorities," *The Pan-American*, October, 1944.

another culture due primarily to the difference in the coloring of the skin.

In the eyes of the Spanish Americans, the Mexican war of 1848 was even less justified. In Mexico itself *corridos* and sarcastic poems and anecdotes aimed against the invader became popular throughout the nation.

As concerns England as a point of contact between the two Americas, we must say that during this period that nation was extremely conservative and most ideas about the United States which came by way of this channel were decidedly anti-republican. There were authors like John Stuart Mill, the great political philospher, who wrote favorably about the United States, but he was the exception rather than the rule. His adversary Lord Macaulay, who in his political essays predicted the early decadence of the great North American Republic, was more in keeping with the spirit of the times,[29] and was considered by his Spanish American contemporaries a typical representative of the European point of view. It is with particular reference to him that the Chilean Lastarria says that the wise men of the old world had conceived a simple formula which had become very popular, explaining the great progress and growth of the United States as a result of certain existing territorial conditions, rather than as the superiority of democratic institutions over the monarchical ones, and that once this favorable circumstance ceased to exist democracy would bring chaos and destruction to the American Republic. Lastarria was not in agreement with this interpretation but he quotes at length, in Spanish, a letter of Macaulay's to Mr. Randall (published in the July edition of the *London Quarterly Journal*, 1861), as a warning to his countrymen against falling under the influence of such likely logic.[30]

All through this period American culture was under attack from European critics. These authors, strongly entrenched in European points of view, condemned it in detail or in general according to their predilections and purposes. Beard, the American historian, says that "criticisms coming from that source were wholly different in animus and intention from the spirit which had inspired domestic critics since 1776. They were directed by interests, passions, and resentments as deep as the conflicts within and among the European nations from which the im-

---

[29] The occasion for these letters—I believe there were three of them—was the presentation to Macauley by Henry S. Randall of his volume biography of Jefferson. Macauley took advantage of this opportunity to point out what he thought were the dangers of Jeffersonian democracy. The particular letter to which Lastarria has reference was dated from Holly Lodge, Kensington, London, May 23, 1857. Concerning Macauley's controversy with Mill and Bentham on this question of democracy see T. Babbington Macauley, "Mill's Essay on Government". *Modern British essayists*, pp. 670-683 (first published in the *Edinburgh Review*, March, 1829); "Benthamis Defense of Mill," *ibid.*, pp. 684-695 (first published in the *Edinburgh Review*, June, 1829).

[30] José Victorino Lastarria, *La América*, Madrid, 1917, I, 38-39.

migrants who had founded and developed America had fled in search of freedom and security, Moreover, they were often deliberately designed to aid parties and causes in Europe or to bend American policy and powers to the uses of European nations locked in death grapple for dominion. In any event, apart from mere captious fault-finding, criticisms from European sources, including British sources, taken collectively, ran to the very roots of life in the old World and the new".[31] On November 12, 1869, Sarmiento wrote to Mrs. Mann from Buenos Aires: "I have not spoken with a Frenchman or an Englishman who has not ridiculed the knowledge of the North Americans, limited according to them to reading, writing, and the few notions they pick up from their newspapers".[32]

These works had considerable influence in both Americas. At this time, the Spanish-speaking countries looked toward France for cultural inspiration, and books published about the United States by Frenchmen and other Europeans were of great interest to them. In the United States conditions were very similar. Beard says that due to an attitude fostered by foreign critics, and by American weakness displayed in reactions to the impact of these ideas, "multitudes of young men and women were brought to such a plight that they derided the whole American scene. Some fled from it and tried to make themselves at home in Paris, London, Berlin, Munich, Vienna, or Moscow. Others remained at home and taking up without social analysis criticisms from Europe, assailed American civilization in the same similar terms."[33]

Sarmiento tells about a conversation that took place between an Englishman and an American farmer which illustrates conditions at the time. It seems that after having discussed the pros and cons of democracy, the Englishman asked the farmer what he thought about education, to which the farmer answered that he was all for public instruction, but that he did not believe in endowing colleges and universities that later became hot beds of aristocracy and European affectations. On another occasion in Washington, Sarmiento met a Mr. Johnson, whose father had been a general in the Revolutionary War, who was horrified at the idea that Sarmiento wanted to promote American democracy in Spanish America. Such an attitude seems to have been common enough. José Milla, who visited the United States in 1871, tells that the year before his arrival a student of Columbia College at one of the public acts of this institution, gave a lecture discussing the advantages of the monarchical form of government over that of the republican.[34]

31 Charles A. Beard, *The American Spirit*, IV, 482.
32 Sarmiento to Mrs. Mann, Buenos Aires, November 12, 1869; in *Boletín de la Academia Argentina de Letras*, IV, 1936, 124.
33 Beard, *op. cit.* p. 484
34 José Milla, *Un viaje al otro Mundo*, I, 265.

There were, of course, as a reaction against this type of literature, Anglo-Saxon and Spanish American writers who wrote essays of various lengths on the positive values of American culture. Although these were intended for home consumption, North American newspaper editorials on subjects of this nature were often translated and quoted by Spanish American authors; for during this period, as in the previous, there was a sense of continental unity in the Americas.

Logically enough, knowledge favorable to the United States was obtained from the works of European authors that chronologically would have fallen in the era of independence but whose influence reached Spanish America with a time lag. Jeremy Bentham, Benjamin Constant, Marcial Antonio López,[35] were among the better known. But by far the greatest influence upon the liberal ideas of Spanish America was exerted by the French contemporary author Tocqueville.

As a whole, it is safe to say that both North and South America looked toward Europe for intellectual guidence, and it is here that we will find the main contact bewteen them.

III. IDEAS OF THE SPANISH AMERICAN WRITERS

During the period we call the nineteenth century, the main literary movement to be found in the Spanish American countries was Romanticism; but unlike the case of Spain and France, where the duration of this school was comparatively short, in Spanish America it remained for the rest of the century, co-existing with other literary elements that came later (Realism and Naturalism) until the appearance of Modernism in 1888.

One of the outstanding characteristics of the literature was its interest in the exotic, a yearning to visit distant lands and to search for that which was little known. This sentiment explains the existence during this epoch of a literary genre we are directly concerned with in this study, namely, "the travel memoir." The contemporary Spanish Americans felt impelled by the spirit of the times to visit numerous places that Spaniards as tourists had seldom seen before: the different countries of Europe, Jerusalem, the Orient, and last but not least the United States. In previous centuries, the Spaniards had maintained themselves isolated from the rest of the world; but with the coming of independence, well-to-do Spanish Americans were to be found in the four corners of the earth. They were suffering from colonial claustrophobia, if we may use such an expression, and were trying to make up all at once for what had been denied their ancestors. Furthermore, they were not satisfied with just seeing new places, they wanted to share their experiences with those who had remained at home. For this purpose,

---

[35] A Spaniard, author of *Descripción de los más célebres establecimientos penales de Europa y los Estados Unidos,* Valencia, 1832.

whether they had literary ability or not, they published numerous diaries and memoirs of their journeys.

Also typical of the times and analogous to Romanticism was a sincere concern with the problems of democracy and the political structure of the new republics. Men such as Lastarria, Bilbao, Alberdi, Sarmiento, Montalvo, and Justo Sierra, all had a common romantic background that is evident even in their purest political writings. In Spanish America, literature was not often divorced from political action; it generally came as a vanguard to political changes. The overthrow of Rosas' dictatorship, for instance, was preceded by countless literary works attacking the tyrant. In most of these, democratic and romantic ideals went hand in hand, for in reality, both elements had a common origin. The Spanish American authors were fully aware of the political force literature represented, and they used it to the utmost of its possibilities. When in August of 1875 García Moreno, the dictator of Ecuador, was murdered, Montalvo, at that time in exile, remarked: "My pen killed him." And he was probably right.

Interest in new literature, as well as new approaches to literary criticism, was another phenomenon common to Romanticism.

1. Travelers

Of the three groups of Spanish American authors who write about the United States during this period, the largest is the one made up of the travellers. We find in it accomplished men of letters—Justo Sierra O'Reilly, Bernabé Loyola, Guillermo Prieto, Camacho Roldán, Benjamín Vicuña Mackenna, Rafael Pombo, etc.—and some of the individual memoirs, as for example Vicente Pérez Rosales' *Recuerdos del pasado,* Santiago de Chile, 1849, or Vicuña Mackenna's *Páginas de mi diario durante tres años de viaje,* 1853-1856, are excellent contributions to Spanish American literature, but judging them all as a group, it must be said that they have very little to offer that is really original. The majority of the writers had read Tocqueville's *Democracy in America*—there is hardly a memoir where its influence is not evident—but the works of the Spanish Americans are quite different from their model. Tocqueville is abstract. In his book he seldom mentions personalities or adduces examples from his personal experiences. D. C. Gilman describes him as having the qualities of a scientific reasoner. "As a naturalist who has collected many flowers or birds or insects classifies and generalizes his knowledge, so the political philosopher notices many social phenomena, and then seeks their lessons, or does not think it desirable, to indicate the concrete illustrations on which his conclusions have been based." The memoirs of the Spanish American travellers, on the other hand, do not seem to follow any definite system and are entirely of a personal nature. They are filled with countless illustrations that may go to prove some irrevocable fact or perhaps just repeat a temporary fad. Nevertheless, it is these very intimate details, regardless of the accuracy of their interpretation, that we find of greatest interest to us. It is to them that we must go to find the spirit of the times and the attitude of the authors.

Many of these travellers came to the United States and confirmed what they already knew, or thought they knew. It seems that it is human nature to find only that which we are looking for. Others, very few indeed, tell us what they saw, free from any ideological or political notions obtained prior to their arrival. All of them were looking for what was of interest to their people, using always as a point of comparison Spanish American culture. Not that they thought that it was superior, for in the majority of cases they did not, but because after all, it was the only point of reference they possessed to judge the people and the things they came upon. The best of these memoirs are not content with just describing the appearance, customs or eccentricities of this nation; they are primarily designed to discover the true meaning of America.

During the period of formation the Spanish American travellers were first attracted toward the United States because of its material and scientific progress. Memoirs reporting on scientific expeditions to the United States date back to 1827. The first visitor of this type was RAMON DE LA SAGRA (1798-1871), a noted economist who was born in Spain but spent the greater part of his life in Cuba. Sagra made several trips to study new scientific discoveries in horticulture. An account of his first voyage, *Memorias para servir de introducción a la horticultura cubana*, was published in New York in the same year. A second memoir of a later trip made in 1835, *Cinco meses en los Estados Unidos de la América del Norte desde el 20 de abril al 23 de septiembre de 1835, Diario de viaje*, was published in Paris in 1837. In 1848, JOSE MARIA DE LA TORRE, also a Cuban, published a work, *Viaje agrícola-industrial a los Estados Unidos*, on a similar subject.

New methods used in the United States for the punishment and care of criminals were first made known in Spanish America by Tocqueville's report of 1831. After this date, Spanish Americans became interested in this field of study. Two authors in particular, VICENTE L. CASTRO and Manuel Payno, came to this country on such a mission. Castro, a Cuban, visited the Philadelphia Penitentiary and gave an account of the essential modifications of prison discipline that had been introduced in America, which was published in the *Revista de la Habana* in 1855.[1] MANUEL PAYNO (1810-1894), who had been Mexican Secretary of Finance and is the author of numerous novels and books of travel, was commissioned and

---

[1] Vicente Castro, "Una visita a la Penitenciaria de Filadelfia," *Revista de la Habana*, 1855.

came to the United States for this purpose in 1843; but he never got around to giving us a report of this investigation.[2]

The day by day development of American sciences was covered thoroughly in the many reviews and periodicals published in this country by refugees from Cuba, Santo Domingo, and Puerto Rico who had taken up their residence here. These periodicals, numbering over one hundred and twenty-five, besides showing interest in American current events and American literature, devoted an entire section to American sciences. We must keep in mind that, although these publications were edited in the United States, they were intended for Spanish American consumption and that they exerted considerable influence there. As the century advanced, interest in American sciences became sufficient to warrant a more specialized type of publication. In 1878 the *Revista agrícola industrial* was published in New York dealing entirely with scientific subjects. All activities along the lines mentioned here are summarized in Manuel Trelles' article "Los Estados Unidos como potencia intelectual" published in the *Revista Cubana*, from May to October, 1894. Trelles, who had lived in the United States for many years, was excellently qualified for this study and his article is by far the best of its kind.

Admiration for North American scientific progress was registered even by those authors who were decidedly anti-American.

Travel memoirs of a broader scope appear for the first time in 1834. During this year there are two works by two Mexicans, published on this subject.

The first of these is RAFAEL REYNAL's *Viaje a los Estados Unidos del Norte*. Nothing is known about the author. Teixidor, who mentions the work in his book *Viajeros mejicanos,* claims that, in spite of a thorough search, he has never been able to discover any fact that might throw light upon the man who wrote it.

As in the case of most other Mexicans, Reynal entered the United States by way of New Orleans and went up the Mississippi. He describes the population of this region as being pale and emaciated due to the presence of malaria and yellow fever.[3] He was surprised at the many classical names given to the cities of this area: Memphis, Rome, Troy.[4] He visited the northeastern states, and was particularly impressed by Philadelphia with its high moral standards and its numerous welfare institutions.[5] He described the average American as being robust, energetic, tolerant, intemperate, and ambitious.[6] He criticized their materialistic attitude toward

---

[2] González Peña, *Historia de la literatura mexicana,* México, 1940, p. 241.

[3] Rafael Reynal, *Viaje por los Estados Unidos del Norte, dedicado a los jóvenes mexicanos de ambos secsos,* Cincinnati, 1834, p. 23.

[4] *Loc. cit.*

[5] *Ibid.,* pp. 99-100, 102.

[6] *Ibid.,* pp. 47, 150-151.

life. "Business is preferred to any other matter."[7] A man was judged not by his moral caliber but by how much money he had in the bank. The most common question was: "How much money is that man worth?"[8] He also disapproved of the way Negroes were treated.[9] His final conclusion was that in the United States, despite some obvious differences, people are fundamentally the same as anywhere else, and that one might find among them good and bad, moral and immoral.[10]

The second memoir, LORENZO DE ZAVAL A S (1788-1836) *Viaje a los Estados Unidos de Norteamérica,* is of particular interest to us because of the author's personality and the prominent part he played in inter-American relations.

Zavala, who came to be the first Vice-President of the Republic of Texas, was born in Yucatán, in 1788, of humble origin. Reared in a revolutionary environment—he was a follower of Rocafuerte and Mier—he was once imprisoned for his political ideas in the castle of San Juan de Ulúa, in Vera Cruz. In 1820 he was elected representative to the Spanish Cortes for the District of Yucatán. Here he identified himself with a radical, extreme left wing. When the news of the Mexican revolution arrived in 1821, he left Spain and on his way home visited France, England and the United States. During the first years after the independence of Mexico he played an important part in the affairs of the nation. He was one of the founders of the lodge "York", the leading anticlerical, pro-American Masonic lodge. A close friend of Poinsett, he was at all times associated with the interests of the United States. He is accused of having acquired large tracts of land in Texas and of furthering his personal interests by sponsoring the establishment of three hundred North American families in that territory. In 1830, due to political reverses, he was forced to leave the country, This time he visited the United States more at length, and was able to observe its institutions and progress with greater care. He then proceeded to Europe where he became established in Paris. There in 1834, he published the impressions of his trip.[11] A second edition of his book, with an interesting introduction by Justo Sierra O'Reilly, was published in Yucatán in 1846. Zavala is also the author of an excellent history of the Mexican Revolution, *Ensayo histórico sobre las revoluciones de México, desde 1808 hasta 1830.*

In 1835, due to the declaration of the Monroe Doctrine and to fear of the political intentions of the United States, Mexico revised its consti-

---

[7] *Ibid.,* pp. 46-47.
[8] *Ibid.,* p. 159
[9] *Ibid.,* p. 21.
[10] *Ibid.,* pp. 160-161
[11] Lorenzo de Zavala, *Viaje a los Estados Unidos del Norte de América,* Paris, 1834; 2nd ed., Yucatán, 1846.

tution making the State of Texas more dependent on the central government. From this time on Zavala started to work more openly for the annexation of Texas to the Union. Since 1826 Poinsett had hoped that some
day he would be able to secure the purchase of Texas through his friendship with Zavala. Having heard that Zavala had refused the appointment
as minister to the United States, Poinsett wrote at the time to Clay: "I
was not sorry that he declined it, he is one of the most efficient leaders
of the party friendly to the United States, the 'Yorkinos', and is more useful
here than he would be in Washington."[12]

After the Mexican War of 1848, Zavala was looked upon by the
average Mexican as a traitor to the nation. Lucas Alamán describes him as
an unscrupulous individual interested only in his personal gain;[13] and Vicuña Mackenna tells that during his trip to Mexico in 1853, he heard reports that "Pedraza, Suárez Iriarte and Zavala, all disciples of the American school, had died poisoned as traitors for being members of the political
faction in favor of the United States."[14] This rumor was not true, but it
clearly reveals the attitude of the Mexican people toward those whom they
considered collaborators with the foreign invader, of whom Zavala was
among the most prominent.

In the prologue to his *Viaje a los Estados Unidos,* Zavala tells us,
as Rocafuerte used to do, that he is writing this memoir because he does
not know of anything "that would be more useful to his compatriots than
to become acquainted with the traditions, habits and government of the
United States, whose institutions they have faithfully copied."[15] He then
repeats most of the pro-American arguments already presented by Mier
and Rocafuerte. He eulogizes the virtues of the American nation, hard-
working, industrious, intelligent, prosperous, religious, tolerant, free, proud,
persevering, etc., and continues to condemn the many defects of the Mexicans.[16]

Disliked as he was by many of his countrymen because of his political
career, even his most ardent enemies had to admit that Zavala was a master
of prose writing. His memoir, written in an unaffected, vigorous Spanish,
flows smoothly and retains the interest of the reader to the very end. The
highlight of the trip was his visit to the President.

Visit to Jackson—

On June 28 we continued on our trip by embarking for Cincinnati on
the Benjamin Franklin, a very small but comfortable steamboat. We paid

---

[12] Poinsett to Clay, Mexico City, Oct. 21, 1826; quoted in William Forrest Sprague,
Vicente Guerrero, Mexican liberator, p. 99.

[13] Lucas Alamán, "Semblanzas e Ideario," *Biblioteca del Estudiante Universitario,*
México, 1939, VIII, 152.

[14] Benjamín Vicuña Mackenna, *Páginas de mi diario,* p. 82.

[15] Zavala, *Viaje a los Estados Unidos,* p. 1.

[16] *Ibid.,* pp. iii - iv, 145, 354.

five pesos and sailed for thirty hours, reaching Cincinnati when they were celebrating the arrival of General Jackson, the President of the United States. It is easy to imagine that there were no lined up battalions, no artillery, no armed people, no bishops nor canons, no priests that came to receive the chief of the government of the Union. There was nothing like that. But one did see large crowds of townspeople who ran down to the edge of the river to receive and see their first citizen, the honorable old man who had liberated Louisiana and given the Floridas to the United States and who today ruled the destinies of the country with prudence, judgement and the purest of intentions. There were musicians, banners, and shouts of joy. Everything was natural and spontaneous. It resembled the 'fiestas' of our towns and cities when they celebrate some saint's day, rather than those ceremonies formulated in the court days, at which no one shows a sincere interest or a real feeling of sympathy. Jackson was received with enthusiasm, especially by the workers, farmers and artisans.

The following day General Mejía and I happened to visit the patriarch president. I had a letter of recommendation for him from Mr. Butler, Chargé d'Affaires of the Legation of the United States to our government. Sr. Mejía had known him since he had been Secretary of the Mexican Legation in Washington. The honorable old man was lodged in a moderately furnished house. He was sitting in a chair surrounded by twenty or thirty persons who appeared to be farmers, and artisans. making it the simplest court in the world. He looked like one of those old heroes of Homer who, in spite of having seen much action in war, retired to live among his fellow countrymen, whom he governs like sons. The General received us cordially, asking us about his friend, General Guerrero. He lamented his bad fortune and expressed his faith in the cause of the Mexican people and their ultimate triumph.

On the 29th of June I embarked on the steamboat Magnolia which left for Wheeling. The third of July was marked by celebrating on board the boat the anniversary of the independence of the United States. The fourth falling on Sunday, which is a holy day, they could not celebrate then, this day being consecrated by religion to the worship of God, each man according to his own belief. The fifteen or twenty persons who were on board the boat were not a sufficient number to give an idea of how this great nation celebrates such a solemn day nor of the noble sentiment with which they behold the ideal of liberty, made possible by such magnificient circumstances. I will not speak therefore, on this occasion, of what happened on this day of general enthusiasm throughout the United States. I have only brought to mind these circumstances to show that even in the most isolated and remote places, the North Americans celebrate with religious, patriotic pleasure the anniversary of their Declaration of Independence, as well as to go on record for the toast that I made on that day which was as follows:

—The Mexican citizens pray to God for liberty wherever they may find themselves. On this solemn day, dedicated to the celebration of the United States of North America, I venture to join my prayers to those of all free men who today celebrate the anniversary of their independence. Here are my wishes: may Providence maintain this nation and its present institutions for many centuries to come, and may Mexico imitate it with success.

Sr. Mejía spoke in a similar spirit, and the North Americans joined their prayers to ours.

In the afternoon of the same day we arrived at Wheeling, a manufacturing town of ordinary glassware, in the state of Virginia where passengers disembarked in order to go to the States of Virginia, Pennsylvania, Maryland, New York, etc. Here I left Sr. Mejía who, in order to reach his destination in Washington, had to continue across the Alleghanies.[17]

Zavala was by no means the only Mexican to participate in the independence of Texas. José Antonio Navarro was also one of the signers of the declaration of independence, and Erasmo Seguin acted as co-commissioner with Stephen F. Austin in the colonists' dealings with the Mexican government. There are historians who claim that one-third of those who opposed the troops of Santa Ana were Mexicans. Nor were pro-American feelings limited to the North American borders of Mexico.

In 1847 JUSTO SIERRA O'REILLY (1814-1861) and Rafael Carvajal came to the United States on a singular mission. The state of Yucatán was at the time torn with internal strife. The Maya Indians had risen and were laying waste the land, and a group of the well-to-do "Yucatecos" had decided that in order to restore peace it was necessary to secede from the Mexican federation. Sierra O'Reilly and his companions were sent to the United States by this group to offer the sovereignty of Yucatán to the American government. The mission failed, but during his trip Sierra O'Reilly kept meticulous notes for his wife and children of all he did and saw. Eventually these impressions were published in a book entitled *Diario de nuestro viaje a los Estados Unidos*.[18] Without doubt Sierra's notes enjoyed considerable popularity in Yucatán. They certainly had a marked influence upon his family, for years later when his son, the well-known author Justo Sierra Méndez, in turn visited the United States he often referred affectionately to his father's earlier visit. Justo Sierra O'Reilly's attitude toward the United States was a friendly one. As in the case of Zavala, he believed the best that could happen to some of the Spanish American territories was to be annexed to the North American Republic as added states.

Other Mexican travellers who visited the United States and left interesting accounts of their sojourn were Luis de la Rosa, Alberto Lombardo, Guillermo Prieto, and Justo Sierra Méndez.

LUIS DE LA ROSA, an able politician who had been Secretary of Com-

---

17 *Ibid.*, pp. 5-9.

18 Justo Sierra O'Reilly, *Diario de nuestro viaje a los Estados Unidos*. Prólogo y notas de Héctor Pérez Martínez, México, 1939. (*Biblioteca histórica mexicana de obras inéditas*, vol. 12) Numerosos documentos incluidos en el apéndice muestran la actividad de Justo Sierra en los Estados Unidos.

merce in 1844, visited the United States in 1848.[19] His stay of two months was something of a social success, and de la Rosa left with an excellent opinion of this nation. That same year he published his book *Impresiones de un viaje de México a Washington*. Being aware of the tremendous differences that existed between the two nations, he was of the opinion that a blind imitation of the United States on the part of Mexico would be a mistake. He sees the essential difference of the two nations symbolized in the careers of Washington and Hidalgo.

> The meditations caused by the sight of so notable a landmark as Mount Vernon, bring to my mind the name of Hidalgo, the leader of the independence movement of my country, whose destiny has been as different from that of Washington as are the circumstances under which each of the two nations declared their independence, and as different also as the two peoples that owe them their nationalities. Washington himself never conceived the idea of independence. This thought was suggested to him by the people. Hidalgo conceived that great idea and prognosticated it among shadows and mysteries, as if it were a sacredly inspired poem. Washington was called by his people to make possible with his courage a glorious revolution. Hidalgo awoke his dormant people and cast a ray of light upon a nation surrounded by darkness. The united people presented Washington with their arms. their valor, and all the resources. Hidalgo created everything with his genius; . . . to his voice the people rose, as some day the generations that are sleeping now beneath the earth will awake at the voice of God. And within a period of a few days, the ailing priest presented before Calderón more than one hundred thousand belligerents, that followed his banner with a fervor, which perhaps will never be reported again in days to come . . . Washington only had to fight the established dominating elements of his country, and thus he could afford to be noble, moderate, and generous. Hidalgo, on the other hand, had to initiate a civil war which turned out to be implacable, bloody, and long. . . Washington understood his people, and they in turn valued their leader. Hidalgo came before his time, and awoke among his people ideas of nationality, liberty, and greatness for which they were not ready. Washington died in the midst of peace, surrounded by the blessings of his countrymen. Hidalgo came to his end on the scaffold, in the midst of the horrors of a civil war, loaded down by the terrible accusations of his fellow clergymen.[20]

As much as Luis de la Rosa admired this nation, he thought that its one great weakness was the Federal System, "because all federations are by nature weak."[21]

---

[19] It is probable but not certain that Luis de la Rosa was in the United States in the early twenties and that he fell under he influence of Rocafuerte.

[20] Luis de la Rosa, *Impresiones de un viaje de México a Washington en octubre y noviembre de 1848*, pp. 52, 53.

[21] *Ibid.*, p. 23. In this he agrees with Mier and Rocafuerte whom he must have known well.

In 1883 the Mexican novelist ALBERTO LOMBARDO crossed the continent by rail. At that time this means of travel still retained some of its original glamour and adventure. In the run between Chicago and San Francisco dining cars were being used. Lombardo was very much impressed by this and other novelties which he vividly describes in his book *Los Estados Unidos. (Notas y episodios de viaje)*, published in 1884. By chance he happened to be in the same train with Oscar Wilde when the famous English author was making his tour through the United States. As they were going over the Sierra Nevada, Rites, one of the fellow travellers, came to tell Lombardo that Oscar Wilde was travelling with them.

—Who is Oscar Wilde? asked Lombardo.
—A person who has attained great popularity in this country by speaking
    ill in public gatherings of all that he has encountered here.
—And what is his criticism?
—The prevailing bad taste. He is an apostle of esthetics and is making a
    crusade to introduce good principles, a crusade that earns for him
    considerable money, for the theaters and halls are always full
    of people who want to see him.
—He will speak, of course, of the buildings?
—He has told the Americans that if they want to build ugly buildings they
    should use bricks, but not waste marble and granite.
—And what more has he added?
—He claims that the habit of littering the streets with goods of all sorts
    destroys their beauty. His reforms extend even to the clothing, and
    he suggests that instead of these two columns called trousers
    they ought to dress themselves with elegant stockings and wear,
    men and women alike, a yellow flower in the lapel.
—But in this matter of the stockings he could not possibly refer to the thin
    ones: at least he would at some time advise them to use cotton
    padding in them?

Lombardo became curious and wanted to meet the apostle of this new creed. He rose from his seat and went to the platform of the following car where Wilde was speaking at the moment. He describes Oscar Wilde as a tall, robust Englishman, with an effeminate manner that contrasted badly with his natural vigor. His hair was long and was parted in the middle. He wore a suit of velvet, stockings, and shoes with buckles. The Americans found revenge by ridiculing the English author. In Reno, a newspaper reported that a gentleman had taken such a strong liking to Oscar Wilde that he had intended to kidnap him. The intervention of the police had been necessary to prevent this singular occurrence from materializing. If Wilde's object was to gain attention and money he had succeeded completely. Lombardo says that the people flocked to his lectures. "They were more eager to meet him than if he had been a prince."

Lombardo's humor turns to serious thought upon beholding the beauty of the state of California and realizing Mexico's great loss.

> We had just come down the mountains and found ourselves in the beautiful state of California. Here is the garden of the United States. The island of Calypso does not have such a perpetual carnival of flowers. The orchards resemble hand-embroidered handkerchiefs and the fields, plushlike bedspreads. The pine trees standing in circular order crown the hilltops, as if they were gentlemen asccending a summit. The rivers, like kings, have reclined on beds of gold. This brilliant region is the greatest loss that Mexico has suffered. Precious jewel! Emerald placed in a valuable setting! Incomparable reunion of all the natural beauties. One could say about it something similar to what Hamlet said of Horace: 'There are more things in heaven and on earth than could be reported.'[22]

GUILLERMO PRIETO (1818-1897)—poet, newspaperman and historian—aspired to be Mexico's national bard. Whether he was or was not is debatable; what we can say with certainty is that he enjoyed great popularity and that he identified himself with the common people of his country.

He visited the United States in 1877. His first impressions, recorded in his *Viaje a los Estados Unidos,* are of particular interest to us because of his strong Spanish point of view, which brings out the contrast between the Spanish and English cultures.[23]

On the whole he is favorably impressed by what he saw. He describes the people as vigorous and healthy, more inclined to social collaboration than to family life! "Here very little importance is given to family life ... In the home you eat, you sleep, you dance, but you cannot say that you live."[24] The original population did not grow; only the immigrant families had children. "If prevailing conditions continue, within 50 years there will not be a single inhabitant of the Anglo-Saxon race."[25] He was shocked to discover that there were such things as birth control clubs. He relates that American women believed children to be a hindrance.[26]

Women were in a privileged position, both in and out of the family circle. "As a rule they are beautiful and captivating."[27] In hotels, restaurants and department stores they had special private compartments.[28] Men, of their own free will, had placed women on a pedestal. "She enjoyed the protection of men and of the law."[29]

---

22 Alberto Lombardo, *Los Estados Unidos* (*Notas y episodios de viaje*), Mexico 1884. pp. 198-200.
23 Guillermo Prieto, *Viaje a los Estados Unidos por Fidel Guillermo Prieto,* Mexico, 1877-78, p. 169.
24 *Ibid.,* p. 170.
25 *Ibid.,* pp. 458-459.
26 *Ibid.,* p. 453.
27 *Ibid.,* pp. 46, 50.
28 *Ibid.,* p. 46
29 *Ibid.,* pp. 46, 47.

Prieto saw very little difference between the way an American treated his own child and that of his neighbor. A child, regardless of who his parents might be, was common seed for the future citizen of tomorrow. The community owed him an education, so that he would be a contributing factor to democracy.[30]

The Americans were by nature independent. From childhood they aspired to be men and economically independent. This they achieved at an incredibly early age.[31]

The different members of the family hardly ever stayed at home.[32]

They had no servants.[33]

Divorce was a common thing. In some states like Indiana, it took only twenty minutes to obtain a separation.[34] Even in the New England States and Pennsylvania, that were supposed to be more conservative, dislike for children and for a long conjugal life were prevalent.[35]

"The greatness of this country," says Prieto, "lies ... in the fact that what in other countries has been called the rabble, in the United States has been called the people." This nation had given the common man a sense of dignity never before acquired by the people of other countries.[36]

Prieto sees "acceleration" as the predominant note in the North American spirit. Open competition kept the people in constant motion.[37] This went along with a deep sense of equality that was based not upon theory but upon actual practice. According to Prieto, in the United States a lackey enjoyed the same privileges as his master.[38]

The strength of the nation, he found, was the result of collaboration and team work. In this country there were thousands of institutions and associations, the members of which were all striving for a common goal.[39] European immigration was another factor that contributed to its stupendous energy.[40]

Prieto observed some aristocratic tendencies within the national character, but he prophesied that these elements would be counterbalanced by the large democratic immigration from the Old World.[41]

The great weakness of the Americans was money. In this country everything was business, including religion and politics. When it came to mone-

---

30 *Ibid.,* p. 218.
31 *Ibid.,* pp. 170-171.
32 *Loc. cit.*
33 *Ibid.,* p. 303.
34 *Ibid.,* p. 458.
35 *Ibid.,* pp. 458, 459.
36 *Ibid.,* p. 204.
37 *Ibid.,* p. 170.
38 *Ibid.,* pp. 48, 49.
39 *Ibid.,* pp. 112, 118.
40 *Ibid.,* pp. 55, 56.
41 *Ibid.,* p. 205.

tary matters he describes the people of the United States as completely unscrupulous. Many were willing to start fires to collect the insurance. Others
habitually went into bankruptcy. "There are some that have had as many
as five and six bankruptcies . . ."[42] Everything that can be sold, is sold."[43]

As concerns inter-American relations Prieto sees the United States as
a threat to the Spanish American countries. Along with his other impressions, he writes a poem, praising America's practical genius at the same
time that he condemns its imperialistic ambitions, which in many ways is a
forerunner of Rubén Darío's poem "A Roosevelt."[44]

At the age of 47 JUSTO SIERRA MENDEZ (1848-1912), one of Mexico's most prolific men of letters, left his native country for the first time.
He himself tells us that since he was a small boy he had always wanted
to visit the United States. His father, Justo Sierra O'Reilly, had fired his
imagination with numerous anecdotes of his own trip of 1848, but it was
not until then that he, Justo Sierra, the son, had the opportunity of coming
to the promised land. It is probable that he knew the United States as well
as most cultured Americans; his knowledge, however, was a literary one.
Having read most of the works written about this country by Spanish and
European writers, Sierra was confronted with the problem of adjusting his
preconceived ideas to reality. He followed the same route as his father, up
the Mississippi, across the Great Lakes, and then to New York and the
eastern coastal states. He went from one familiar landmark to another,
always accompanied by the ghost of those who had preceded him. His
arrival at Niagara was particularly touching. He had read almost everything
that had been written on the subject. His father's description and Heredia's
poem he knew practically by heart. It is not surprising that the actual sight
of the Falls, in spite of their great beauty, came to him as a slight disappointment.

---

42 *Ibid.*, p. 205.
43 *Ibid.*, p. 205. He uses almost the same words as Foronda.
44 *Ibid.*, p. 124.

   "Que alce el Yankee palacios en los mares
Que de férreo tendón doten los vientos,
Para que tenga cuerpo el pensamiento
Rieles el éter, el espacio voz.
   Que entre el triunfal hosanna del trabajo
Levanten los alcázares su frente;
Que pase sobre el cuello del torrente
Envuelto en humo ráp do el vapor
    Todo lo pueden ellos, ellos pueden
Convertir en espléndidas naciones
de mi patria infelice los girones,
   Botín de engaño, presa de baldón.
    Todo lo pueden ellos! mas no pueden
Arrancar a mi patria su nobleza!
Ni robar a su espléndida belleza
Su heroico, su divino corazón."

Niagara — "The train slowed down and we could see better the tobacco colored forest, the groups of houses with symmetrical patches of snow on their roofs, and below, here and there, neat white puddles on the wet and muddy ground. The train stopped and it was seven o'clock in the morning.

From the temperature of twenty-five centigrade in the Pullman we changed to three or four degrees below zero in the station; we passed rapidly, as everything is done there, without transitions, without shadings, *en bloc*.

A great gust of polar wind penetrated us to the marrow; the dense sky, quilted with enormous fleeces of gray wool, was above us and the rain touched us in the form of a shower of molecules of ice.

It would be a hyperbole to say that the sensation was pleasant; the truth is that at that moment I was not thinking about it; while my companions were arranging for our transfer to the Niagara House, the only hotel that remained open on the American side, I looked slowly around, as if wanting to convince myself that I was indifferent. I was determined not to be surprised by anything. I had seen photographs of the big waterfall so many times! It had been mentioned so much to me that complete surprise was impossible! On the contrary I felt beforehand the proud melancholy of disillusionment. I had read many descriptions of Niagara; that of Chateaubriand, that of Tyndall (I only speak of those which had impressed me most) and that one which was more familiar and intimate to me, written by my father in '48, exactly at the time when I was born. I did not remember them at that moment, nor did I want to. Of the poem of Heredia I could only recall one phrase: 'Niágara undoso . . .' Can Niagara be called *undoso*, my God!

Impatience devoured me, as the fox the entrails of the Spartan youth, without letting my face show anything. The faces of fat people, composed of more or less ample curves, are very suitable for feigning emotions. They would be thick, perfect masks if the facility with which we change color did not expose us. One thing disturbed me profoundly, the noise, the famous perpetual thunder of Niagara, that can be heard at a distance of 20 kilometers, and that there at 200 yards was not audible. Where was the thunder? I asked my companions, and we all stopped and listened . . . Nothing! Niagara was not thunderous that day; the lion did not roar. He was cold.

In a vehicle that was almost comfortable, we went through some streets of the city; the same American city as always. These cities of very tall houses, with window grates devoid of decorations, constructed of the same material, painted the same colors, lined up in an identical way, appear to be factory-made by the same pattern, like hats or suitcases. We arrived at the hotel. We installed our belongings rapidly, and then we ran to the stoves. Immediately after that we ate a bad lunch with gusto.

Then, while the excursion cars were arriving, we quickly visited a place where they sold trinkets of Niagara. 'Niagarities' I will call them.

There at the farthest end of the hall was a window, and from there a good part of the river could be seen . . . But I did not want to see it.

The charming girl who took care of the 'Niagarities' and gently sold them for what I thought a very high price, showed me some photographs, very good ones to be sure, some dolls dressed as the Indians of that territory, tobacco pipes of all sizes, moccasins of silky fur, rosaries of Niagara stone, hundreds of crystal paper weights with Niagara Falls inside, paper cutters and everything imaginable. It was all very pretty and quite tiresome. I was already bored with Niagara.[45]

In Central America the best travel memoir having the United States for its subject was written by JOSE MILLA (1822-1882), one of the most prolific writers Guatemala has ever produced. This author, also known by the pen-name of Solomé Jil, was for many years the editor of the *Gaceta Oficial,* and the author of a history of Guatemala and of several historical novels.[46]

Milla visited the United States in 1871. As in the case of other travellers who came by way of the Pacific, he landed in San Francisco, crossed the continent by train and visited the large cities of the eastern coast. From New York he sailed for Europe where he continued with his journey to France, Italy and England.

In his three-volume memoir, he is accompanied by an imaginary character, Juan Chapín, who represents the common man of Guatemala. As in the case of Don Quijote and Sancho, these two characters share many adventures and visit strange, distant lands. The two are in reality a unit, opposing each other, yet bound together by a common need for one another. Milla's companion represents the instincts, traditions and prejudices of the Spanish American people. Opposing this attitude is the rational, worldly outlook of Milla, trying to make Chapín understand why things are as they are. In creating, out of his own mind, what he believes would be the typical attitude of his fellow countrymen under a given situation, Milla reveals for us part of his own conscience and in a way his own limitations in interpreting both the culture of Spanish America and that of the United States.

Chapín — who is at the same time shrewd and naive, but always ignorant — is critical of many of the things he found in this country, particularly the position enjoyed by women in society.

He cannot understand how a woman can possibly be a medical doctor and much less a newspaper reporter. Milla, who is on the inside of things and knows the secret, explains that in the United States women are that and much more. "There are even congresswomen and secretaries of state,

---

[45] Justo Sierra, *En tierra yankee* (*Notas a todo vapor.*), México, 1898, pp. 171-173.
[46] Coester, *The literary history of Spanish America,* p. 447.

in short, everything a man can be."[47] This, he explains, is due to a great degree to the general upbringing and education given women in this country. Both boys and girls are reared together and receive the same instruction. From childhood students of both sexes go to the same schools, enjoying the same freedom and the same outlook on life. Milla is of the opinion that this excellent relation would not work in Europe or in Spanish America, due to the temperament and traditional culture of those peoples.[48] Vassar College, in Poughkeepsie, he believes to be the epitome of education for women. "Vassar College created in 1861 for the education of women is perhaps the finest institution of its type in the world. A wealthy retired brewer gave a half million dollars for the construction of a magnificent building on the same style as the Tulleries in Paris. He appointed 28 trustees, and in a solemn act he presented the $500,000 that went to pay for the founding of the college that today carries his name." Milla explains that in order to be admitted to this institution the young women had to at least be able to translate Caesar, Cicero and Virgil; and to have studied rhetoric, algebra and general history.[49]

He was much impressed by education in the United States in general. He remarked that Spanish was taught in many colleges. He was surprised, however, to find out how poor the libraries were when it came to books on Spanish America. In the New York Public Library, at that time located in Lafayette Place, he did not find a single book that had to do with Central America. "Here there is very little interest in getting to know us, and we, on our part, are even less interested that they should."[50]

Of the South American writers who visited the United States, VICENTE PEREZ ROSALES (1807-1886), Simón Camacho, Salvador Camacho Roldán, Benjamín Vicuña Mackenna and Domingo de Pantoja, have left us the best travel memoirs. The Chilean Pérez Rosales is the only one of this group who writes about the California gold rush. The others visited the eastern costal states.

Pérez Rosales was born in Chile, in April, 1807. His early family background and education represented the best that Chile had to offer during the early years of the nineteenth century. Once his elementary studies were completed, he spent three years in Paris, for in those days, by Chilean standards, one was not an accomplished gentleman without having visited that city. Here he studied in the academy of don Manuel Silvela, a Spanish liberal well known in Spanish America. He met among other people San Martín, Egaña, Irizarri, Olmedo, and Bello. For two years after his return he lived in Santiago until the loss of the family fortune forced him to lead

---

47 José Milla, *Un viaje al otro Mundo.* I, 29-30.
48 *Ibid.,* I, 266-268.
49 *Ibid.,* I, 263.
50 *Ibid.,* I, 93. Milla's observation on this matter is far from being exact.

a life of adventure, that widened his outlook on life but did not improve his economic situation. He was among the first to arrive in California when gold was discovered.[51] The account he gives of his experiences there, in his book *Recuerdos del pasado,* is comparable to any other description, in any language, of the California gold rush of 1848. After his failure as a gold miner, he again returned to Chile where he became an immigration agent for the government of Montt-Varas. He was instrumental in bringing large groups of German colonists to southern Chile.

The predominating characteristic of American civilization, as seen by Pérez Rosales, is acceleration.[52] This phenomenon consisted in the hastening of the tempo of life and in the intensification of the individual and collective initiative. California found itself transformed overnight by people that came from the four corners of the earth, all of whom shared the American spirit: daring, constancy and faith in the immediate future. The activity of these peoples and the conquest of California in general was motivated by material, practical purposes, rather than by spiritual values. "No one walked, they flew."[53]

The unifying force of this whole movement was the press. "One could always see travelling, among the cannon of the army, the wagon of the printing press. From each army headquarters there came every day thousands of printed sheets that disseminated everywhere news concerning the progress of the campaign or presenting the advantages of a peaceful annexation to the American Union."[54]

As soon as John D. Sloat had taken possession of Monterrey in the name of the United States, there appeared, in that same town, the newspaper *Californian,* along with the foundations of a temple acclaiming liberty of faith, and two schools the "elegance of which contrasted with the heavy Spanish colonial buildings." The following year, the modest village of Yerbas-Buenas, today San Francisco, could boast of the *California Star.*

Two years later there were five newspapers published in upper California: the *Pacific News,* the *Journal du Commerce.* the *California Courier,* the *Herald* and the *Evening Picayune.* Sacramento had the *Transcript* and the *Placer Times,* and Stockton, the *Journal Times.*[55]

There was nothing theoretical about the program that was being carried out. The Yankees started by building roads and making the place they wanted to colonize accessible; they constructed works that led to the stability and security of the settlers such as schools and churches. Land was

---

51 Concerning Pérez Rosales' life see "Introduction", *Recuerdos del pasado, 1814-1860;* Santiago de Chile, 1886; also: Guillermo Feliú Cruz, *Vicente Pérez Rosales, Ensayo crítico,* Santiago de Chile, 1946.

52 Vicente Pérez Rosales, *Recuerdos del pasado, 1814-1860,* pp. 263, 264, 265.

53 *Ibid.,* p. 303.

54 *Ibid.,* p. 264.

55 *Loc. cit.*

to be had for the asking. In return for these advantages they demanded of the people only that they remain in a permanent place. Pérez Rosales was offered excellent sites, but since he had not come to settle but to gather gold, he answered smilingly: "Try another dog with that bone."[56] Nevertheless, Pérez Rosales realized that the greatest wealth of California was not its gold but its infinite agricultural and industrial possibilities.[57]

The towns were all cut from the same pattern. All were possessed by the same excitement and feverish activity. "To see one town was to see them all."[58]

Within the heterogeneous multitudes that made up the population of California, he found several types that predominated. There were the Chileans, with their toasted flour, their knapsacks, their shovels and crowbars, their pans for washing gold, and a dagger at their side. There were the Oregonians, rough and quarrelsome, with their long rifles and six-shooters, powder bags, knives, mountain boots and abundant supply of brandy bottles. There were the sons of the celestial empire, the Japanese, with large varnished parasol hats, a large handkerchief around the neck, an Arabic dagger at their waist, shoes with soles of ten layers of cardboard, and two sacks of rice suspended from the end of a stick that hung over their shoulders. Only the Yankees and the Europeans showed in their dress no signs of regionalism.[59]

The Indians, many of whom spoke Spanish, had at first befriended the Americans; but soon, smarting under the rough treatment received at the hands of the newcomers, they started to murder and rob. These same Indians treated Rosales and his group with all manner of courtesies and attentions once they found out they were Spanish. He describes them as dark and not as strong as those of Chile. Their dress was an indescribable mixture, half savage and half European.[60]

The native whites he depicts as completely bewildered by what was taking place. Pérez Rosales travelled with some of them and found them to possess the characteristic Spanish kindness and generosity.[61] On one occasion, while approaching a Spanish village, he was mistaken for an American and almost shot. "God forgive you, my friend," said his host once he had identified himself, "for the scare you have given us. When we saw you approach, we thought that you were one of those scoundrels who infest our roads and towns since the peace made us change masters! Come in, Sir, come in!" "And he had a right to be afraid," says Rosales, "only the native proprietor knew of the many injustices, without appeal, to which

---

56 *Ibid.*, p. 301.
57 *Ibid.*, p. 320.
58 *Loc. cit.*
59 *Ibid.*, p. 304.
60 *Ibid.*, pp. 311-312, 325-326.
61 *Ibid.*, pp. 358-359.

he had been subjected since the invasion of those they called 'the barbarians from the North' started." His host then begged Pérez to take off his rough mining outfit and change into some of his own clothing, so as not to continue reminding him "of those intruders whom he hated so much."[62]

Friction with the Americans was not limited to the Indians and the native Californians; the Chileans and other Spanish Americans who were present did not get along with them any better. Pérez accuses them of being prejudiced against everything Spanish. There seems to have been an open feud between the Americans and the Chileans that cost many lives on both sides and that finally forced most of the latter to return to their own country. Pérez tells of an incident, when a group of Americans almost hanged a friend of his, by the name of Alvarez, for an insignificant motive. "Some shovels were misplaced, and there being in their midst no other suspect than that descendant of an African (for thus they called the Chileans and the Spaniards), they accused him of the theft, and without any loss of time, that group of barbarians formed a jury and were going to do to Alvarez what they frequently did with the well known robbers."[63] Fortunately, for Alvarez's sake, Pérez Rosales and some American friends intervened and the execution never took place.

According to Rosales this attitude, on the part of the Americans toward the Chileans, was totally unwarranted. The Chileans contributed in many ways to the development of California during its early stages. Many of the cereals and other goods used by the first wave of colonists were Chilean, and Chileans were the founders of some of the new towns. The first charity hospital was built by the Chilean brothers, Manuel and Leandro Luco, who sold their boat Natalia with its entire cargo for this purpose.[64] "There was not a family in Chile that did not have at least one representative in California."[65]

Drinking was so common that you could trail the Yankees by the empty bottles they left behind.[66]

The population was made up of a few good people and a multitude of bandits, "men whose only God was gold, who understood only the justice of force."[67] Anarchy prevailed throughout the land. In Stockton Pérez Rosales saw the first gibbet, the first sign of civilization he saw in California.[68]

While he was mining gold in California another South American author, Domingo Faustino Sarmiento, was sent to the east of the United States by the Chilean government to study the educational system. He was

---

[62] *Ibid.*, pp. 360-361.
[63] *Ibid.*, p. 277.
[64] *Ibid.*, pp. 265-266.
[65] *Ibid.*, p. 363.
[66] *Ibid.*, pp. 298, 310.
[67] *Ibid.*, p. 330.
[68] *Ibid.*, pp. 335-336.

followed in 1862 by SIMON CAMACHO, known by the pen-name of Nazareno. Camacho's book *Cosas de los Estados Unidos,* published in New York, 1864, is primarily concerned with the behavior of American women. He finds them to be free, beautiful and fully masters of the situation. In complete agreement with most Spanish Americans who visited this country, he believed that women and children enjoyed a privileged position.[69] "Here women are the queens, the kings are the children."[70]

Later come other authors: Salvador Camacho Roldán, Benjamín Vicuña Mackenna and Domingo de Patoja.

SALVADOR CAMACHO ROLDAN, Colombian essayist and student of social problems, is the author of two books on the United States. The first of these is *The Life of Lincoln,* first published in the *Opinión* of Bogotá and later translated into English and printed in book form in New York, 1925. Lincoln, a timely popular subject, became for the Spanish Americans what Washington and Franklin had represented during the previous period. In the second book *Notas de Viaje,*[71] Camacho Roldán makes a favorable evaluation of the civilization of this country. During an interview held with a newspaper reporter, he summarizes his attitude toward the United States in the following manner:

"What do you think of the United States?", asked the reporter.

"It is a very large country, very rich, very free and very happy." answered Camacho Roldán.

"What have you found most striking?"

"Its numerous means of communication: its railroads, its steamships in the rivers, its tremendous production, and the immenseness of its cities."

"Have you found anything unpleasant or that might be worthy of censure?"

"I have been surprised only by the attitude of contempt that the white population has for the races of a darker color."

"And why are you surprised by that?"

"Because, having to live with colored people, needing and receiving their cooperation, as you do, it seems only natural that you would do them justice by accepting them, without prejudice, in your theaters, hotels, churches and schools, which I see is not the case."

"And what do you think of Mr. Cleveland?"

"I like Mr. Cleveland. His public acts seem to be motivated by the highest American ideals."

"What acts?"

"Those relative to the protection of the Indians and the preservation of their lands; his message to Congress concerning attacks against the Chinese; and his veto of laws intended to plunder the treasury on pretext of pensions for the veterans."[72]

---

[69] Simón Camacho, *Cosas de los Estados Unidos,* New York, 1864, pp. 17, 33, 47, 95.

[70] Justo Sierra, *En tierra yankee,* p. 88.

[71] Salvador Camacho Roldán, *Notas de viaje (Colombia y Estados Unidos de América),* Bogotá, 1890.

[72] *Ibid.,* pp. 595-597.

BENJAMIN VICUÑA MACKENNA[73] was scarcely twenty years old in 1852, when, due to political reasons, he was forced to leave Chile. During the next three years that his ostracism lasted, he visited California, Mexico, the United States, Canada, England, France, Italy, Germany, the Netherlands, the coast of Brazil, and Argentina. Upon his return (1856) he published the notes of his diary, first in serial form, in the gazette *Ferrocarril,* and later that same year in book form, entitled *Páginas de mi diario durante tres años de viaje: 1853-1854-1855.*[74] Vicuña's work enjoyed great popularity in Chile. For a long time after its publication it was the leading topic of discussion in social and intellectual circles. Its popularity is unquestionably well deserved. With the exception of Sarmiento's *Viajes,* there is no other contemporary travel memoir written by a Spanish American about the United States that possesses a greater wealth of information. Years later, Vicuña came to play an important role in the political life of Chile, and in 1865, during the Chilean war with Spain, he was sent to the United States as a confidential agent. In New York he founded *La Voz de América,*[75] the first periodical dedicated to promoting the unity of the Americas. He was aided in this work by Domingo Faustino Sarmiento, who was then the Argentine Ambassador to the United States.[76] Vicuña also participated in several schemes to free Cuba and Puerto Rico. Besides a memoir of his second trip, *Diez meses de misión a los Estados Unidos de Norte América,*[77] he is also the author of several books on inter-American subjects.[78]

While in California, at the time of his first visit to the United States, Vicuña Mackenna became acquainted with James Curtis, a young man of a well-to-do Boston family. In his company and that of other gold miners he sailed from San Francisco to Acapulco, went across Mexico to Vera Cruz, and then by way of New Orleans and the Mississippi all the way to Boston. Upon their arrival Curtis took him to his home and presented him to his family. Vicuña was particularly impressed by his sisters; they were

---

[73] While in the United States he sometimes wrote under the pseudonym of D. J. Hunter.

[74] Santiago, 1856.

[75] New York, 1865.

[76] Vicuña Mackenna, *La Argentina en el año 1855,* Buenos Aires, 1936, p. 10

[77] Santiago, 1867.

[78] The political relations between the United States and Chile about the year 1819 are excellently studied by Mackenna in his work *El ostracismo de los Carrera,* Santiago, 1857; *Obras completas de Vicuña Mackenna,* V, 56-65. He is also the author of a collection of essays and lectures that goes by the title of *A Sketch of Chili, expressly prepared for the use of Emigrants, from the United States and Europe...with A Map and...Papers relating to the...War between that Country and Spain, and The Position assumed by the United States...By Daniel J. Hunter,* New York, 1866. (The second part of this work is entitled: "Chili, The United States and Spain: a series of lectures...on the position... of Chili in the pending war with Spain, New York, 1866".)

intelligent, attractive and completely free. To his utter amazement they accompanied him everywhere unchaperoned.[79]

In Boston he also met Prescott and Parker, both personal friends of Curtis. He had wanted to meet Ticknor, but their meeting could not be arranged at the time.[80]

From Boston he returned to New York where he got to know some of the outstanding Spanish Americans of his day. Indeed the public diversions of New York offered him very few attractions, but he found an agreeable pastime in the relations he cultivated with the South American circle, composed mainly of business men and exiles who had taken refuge in this country. Among the people he met there were the Mosquera family, General Páez, Mr. Irizarri, the family of Mr. Tracy, and the consul of Chile, Mr. Reily.[81]

> It was a fruitful source of mediation for a South American to attend a meeting where so many distinguished refugees were present. In the family of the Mosqueras alone there were two defeated presidents, General Tomás Mosquera and his son-in-law and successor, General Errans. The other two brothers of Mr. Mosquera were the recently expelled Archbishop and Mr. Manuel María, who had been the Ambassador of New Granada in Europe for fourteen years with a salary of twelve thousand pesos. What has happened, one asks with surprise, to the organization of the Spanish American Republics, at the sight of these family oligarchies that are almost as powerful as the royal houses of Europe?[82]

Vicuña describes General Mosquera as a man about 55 years of age, dark in color and of medium height. A bullet wound that had crossed his mouth, from gum to gum, when he was aide-de-camp to Bolívar had sunken his cheeks, and he would have appeared somewhat younger without the thick mustache he wore. He divided his time between his office on Broadway and his study, because according to Vicuña he was one of the most prolific and untiring writers of South America. At the moment he was writing the *Memoirs of Bolívar*. Señor Mosquera spoke of Chile as an expert who knew the country. He had originally come to the United States to promote a South American alliance with the North American Federation, in opposition to the tyranny England was imposing upon the shores of the southern continent in the interests of her commerce. In his conversation, in his manners and in his general approach Mosquera gave the appearance of a distinguished person. He admitted to Vicuña that he was the author of all the liberal reforms and industrial advantages that his country had acquired, such as the

---

[79] Benjamín Vicuña Mackenna "Páginas de un diario", *Obras completas de Vicuña Mackenna*, Santiago de Chile, 1935, I, 155.

[80] *Ibid.*, pp. 159-162.

[81] *Ibid.*, p. 226.

[82] *Loc. cit.*

navigation of the Magdalena River and the construction of the railroad at the Isthmus.[83]

As to physical appearance, he describes General Errans as the reverse of his father-in-law, lean and sullen of figure; he resembled him, however, in character and ideology. Vicuña heard him speak very few times, but in his political ideas, in his concepts of inter-Americanism and in the monomania of writing, he seemed a disciple of his father-in-law. His young wife, the former Amelia Mosquera, ex-first lady of New Granada, devoted herself entirely to her family and to the education of their children.[84]

The ex-minister Manuel María revealed, according to Vicuña, more capacity than the rest of the brothers; and the other, the Archbishop, emaciated by sickness and sorrow, seemed to be slowly dying.[85]

In the home of Sr. Mosquera, Vicuña used to see frequently another noted personality of Spanish American history, José Antonio Páez, hero of the war of Independence and ex-president of Venezuela. Vicuña found real pleasure in speaking with this man. He describes him as an extremely agreeable person, simple and manly — a man of the people. Many times he told him how he had risen from a private soldier under Bolívar and Sucre, to first general of the land. General Páez was president of Venezuela in the epoch of its greatest prosperity, until his own favorites, the Monagas brothers, had him exiled. He was living peacefully in New York when news of assassinations perpetrated by Congress reached his ears, he reunited some scattered auxiliaries and invaded his native land at the head of 700 men. After a campaign of seven months of defeat he finally had to surrender, and was made prisoner and taken to Maracaibo. Nine months later he returned to New York. The city received him with great honors. If he had been a native son more could not have been done for him. They even offered to help him economically but Páez graciously declined this aid.[86]

At the time Vicuña knew him he was writing his memoirs, an important document on the formation of South America.

> General Páez is one of those loyal, strong-hearted men, but without malice or intellectual education, of whom intrigues and political parties have taken possession. One is able to compare him with our illustrious General Reire, whose physique he also possesses: broad of shoulders, of middle height, elegant in his dress, with a kind smile, while his large and ardent eyes reveal internal strength. Like that Chilean general, Páez began as chief of the "guerrillas" and was afterwards general of the cavalry, and finally liberal president. He was disgusted with politics and speaking of his native

---

83 *Ibid.*, p. 227.
84 *Loc. cit.*
85 *Ibid.*, p. 228.
86 *Loc. cit.*

land he would exclaim: 'Thieves! Thieves!' He told me that he did not like to remember the epoch of the war, except as regards the memory of the brave companions in arms sacrificed at his side. In spite of his wounds and his campaigns, he was still fresh and active. He is very much loved in New York and has a particular taste for dressing with care and elegance. Many times I have met him on Broadway on Summer mornings all dressed in white, with a large chain of gold, blue spring paletot, and his hat somewhat inclined over his ear—a hangover from his days on the plains. In spite of his recognized goodness, General Páez has been a man of passions and even of vices; gambling was his great passion. His last attempt to invade Venezuela in 1854 was frustrated by the embargo of the SS Franklin by the American government in New York.[87]

He also visited José Antonio Irizarri, who was living in New York with a fellow-refugee, Sr. Arboleda, a distinguished writer from New Granada. Irizarri was at that time writing his famous English-Spanish grammar. The nature of such intellectual activities disgusted Vicuña.

How much more preferable, useful and worthy of his talent it would be for him to spend his old age writing his memoirs; then the life of his person would be bound to the history of South America in all its phases. Truly Sr. Irizarri is a typical product of South American politics and history. First journalist of Chile in 1812, he removed the mask of the revolution with his *Semanario Republicano*. In 1814 when he was only 25, he was dictator for a few hours. A little after that he was outlawed, and ever since then he has been an indefatigable and errant emissary of the reaction. From Chile and the Plate River to the Antilles and his native soil of Guatemala, he has been an apostle and a soldier of the restrictive system of which he still confesses to be an advocate. In Chile, in the region of the Plate, in Peru, in the three republics of Colombia, in all of Spanish America, with the exception of Mexico, he has supported his cause with ardor, but a bad star has guided him in these parts. He met with failure in Chile, Peru, Venezuela, New Granada and Guatemala consecutively. Today, old, sick and a refugee in a strange city, he still maintains that Cuba, the last colony of Spain, is worth more than the rest of the republics of South America. A very sad conviction indeed.[88]

Every one of the refugees Vicuña met in New York was a prolific writer, but unlike those from the region of the Caribbean who were still looking forward to the day of their independence, these men were concerned with the past. They had fought their battle and won, and after enjoying a few years of triumph they now found themselves exiles in a foreign land. At present they were occupied in writing their memoirs, trying to record for posterity the events that led to the independence of South America. In their works there are few references to the United States. This country

[87] *Ibid.*, p. 229.
[88] *Ibid.*, pp. 230-231.

had taken them in and given them shelter and protection, and they were grateful for it. Their attitude was friendly. They were not interested, however, in interpreting this civilization so it could be used as a model by future South American generations. Their hearts were still in the battle-fields of Venezuela and Chile.

Memoirs describing life in the large cities of North America are many during this period. G. F. DE VIGUNT, a Cuban, gives his impressions of New York in an article "Paseo por Nueva York" published in the *Revista Habanera* in 1861.

RAFAEL POMBO (1833-1912), the Colombian poet, paid tribute to the great city by devoting one of his poems to the beauty of its women.

In 1854, Pombo was sent to New York as Secretary of the Colombian Legation, and remained there for five years. During this time, he successfully mastered the English language and wrote several poems in English that were published by Bryant in *The New York Evening Post*. The poem with which we are concerned, "Las Norteamericanas en Broadway", has to do with a young man, presumably Pombo himself, standing beneath the portico of the Saint Nicholas Hotel admiring the passing throngs of American beauties. He compares them with the different Spanish American types, and though he appreciates the beauty of his compatriots, he admits that he is bewitched by the brilliance of the blue eyes and the crimson of the cheeks of the New Yorkers. He concludes the poem by warning against falling prey to their charms, "woe to him that sees this fascinating array!" "Their hearts, like the swirling waters of the Niagara, are cruel, insatiable and cold."

Other books concerning New York are: EUSEBIO GUITERAS' (1812-1893) *Un invierno en Nueva York* published in Barcelona in 1885; and RICARDO RODRGUEZ's (?-1906) *Impresiones y recuerdos de mi viaje a los Estados de Nueva York, Nueva Jersey y Pennsylvania,* published in Sagua la Grande in 1887. This second work in spite of its comprehensive title deals almost exclusively with New York City.

Chicago too had its share of publicity. The Chicago Exposition and other important events that took place in this city were given much attention by the Spanish American press. In 1885 ALBERTO G. BIANCHI, Manuel Caballero, and Arroyo de Anda, three Mexican newspapermen, came to Chicago where a banquet was given in their honor. As a remembrance of their sojourn Bianchi published *Los Estados Unidos. Descripción de viaje,*[89] which included, besides Bianchi's impressions of Chicago, speeches given by himself, Manuel Caballero,[90] and Arroyo de Anda. It is needless to say that these speeches were in keeping with the best Rotarian traditions. They consisted of a series of exchange of compliments between Mexico

---

[89] Mexico, 1887.
[90] *Ibid.* pp. 93-94.

and the United States, and included a poem exalting the glories of George Washington written by Bianchi himself[91] In 1893, MANUEL CABALLERO published *México en Chicago,* which was a rehashing of his companion's previous book.

But the best book describing the immense growth and material wealth of that city, as it changed from a great village into an imposing metropolis, is RAIMUNDO CABRERA Y BOSCH's *Cartas a Gorín. Impresiones de Viaje,* published in Havana in 1892. Cabrera explains the change undergone by American civilization in its progress westward. He points out certain aristocratic characteristics of refinement and culture inherent to New Englanders that disappear as the Americans go westward. For him the symbol of this new, dynamic, materialistic civilization is Chicago.[92] Cabrera is also the author of another book on the United States, *Los Estados Unidos, con notas, aplicaciones y comentario,* published in Havana in 1889.

Concerning Philadelphia, Baltimore and Washington, there are: RAMON ZAMBRANA's (1817-1866) article "Baracoa, y de Filadelfia a Baltimore" published in the *Revista del Pueblo* in the April and May issues of 1865; EMILIO BLANCHET's (1829-1915) "La ciudad de Washington", published in the review *Nuevo País,* on August 9, 1899. Blanchet is also the author of an article describing Yellowstone National Park.

As a conclusion to this survey of Spanish American travellers who wrote about the United States we should not fail to mention those whose primary interest was to visit Europe and the Holy Land, but who found it convenient to go by way of New York or some other part of the United States. These authors, although their main interest was in the Old Continent, often dedicate a chapter of their diaries to this country. This is the case of Nicolás Tanco Armero, José López Portillo y Rojas, Ignacio Martínez, Felipe S. Gutiérrez, José María de Jesús Portugal, and many others.[93] Spanish American visitors to the United States became so numerous that

---

[91] *"A Washington"*
Un pueblo entero se esforzaba en vano
Por no sufrir la vida del colono,
Ni soportar la saña y el encono
Siempre sujeto al yugo del britano.
Libertad anhelabas, y tu mano
Pedazos hizo el vacilante trono,
y la santa virtud te dió su abono,
Y libre hiciste al pueblo americano.
Hoy ese pueblo canta tus loores
Y repite doquiera tu victoria
Tu altar regando de fragantes flores.
Yo que sé de tus hechos la memoria
Recuerdo nuestro grito de Dolores.
Y elevo un canto a tu perenne gloria.
Ibid., p. 132.
[92] Raimundo Cabrera y Bosch, *Cartas a Gorín,* Habana, 1892, pp. 200-201.
[93] See bibliography.

Vicuña Mackenna relates how in 1853 seven Chileans, including himself, came together by chance at the theater in Philadelphia.[94] The presence of these Spanish Americans in the United States shows, on their part, a decided interest in the progress and affairs of this country, but we should keep in mind that this group was small compared with the number of Spanish American travellers who visited France and Spain, and other European countries.

2. Political Writers

The primary political theory to be discussed by the Spanish American authors during the earlier part of the nineteenth century was Federalism, or if seen from the opposite point of view, Centralism.

Those republics where the seat of government resided in a central capital, and where each of the divisions of this nation—province or state—was administered by individuals delegated by the central government, as opposed to the doctrine of State Rights, were considered by the Spanish Americans as having a centralized or unitarian government. The French and Chilean Republics are good examples of this type.

Those republics in which each of the divisions of the nation was independent—except for matters that were of an international nature—but united into a league by a common constitution or compact were considered by the Spanish Americans as a federal government, as for instance the government of the United States of America and that of Mexico.

In Mexico, where the political life of the country was closely affected by the policies of the United States, this issue dominated the political scene from 1823 to 1848. When Iturbide fell, Rocafuerte, Mier and de la Rosa advised the Mexican liberals to adopt a centralized form of government that would eventually unite and strengthen the nation against foreign intervention. Unfortunately for Mexico they did not take this advice and instead founded the Federalist movement. As a result the nation became divided into two political camps, the actions of which did not always consider the best interests of the republic.

On one side were the Centralists or Unitarians, a group made up of the old Spanish party, the well-to-do "criollos" and most of the clergy. This party which was under the leadership of Lucas Alamán, Nicolás Bravo, and Anastasio Bustamante, was anti-American, pro-Catholic, and believed that the activities of the new government should be channeled along the line of the traditional Spanish institutions. Many of them joined the Masonic order of "York" and looked toward England for aid against North American aggression.

---

[94] The names of the gentlemen involved were: Señor Echevarría, the two Tocornales brothers, don Ramón Undurraga, don Ladislao Larrain, and Señor Alvarez, of Valparaíso.

Distrust of the intentions of the United States became the favorite topic of this group. The Mexicans had reasons to be afraid. Zozaya, the Mexican Ambassador to the United States during Iturbide's government, shortly after presenting his credentials sent a note which received considerable publicity, anticipating the future hostilities between the two nations. He warned that "these republicans whose arrogance does not permit them to consider us as equals but as inferiors would in the course of time become our declared enemies." With this in mind, he advised the Mexicans to be wary of the United States and its people, "even though today they might appear to be their friends." He added that in the sessions of the general congress of the United States as well as those of the local legislatures of the different states, "one hears constant talk of military preparations which evidently have no other purpose than the ambitious designs over the province of Texas."[95]

A few years later, in 1829, Terán wrote his famous report accusing the Americans of acting in bad faith toward Mexico and advising the creation of a strong central government to prevent the dismemberment of the nation. "They begin by assuming rights, as in Texas", says Terán, "which are impossible to sustain in a serious discussion, making ridiculous pretensions based on historical incidents which no one admits—such as the voyage of LaSalle, which was an absurd fiasco, but serves as a basis of their claim to Texas. Such extravagant claims as these are now being presented for the first time to the public by dissembling writers; the efforts that others make to submit proofs and reasons are repeated by these men, in order to attract the attention of their fellow countrymen, not to the justice of the claim, but to the profit to be gained from admitting it. At this stage, it is alleged that there is a national demand for the step that the government meditates. In the meantime, the territory against which these machinations are directed, and which has for the most part remained unsettled, begins to be visited by adventurers and *empresarios*. Some of these take up their residence in the country, pretending that their location has no bearing upon their government's claim or the boundary disputes; shortly afterwards, some of these trail blazers develop an interest which complicates the political administration of the coveted territory . . ., and the matter having arrived at this stage—which is precisely that of Texas at this moment —we have diplomatic manoeuvers . . ." Terán concludes his report by stating that "he who consents to or does not oppose the loss of Texas is an execrable traitor who ought to be punished by death . . ."[96]

---

95 Quoted in Francisco Castillo Nájera, *Future relations between Mexico and the United States*, Washington, D. C., 1942, p. 8.

96 Quoted in Alleine Howren "Causes and Origin of the Decree of April 6, 1830," *The Southern Historical Quarterly*, XVI, 1913, 395-398. There are several memoirs concerning Mier y Terán's expedition: two by J. M. Sánchez, one by a French scientist named L. Berlandier, and another by Terán himself. There is also an extensive correspondence

In the meantime Butler, Poinsett's successor, was advising President Jackson to conquer Texas without further delay. For this reason he quarreled with Lucas Alamán, Mexican Secretary of State, and was recalled to Washington. In the United States, Manuel Eduardo de Gorostiza, the Mexican Ambassador and a noted author in his own right, published a pamphlet summarizing the relations between the two nations and defending the Mexican point of view.[97] The attitude of the Mexicans toward the United States during this period, however, can best be seen in the writings of Alamán himself, who for many years served as the principal spokesman for the anti-American party.

There are few figures in Spanish American literature whose personality has caused more controversy than that of LUCAS ALAMAN (1792-1853). A conservative of aristocratic antecedents, who came to be the defender of everything Spanish and a deadly enemy of the United States and its friends, he has been exalted or condmned by the Mexicans for the last one hundred and twenty-five years. Among his particular enemies were Mier, Zavala and Poinsett. The first two he accuses of being unnatural sons, who were bringing destruction and shame upon themselves and their nation. As concerns the third, he was instrumental in having him recalled to Washington. They in turn looked upon Alamán as the arch-conservative of his day.

While attending the Spanish Cortes he had met Luis de Onís, and upon his return to America he followed closely Onís' reports to the Viceroy. He was also closely associated with Zozaya, Terán and Gorostiza. Years of observation and careful study of the foreign policy of the United States had brought him to the conclusion that sooner or later that country would take possession of Mexico. In order to prevent this he advocated a highly centralized government, free from internal ideological strife. His followers, among whom are to be included some of the outstanding authors of today, Antonio Caso, Carlos Pereyra, Esquivel Obregón and José Vasconcelos, point to the fact that most of Alamán's predictions came true and that by 1848 the most sincere Mexicans, whether they had agreed with Alamán's political ideas or not, came to the realization that he was a true patriot and a man of considerable vision. Anthony Butler, the American representative who followed Poinsett, describes him as "a wise and astute man."[98]

Alamán appears in history as a tragic figure, who, aware of the adverse fortune of the Mexican nation and often misunderstood by his own

---

between Terán and Austin, and Terán and other Mexican officials. Please see Vito Alessio Robles, *Coahuila y Texas*, 2 vols., Mexico, 1945, I, 271-375; also C. E. Castañeda. "A Trip to Texas in 1828," *South Western Historical Quarterly*, XXIX, 249-288. An excellent account of the intentions of the United States concerning Mexico's northern provinces is to be found in Flagg Bemis, *John Quincy Adams and the Foundation of the American Foreign Policy*, New York, 1944, pp. 562-564.

[97] *Examination and review of a pamphlet printed and secretly circulated by M.E.A., late envoy extraordinary from Mexico.*, Washington, 1837.

[98] Arturo Arnaiz y Freg, in Alamán, *Semblanzas e ideario*, México, 1939, p. xviii

countrymen, fights back against historical forces uncontrollable by men. In his introduction to Alamán, *Semblanzas e ideario,* Arturo Arnaiz y Freg tells us how from the balcony of his home Alamán watched as the battle of Padierna progressed and of his intense suffering. "He was, before the invader, a Mexican watching with his binoculars the fulfillment of his most dreaded predictions."[99]

Alamán's ideas are not unlike those of the great precursors: Miranda, Simón Rodríguez, Bolívar, San Martín, Rivadavia and the others. In a way he was an innovator. He considered himself the outstanding economic philosopher in the Mexico of his day, and it may be that he was. His training in this field was along the same lines as that of Cabarrús, Campomanes, Jovellanos, Casa Yrujo, and Foronda, all outstanding liberals who held the United States in great esteem and admiration. It is possible that under different circumstances Alamán, too, might have looked with favor upon the United States. However, imperialistic ambitions on our part and fear of internal chaos, as far as Mexico was concerned, were two important factors that had a marked influence on his attitude.

He used to say that it is very difficult in itself to free a nation, but if at the same time this is taking place, one tries to change all the established forms of government and social customs, the difficulties become unsurmountable. He pointed out that in the United States the winning of independence was the primary goal. The success and prosperity of this nation he attributes to the fact that they did not destroy their institutions and that they were able to maintain law and order. He agrees with Iturbide. He says that the emperor believed "that a true imitation of the United States did not necessarily consist in copying its constitution, for which the Mexicans had less need than the Russians or the Turks, but rather in following the same policy of obtaining their independence and at the same time allowing the form of government to which the nation had been accustomed to remain."[100]

He was of the opinion that it was because they had departed from this norm, and because they had wanted to establish the most exaggerated liberal theories, that all the calamities imaginable had suddenly fallen upon the Spanish American nations. "They have frustrated all the advantages that independence should have obtained. It is interesting to note that the two great men America has produced, Iturbide and Bolívar, have coincided in the same idea. The first, in the Plan de Iguala, provided for a monarchy for the Spanish royal family; the second had intended to invite the family of Orleans to occupy the monarchy he wanted to create in Colombia.[101]

As an author Alamán has not been widely read in Mexico and is almost unknown in the rest of Spanish America. This is due to the fact that

---

99 *Ibid.,* p. xix.
100 Lucas Alamán, *Semblanzas e ideario,* p. 118.
101 *Loc. cit.*

most of his books, like his *Historia de México,* are historical essays, a literary genre that has never enjoyed much favor in romantic Spanish America. The short sketches describing the personality of his contemporaries are small jewels of psychological analysis. The history of Mexico passes before our eyes, as though it were a colorful pageant. Today, because of their subjectivity, there are many critics who are not willing to accept their value as an interpretation of history, but their personal, literary qualities are beyond doubt.

During the presidency of Paredes y Arrillaga, there was published a monarchical proclamation in the periodical *El Tiempo,* that Arnaiz y Freg attributed to Alamán, and that we believe summarizes his attitude.

> We desire a constitutional monarchy, that would be able to protect the
> different departments, to defend them from the savages who run them to
> the ground, and to extend the frontiers of civilization that are falling back
> before an overwhelming avalanche of barbarism. We wish a stable govern-
> ment that will inspire confidence in Europe, and that will obtain for us
> alliance with foreign countries, in order that we may fight against the
> United States if they persist in destroying our nationality.[102]

Opposing the Unitarians were the Federalists, the reform party that formulated the federal constitution of 1824. They believed that by closely imitating the United States they would achieve a similar growth and prosperity. They were anti-Spanish, anti-British and aimed at curbing the wealth and privileges of the church. The organization of the party was constructed around the York lodge of the Masonic order, which, as we have already stated, was under the direction of the American Ambassador, Poinsett. Among the leading Mexicans who made up this group were: Vicente Guerrero, Lorenzo de Zavala and Justo Sierra O'Reilly. At the end of the presidential term of Guadalupe Victoria, the "yorkinos", not satisfied with the election of Gómez Pedraza, provoked a revolution and seated their own candidate, Vicente Guerrero. Historians like Francisco J. Gaxiola blame Poinsett for this disturbance which interrupted the continuation of a legitimate government. During his presidency Guerrero expelled most of the Spaniards from the Mexican territory, and launched a progressive program of education aimed against the church. Under the direction of Gómez Farias, who followed Guerrero, freedom of faith and the abolition of religious educational institutions was planned, but these attempts never did succeed.

Typical of the attitude held by the "Federalists" is JOSE MARIA BO-CANEGRA, who published a book on the federal system, *Disertación apologética del sistema federal.*[103] Bocanegra believed that the constitution of the

---

102 Quoted in prologue to Lucas Alamán, *Semblanzas e ideario,* México, 1939, p. xxxiii.
103 México, 1825.

United States had proven its worth after bringing the nation through a series of political crises as formidable as the war of 1812. The progress and good fortune of the new republic he attributes to its constitution, which he says fostered education, the publication of books and periodicals, the arts and sciences, navigation, agriculture and commerce.[104] He points out that the position of Mexico now—at the time of its birth as a nation— was even more favorable than that of the United States in 1776. "It's with-out doubt, therefore, that finding ourselves, without any dangerous neigh-boring enemies, but on the contrary, with powerful friends who are stimu-lated by their own interest to protect ours—that we the Mexicans are in a more advantageous position than were our neighbors and natural allies the Anglo-Americans to the north."[105] We must say on behalf of Bocanegra that he was a true Mexican patriot and that his idealism was a disinterested one. As secretary of State it was his task to defend the interests of Mexico after the conflict provoked by the Texas affair. He fulfilled his duties with ability and impeccable patriotism.[106] It is ironic, however, that of all people, fate should have selected Bocanegra for this painful task. There is an old Spanish proverb that says: "Quien vive de ilusiones muere de desengaños."

As anti-American feeling mounted in Mexico, the popularity of the "Federalistas" diminished. There were many Mexicans who at the begin-ning sympathized with the United States, but were now convinced that an invasion of the Mexican territory by that country was imminent, and that the only way to save Texas and the inner provinces, and perhaps Mexico proper, was to create a strong centralized government. This opinion was shared by all Mexican patriots both liberals and conservatives.

The change came too late to save Mexico from mutilation and a humil-iating defeat, and when the crucial moment arrived, Zavala and some of the leading Federalists joined the American camp.

The Texas incident and later the war between the United States and Mexico served as a literary topic for many Mexican authors of this day. José Fernando Ramírez, Carlos María Bustamante, Roa Bárcena, José María Bocanegra, and even Santa Ana himself wrote books on this sub-ject.[107] It would not be necessary, however, to read the works of all these authors to become acquainted with their attitude toward the United States, for their opinions are all more or less alike. AGUSTIN A. FRANCO in his essay "Ojeada sobre Texas" synthesizes the Mexican point of view when he says:

From the moment our imprudent frankness gave a generous welcome to

---

[104] José María Bocanegra, *Disertación apologética del sistema federal*, México, 1825, pp. 25-26.

[105] *Ibid.*, p. 19.

[106] J. M. Vigil, "Prólogo" in Bocanegra, *Memorias para la historia de México independiente*, 1822-48, México, 1892, p. vii.

[107] Concerning **works** written by these authors consult the bibliography.

the Anglo-American colonists, when the communications of the celebrated Austin came asking us for an asylum with calculated humility, it was almost certain that, seduced by deceiving appearances, we were going to allow ourselves to fall into a lethargy of dangerous tranquility. Moved by sincerity and good faith, which are inherent to all new and inexperienced nations, we believed that we had done a great thing by introducing into the beautiful regions of Texas a persevering and hard-working race; but we were forgetting that this same race has an insatiable thirst for land and that the sons of the conquerors of the forests also had invaded with inexhaustible constancy and firmness the possessions of the original natives, and had expelled them from their homes all the way from the vast meadows of the Missouri to the forest of the state of Oregon. Why should they then behave in a different manner on our own soil? We were forgetting that this country is a nation of contradictions, that many times the very orator who is soiling his lips with the sacred name of liberty, the very man who preaches from the tribune in Washington, is one of those who holds in his possession hundreds of unfortunate negroes, subject to the barbarous sufferings of slavery. We were mistaken, and the simple settlers who came meekly to ask for our hospitality before long took roots and demanded as a right that which at first they had asked as a favor. Not unlike a viper that sinks her venomous fangs in the breast of the one who has given back to it its life... [108]

The people of the streets of Mexico were no less eloquent than the authors. Numerous *corridos*, humorous poems and derogatory anecdotes about the Americans circulated through the nation. The following poem, which we purposely have not translated so as to retain its full flavor, will serve as an example:

El Padre Nuestro de los yankees, que rezan los mexicanos:

El anciano y vil Scott,
Como en maldades tan diestro,
Sin más ley que su ambición
Quiere ser el *Padre nuestro*.

Oh yankee! vuestra codicia
Os ha traído a nuestro suelo,
Como aquí matáis el hambre,
Decis *que estáis en el cielo*.

Este suelo respetable
Con sangre ha sido regado,
Y los héroes de la patria
Lo han hecho *santificado*.

¿Qué diremos de Taylor?
Que es monstruo, efigie de hombre,
Inhumano, cruel, infame,
Detestado *sea tu nombre*.

Con la más torpe malicia
Encareces tu gobierno
Y pretendes que digamos
Que venga a nos el tu reino.

Aunque ejerzas con nosotros
La más inicua maldad,
Jamás nos oirás decir
Hágase tu voluntad.

Si no pudiéramos ya
Defendernos en la guerra,
Preferiremos andar
Errantes *así en la tierra*.

En querernos conquistar
Has puesto todo tu anhelo:
Dices que si lo logras
Estarías *como en el cielo*.

---

108 **Agustín A. Franco** "Ojeada sobre Texas", in Bocanegra, *Memorias*, II, 663. (cover of vol. II dated 1897).

Infelices de nosotros
Si ellos logran su intento!
Pues con sus artes e industrias
Nos quitarían *el pan nuestro*.

Nos pondrían contribuciones
Con la mayor tiranía,
Y héte aquí ya duplicados
Los males *de cada día*.

Esos pillos voluntarios
Que conducen en convoy
Nos dirán: Ese dinero
Por bien o por mal *dádnosle hoy,*

Hoy el yankee es generoso
Aparente y no de veras,
Protege a los prisioneros
Y *perdona nuestras deudas*.

Pero en llegando a triunfar
Nos marcarán nuestro rostro
Pues son hipócritas falsos
Y no *así como nosotros*.

Ellos pretenden tratados
De paz, por lo que no estamos;
Váyanse todos del país
Y tal cual los *perdonamos*.

Mas si llevan adelante
De le guerra los horrores
Los trataremos de infames
Y como *nuestros deudores*.

Vete, pues, yankee malvado,
Fuerza es que de aquí te alejes,
Y tus infames costumbres
Te pedimos *no nos dejes*.

Porque aunque tú subyugaras
A nuestra amada nación
Siempre al fin los Mexicanos
Han de estar *en tentación*.

Y tú, General Santa Ana
De la Patria héroe inmortal,
Líbranos de estos malvados
Y *mas líbranos del mal*.
Amén.[109]

The Protestant religion was regarded by many Mexican authors as a pretext used by the United States to penetrate their nation.[110]

With all fairness of mind, we must say that in Mexico there is very little analysis of "Democracy" as a political entity. This ideal is overshadowed by the political and territorial ambitions of the United States. The Mexicans were divided into pro- or anti-Americans, not so much according to their political beliefs as to their personal interests. Emotional elements such as religion, patriotism, traditional prejudice, and even personal gain on the part of a few, played an important part in determining the ideas of the political thinkers of this nation.

In South America the struggle of Federalism versus Unitarianism took on a different aspect, for there Federalism was not associated with North American aggression as it had been in the case of Mexico. It is true that there were no movements as spontaneous or as democratic as those led by Hidalgo or Guerrero; yet the South Americans, due to the fact that they were not menaced by a powerful democratic neighbor, were able to study the problems of democracy more objectively.

The issue of Federalism varied from country to country. In Venezuela it became a political football. A. L. Guzmán stated that he did not know how the people of Venezuela had come to have a love for federation, since they

---

109 Quoted by Vicuña Mackenna, *Páginas de mi diario*, pp. 53-54.

110 Don Francisco G. Cosme dice en su libro, *Historia general de México.* que el catolicismo es en México una religión que favorece la obra de integración nacional, mientras que la propaganda protestante es empresa anti-patriótica y verdadera vanguardia de la anexación del país a los Estados Unidos. Dice que la propaganda protestante siempre ha sido considerada por los mejicanos perspicaces como la vanguardia de la conquista pacífica de México por la absorbente nación vecina.

did not understand what the term meant. "This idea came from me and from others when we said to ourselves: Supposing that every revolution needs a watchword, and given that the convention of Valencia did not choose to baptize the constitution with the name 'Federal', let us invoke that idea, because, señores, if our opponents had said 'Federation', we would have said 'Centralism'."[111]

In Argentina the problem was even more complex, for there the Federalists very often were dictators, *caudillos* who ideologically represented the very opposite of American democracy.[112] The Unitarians on the other hand were generally progressive liberals who had a friendly attitude toward the United States. In most countries this idea became subsidiary to other problems that were more vital to the existence of the nation.

The whole problem of Federalism versus Unitarianism in South America is explained by Sarmiento in a letter to Mrs. Horace Mann. [113]

> Your last question concerning the word 'unitario', says Sarmiento, comes at a most opportune time, for it is truly representative of our difficulties. We speak of unitarian government as opposed to federal government. All the South American republics were organized under the system of the French Republic, with a central government. You remember the turmoil that the idea of federation caused in France, attributed as a crime to the Girondists. Our men of state, Bolívar, San Martín, and Rivadavia, had the same aversion to this idea of federal government. Argentina had a first hand example of it as early as 1814 with the secession of Paraguay under the tyranny of Dr. Francia. Later, Uruguay also separated with Artigas in the name of Federation and fell into the hands of the Portuguese.

Sarmiento continues to relate how this was followed by civil war with the guerrillas in the interior and the disruption of the central government, making each province almost independent with its little tyrant at the head. In 1825, Rivadavia called for the meeting of a Constituent Congress, which provided the Unitarian constitution. But the guerrillas of the provinces refused to accept it, and Rivadavia was forced to resign. In 1829 civil war began again, and resulted in the promotion to power of Rosas, "chief of the barbarous and tyrannical party of the entire republic." "I belonged to the Unitarian Party," says Sarmiento, "because of education and antagonism to the ideas and tendencies of Rosas and the guerrillas." In 1847 he was in the United States and saw at first hand the workings of the federal institutions. In Argentina, forty years of dispersion and separation, each province governing itself, had broken the national links and actually created states that could not reunite except under the federal government, such as

---

111 Quoted in William Whatley Pierson, "Foreign Influence on Venezuelan Political Thought." *The Hispanic American Historical Review*, XV, 1935, 24.

112 An exception to this is Manuel Dorrego.

113 Sarmiento to Mrs. Mann, Chicago, February 2, 1868, "Cartas de Sarmiento," *Boletin de la Academia Argentina de Letras*, IV, 1936, 338-343.

the guerrillas had proposed against Rivadavia. Rosas had triumphed in
the entire republic against the unitarian forces. The coastal cities, "in order
to free themselves from the horrible and barbarous tyranny," had reunited,
but only within the ramparts of Montevideo, which Rosas besieged, where
the Unitarian immigrants, aided by the liberal party of Montevideo, were
able to defend themselves.

Such was the condition when Sarmiento returned from the United
States in 1848. In order to combat it, he founded in Chile the *Crónica*,
a weekly intended to proclaim the federal government as a means of establishing the republic according to the system and constitution of the United
States. "In this manner we were able to attract the provinces to our party,
accepting the federation as an existing fact." Later he established another
weekly publication, also in Chile, entitled *Sud América*, which up to 1850
set forth the main characteristics of the federation, as Sarmiento had observed
it in the United States. The result of the articles published in this periodical was that free navigation on the rivers and the use of ports were
granted to the provinces.

Sarmiento's efforts were crowned with the most complete success. The
Unitarians finally accepted the idea of a federal organization. In
1850 Sarmiento wrote *Argirópolis*, a pamphlet urging the reunion and alliance against Rosas of the Unitarian and the Federalist chiefs. Argirópolis,
city of silver, was to be the future capital of the federation. It was to be located on the island of Martín García; thus with the prospect of the creation of
this imaginary capital the question of whether Buenos Aires would dominate
the nation was eliminated.

This pamphlet, *Argirópolis*, had the greatest effect upon the populace
and was the undoing of Rosas, even among his very own supporters. Bon-
pland, the celebrated naturalist friend of Humboldt, presented it to Urquiza,
principal lieutenant of Rosas, who, convinced by the arguments presented
therein, refused to submit further to Rosas' orders, accepted the idea of a
federal constitution and allied himself with the Unitarians, who were
at the time defending themselves at Montevideo. The result of all
this was the battle of Caseros and the fall of Rosas. Sarmiento was present
at this memorable occasion, having come from Chile to be with the allied
army, which under the orders of General Urquiza marched upon Buenos
Aires.

"In this way," says Sarmiento, "the Unitarian Party itself agreed to
give the country a federal constitution." The movement was initiated by
Sarmiento without any cooperation at the beginning, and was the result of
his visit to the Unied States and of his desire to put an end to the war and
establish a civilized government. But when Urquiza had triumphed over
Rosas, the third of February, 1852, "seeing himself at the head of a powerful army, and incapable, because of his ignorance and customary habits

of violence, of understanding the work of which he had become an instrument, he tried to continue his old system of arbitrariness." Then Sarmiento left him and returned to Chile, a voluntary exile, rather than support this new tyrant, thus abandoning all hope of honor or recompense for his participation. Buenos Aires finally freed itself from Urquiza and established itself as a separate state under the leadership of the former Unitarians; Urquiza governed the provinces which before had been Federalist. Sarmiento was then named deputy to the legislature of Buenos Aires, which he did not accept. He dictated instead a letter to the electors and to the people of Buenos Aires reproaching them for having separated from the republic. Sarmiento was at once nominated deputy to the Congress for the Province of Tucuman, and once more he refused to serve because they had established themselves without Buenos Aires. In 1856 Sarmiento went to Buenos Aires from Chile, and from then on began to work for the union and for the incorporation of Buenos Aires into the rest of the republic. All of Sarmiento's writings of this period were for this primary object. The address in honor of the ashes of Rivadavia, which had been brought back from Europe and were received with great ceremony on the wharf of Buenos Aires, was an appeal to the national sentiment for the union. In 1869 a convention was called in Buenos Aires to propose corrections to the Federal Constitution; Sarmiento, acting as delegate, introduced all those changes that contributed to making this constitution like that of the United States. He was also named the delegate for Buenos Aires to the National Convention which was to accept or reject the said corrections. "In the first and the other convention," says Sarmiento, "I took an important part in the business and in the direction of the debates, as can be seen from the Diary of the Sessions which has been published." "This has been my part in the federal organization of the republic, executed by the old Unitarians. Afterwards I went to San Juan, and as governor of that province I tried to found the government of a state since I had done so for the national and federal. I encountered difficulties on the part of my friends, the Unitarians, who were now running the federal government, thinking that I gave or hoped to give more power to the provinces. Disastrous results have later shown them that I was right."

As we have seen in the analysis of the struggle between the Federalists and the Unitarians, these two schools of thought were definitely affected by the example of the United States, yet due to their many inconsistencies they can hardly be used as a yardstick to determine the attitude of the South American writers toward North American political institutions. As a whole their attitude was of a much more general scope and responds to a complex personal and ideological pattern, rather than to a like or dislike of the federalist system. There are, nevertheless, three general groups into which most of the South Americans fall.

With the advent of independence, the South American States found themselves in a position where they had to choose a course between the following possibilities: first, to return to colonial ways; second, to modern-ize their nations retaining in part the Spanish traditional culture; third, to make a clean break with the past and assume new cultural and moral values.

To this first group belonged most of the clergy and all those who wanted to prevent the spread of irreligiousness, which they felt was intro-duced along with foreign liberal ideas; also those who believed that the struggle for independence was in reality a civil war and that sooner or later it was bound to have disastrous repercussions. They were pro-European and anti-American Representative of this group is JUAN DE EGAÑA, the author of a small volume *Memoria Política*[114] written in answer to Blanco White and other liberals who had criticized the Peruvian Constitution of 1823 on the grounds that it declared the Catholic church the only national religion.[115] Egaña was of the opinion that freedom of religion might have some advantages in a country like the United States or England where religious sects were numerous, but he finds no use for it in a country where only one religion is professed.[116] By using the United States and England as examples he comes to the following conclusions: first, that a multitude of religions in one state leads to no religion; second, that the existence of only two religions will inevitably lead to civil war and the destruction of the state; third, that uniformity of religion is a consolidating force that brings tranquillity to the nation.[117]

To the second group belonged the moderate liberals who realized that changes were necessary if the Spanish American states were to take their rightful place among the other nations of the world. They preferred to accomplish this change, however, without destroying whatever positive qualities were still to be found in their traditional civilization. The majority were Catholics and were willing to imitate the United States in political but not in religious matters. As in the case of the first group they were aware of existing racial rivalries and had misgivings as to the good inten-tions of the United States toward South America. MANUEL CARRASCO AL-BANO (1834-1873) and Benjamín Vicuña Mackenna are typical of this group.

Carrasco Albano is a noted Chilean statesman, the author of several notable works in the field of political science and literary criticism. Unfor-tunately, his last studies were destroyed by himself during a period of ill-

114 *Memoria política* was first published in the *Abeja de Chile* (circa 1826); republished in Caracas, 1829.

115 Blanco's article appeared in the *Mensajero de Londres,* and was reprinted in the *Peruano,* August 9, 1826, no. 20.

116 *Memoria política,* Caracas, 1829, p. 3.

117 *Ibid.,* pp. 10, 20.

ness. Among them was a critical study of John Stuart Mill's essay *On Liberty*, that at one time he had read before the "Círculo de amigos de las letras."[118]

In spite of the fact that he was friendly toward democratic ideals and that he admired the progress of the United States, he saw in this nation the principal enemy of the Spanish American republics. He was of the opinion that in America there were two races, each possessing hatreds inherited from the mother countries that made them incompatible.[119] To check the growing power of the United States he proposed an alliance of the Spanish American countries and a program of cultural and industrial development similar to that which had proved so profitable in the Anglo-Saxon republic. He attributes the success of our nation to industrialization; to its numerous ways of communication; particularly the railroads; and to immigration.[120] With Pérez Rosales he was the primary exponent of German migration to Chile.

Vicuña Mackenna had similar ideas. He believed that the primary problem confronting the Spanish Americans was the growing power of their northern neighbor. "That the Americans acknowledge the proximity of their universal domination," he stated, "is a theory accepted by all; but with regard to their domination of Spanish America they consider it an accomplished fact since their war with Mexico. North America does not accept the brotherhood of the continent to the south, not even in name." He realized that there were great differences between the different sections of the United States. "But if there were discrepancies in points of topography, the Saxon race was unanimous in its insolent contempt for the peoples of Latin origin, the contempt of the Vandal in the presence of the Roman, but alas!, a bent and senile Roman..."[121] Vicuña proceeds to tell an anecdote he considers characteristic of the attitude of North Americans toward them. It seems that during the war with Mexico, an American rifleman broke into the assembly room of the Mexican Congress, set aside his trappings and below the very symbol of sovereignty of that conquered nation proceeded to relieve himself. "This characteristic deed," says Vicuña, "I have heard many Americans refer to and it was for them one of national significance, a spontaneous display of their attitude concerning the invaded country and the subdued people. It was, in truth, a natural manifestation..."[122]

Concerning North American imperialistic ambitions he says that America recognized its territorial boundaries as the border of Panama. No one in the United States recognized any political boundaries on the entire surface

118 Manuel Carrasco Albano, *Comentario sobre la constitución política de 1833*, Valparaíso, 1858 (second ed., Santiago, 1874) p. xiii.

119 *Ibid.*, p. xvii.

120 *Ibid.*, xx, xxi, xxii, xxxv.

121 Benjamín Vicuña Mackenna "Páginas de mi diario," *Obras completas*, I, 260.

122 *Ibid.*, p. 261.

of the globe. Mexico, which had just sold them a new tract of land, they considered as their province. They had not yet made up their mind whether they would take her in now or a little later, in part or entirely. Vicuña quotes from the *New York Herald,* April, 1853, "Mexico must fall. In a word, Mexico must be ours." The domination of the United States over Nicaragua was, for the time being, entrusted to Walker and his cohorts. In Panama, its power was its railroad line and its colonies. The port of Colón had lost its name, and in Panama the "Calle Real" was called "Main Street" and that of "La Merced," "Mercy Street". Cuba was the lone star that shone brilliantly in the constellation of the northern flag. With its possession the American geographic system would be complete, "it is thus that they wish to think about it today."[123]

With respect to the southern continent, Vicuña said that they only desired a supreme, irresistible influence, such as the protectorate of Ecuador, for example. When the government of Chile, in 1853, refused the extradition of an American criminal, the *Herald* came out with headlines that read *Blockade of Valparaiso,* adding that the American squadron was prepared to blockade that port if the delivery was not made immediately. "Its principal accusation against South America is that of 'Indolence, laziness, race pride, and the eternal danger of revolutions and bloody discords'."[124]

As to political parties in North America he said that the several that were in existence had been divided into factions during the present administration (Pierce was president at the time), but that the Whigs and the Democrats continued to be the most important. They were in discord only as to the way progress was to be realized, but fundamentally they were in agreement on all important issues: the Union, the slavery question, etc. The only discrepancy at the time was the acceptance of the Monroe Doctrine. While the Whigs were satisfied with the territory already acquired and denied the right of conquest, the Democrats not only affirmed it, but authorized and practiced it. The Democratic party was the most considerable. It was composed of the majority of the working classes, of the immigrants that came fleeing from tyranny in Europe, and of youth in general. The Whig influence was limited to certain families, to the aristocracy of New England principally. The Abolitionists or Free Soilers, who wished the elimination of slavery, were more than a party, a semi-religious sect that did not possess an immediate political plan, unless it was to send the Negroes back to Africa, not for their benefit, but to rid themselves of their association as well as to impair the interests of the South. The modern party of the Know Nothings was not exactly a political faction, it was society itself, united to defend its material interests: stopping immigration, pre-

---

123 *Ibid.,* pp. 261-262.
124 *Loc. cit.*

scribing religious liberty, nationalizing the country, "that is to say, to do in fact that which existed in theory."[125]

The third group of authors was made up of the extremists. They were dominated by a strong French anti-clericalism and often wanted to change everything Spanish regardless of its merits or defects. This group was strongly pro-American and chose to follow what they thought were this country's political and religious ideas, not always realizing that the United States was in reality a religious and conservative nation.

In Chile, JOSE VICTORINO LASTARRIA (1817-1888), outstanding political thinker and author of numerous books on constitutional government, was one of those who believed that through education and enlightenment the customs of Spanish America could be changed so as to make these countries suitable for the transplantation of North American institutions. Lastarria wanted to make a clean break with the past and with Europe. He believed that the differences between the Old and New Continents were more than just the political institutions. There were moral, religious and psychological differences that Spanish America had not yet quite mastered, but that in the case of the United States were supreme and victorious.[126] With this approach in mind and armed with arguments taken from J. Debrin[127] and Tocqueville,[128] he launched an attack upon the European critics of America which represents one of the finest defenses of the American institutions by a Spanish American.

> The most presumptuous wise men of the Old World have the touchstone, which has become very popular, for explaining the existence and progress of the republic of North America, and it is to assume that special conditions of territory and population have produced such a prodigy.[129]
> Lord Macaulay, the great English historian, who with his lofty talent and high judgement not only gained fame but acquired a title of nobility, wrote to Mr. Rand, of the United States, giving his opinion of the democratic institutions under the domination of that paralogism:
> "I have long been convinced that institutions purely democratic must, sooner or later, destroy liberty or civilization, or both. In Europe, where the population is dense, the effect of such institutions would be almost instantaneous. What happened lately in France is an example. In 1848 a pure democracy was established there. During a short time there was reason to expect a general spoliation, a national bankruptcy, a new partition of the

---

125 *Ibid.*, pp. 255-257.

126 José Victorino Lastarria, *La América*, Buenos Aires, 1865, p. 173.

127 Lastarria cita a J. Debrin que escribe desde Nueva York, agosto, 1863, para defender a los Estados Unidos y su forma de gobierno de los ataques y propaganda europeas. Debrin hace un resumen del desarrollo adquirido por las ideas e instituciones democráticas en el continente americano, con referencia particular a los Estados Unidos, *Ibid.*, pp. 21-32.

128 Quotes *De la Démocratie en Amérique, Ibid.*, p. 110.

129 *Ibid.*, p. 38.

soil, a maximum of prices, a ruinous load of taxation laid on the rich for
the purpose of supporting the poor in idleness. Such a system would, in
twenty years, have made France as poor and barbarous as the France of the
Carlovingians. Happily the danger was averted; and now there is a despotism,
a silent tribune, an enslaved press. Liberty is gone, but civilization has been
saved. I have not the smallest doubt that, if we had a purely democratic
government here, the effect would be the same. Either the poor would
plunder the rich, and civilization would perish, or order and prosperity would
be saved by a strong military government, and liberty would perish. You
may think that your country enjoys an exemption from these evils. I will
frankly own to you that I am of a very different opinion. Your fate I believe to be certain, though it is deferred by a physical cause. As long as you
have a boundless extent of fertile and unoccupied land, your laboring
population will be far more at ease than the laboring population of the
Old World, and, while that is the case, the Jefferson politics may continue
to exist without causing any fatal calamity. But the time will come when New
England will be as thickly peopled as Old England. Wages will be as low,
and will fluctuate as much with you as with us. You will have your Manchesters and Birminghams, and in those Manchesters and Birminghams
hundreds of thousands of artisans will assuredly be sometimes out of work.
Then your institutions will be fairly brought to the test. Distress everywhere
makes the laborer mutinous and discontented, and inclines him to listen
with eagerness to agitators who tell him that it is a monstrous iniquity
that one man should have a million while another cannot get a full meal.
In bad years there is plenty of grumbling here, and sometimes a little rioting.
But it matters little. For here the sufferers are not the rulers. The supreme
power is in the hands of a class, numerous indeed, but select; of an educated
class; of a class which is, and knows itself to be, deeply interested in the
security of property and the maintenance of order. Accordingly, the mal-
contents are firmly yet gently restrained. The bad time is got over
without robbing the wealthy to relieve the indigent. The springs of national
prosperity soon begin to flow again: work is plentiful, wages rise, and all
is tranquillity and cheerfulness. I have seen England pass three or four times
through such critical seasons as I have described. Through such seasons the
United States will have to pass in the course of the next century, if not
of this. How will you pass through them? I heartily wish you a good deliv-
erance. But my reason and my wishes are at war, and I cannot help fore-
boding the worst. It is quite plain that your government will never be able
to restrain a distressed and discontented majority. For with you the majority
is the government, and has the rich, who are always a minority, absolutely
at its mercy. The day will come when in the State of New York a multitude
of people, none of whom has had more than half a breakfast, or expects
to have more than half a dinner, will choose a Legislature. Is it possible
to doubt what sort of Legislature will be chosen? On one side is a statesman preaching patience, respect for vested rights, strict observance of public
faith. On the other is a demagogue ranting about the tyranny of capitalists

and usurers, and asking why anybody should be permitted to drink Champagne and to ride in a carriage while thousands of honest folks are in want of necessaries. Which of the two candidates is likely to be preferred by a working-man who hears his children cry for more bread? I seriously apprehend that you will, in some such season of adversity as I have described, do things which will prevent prosperity from returning; that you will act like people who should in a year of scarcity devour all the seedcorn, and thus make the next a year not of scarcity, but of absolute famine. There will be, I fear, spoliation. The spoliation will increase the distress. The distress will produce fresh spoliation. There is nothing to stop you. Your Constitution is all sail and no anchor. As I said before, when a society has entered on this downward progress, either civilization or liberty must perish. Either some Caesar or Napoleon will seize the reins of government with a strong hand, or your republic will be as fearfully plundered and laid waste by barbarians in the twentieth century as the Roman Empire was in the fifth, with this difference, that the Huns and Vandals who ravaged the Roman Empire came from without, and that your Huns and Vandals will have been engendered within your own country by your own institutions.

Thinking this, of course I cannot reckon Jefferson among the benefactors of mankind, I readily admit that his intentions were good and his abilities considerable. Odious stories have been circulated about his private life; but I do not know on what evidence those stories rest, and I think it probable that they are false or monstrously exaggerated. I have no doubt that I shall derive both pleasure and information from your account of him."[130]

We are pleased with ourselves in copying the opinion of the most characteristic writer of England, because it is the opinion which predominates in all the great men of that nation, the opinion which appears paraphrased and explained in all forms in the English press and in her speeches. But as the noble Lord has so fortunately misunderstood the situation, so have all the rest. The press and the statesmen of this country have had so great a disappointment with the ending of the North American war, that they still have not recovered from their fright.

Shall we have to demonstrate in America that these ideas are mistaken? Will it be necessary to say that the republican form of government has triumphed in a prodigious crisis which has no comparison in magnitude and power, that it has overcome those crises which produce the mutinies which so often threaten the monarchy and the aristocracy in Great Britain?

And why didn't the fears of the learned historian come true during the crisis produced by the war and the election of a new president? Then there was a numerous hungry class which the demagogues of the democratic party exploited to the full aided by the authority of the governor of New York and by the gold that the slave party and the English and French protectors of slavery spread with open hands.

Then came the time the Lord of English literature had expected to

---

[130] *Ibid.*, pp. 38-42; quoted from *The London Quarterly Journal*, July 1861.

come later; then the democratic institutions were put to the test which he had feared. The American government did not find it necessary to restrain a majority agitated by misery and by corrupting gold. It trusted in the power of its institutions and in the judgment of the people. The institutions triumphed, with the re-election of Abraham Lincoln the people proved that they wanted the abolition of slavery. They also proved that government founded in liberty and the rights of the individual will not be swayed by demagogy nor mutiny.

Mutiny is a manifestation of the democratic spirit in North America. The authorities almost never attempt to restrain it. It leaves the defense of its institutions to a free people, that have no king who lives from the public fortune and that have no aristocracy to exploit them ... [131]

In Colombia, FLORENTINO GONZALEZ, who for many years was professor of constitutional law in Venezuela and Argentina, came to the conlusion, after many years of studying the development of democracy in North America, that the Spanish American states should break with the past and imitate the United States. Realizing that the traditions of the two peoples were different, he proposed a change in Spanish American customs to make suitable the transplantation of the institutions of the United States. This transformation was to be done through education, and with this purpose in mind he wrote the *Lecciones de derecho constitucional,* used even today as a textbook in government in some of the Spanish American countries. For many years he enthusiastically delivered lectures on the fundamental values of the North American institutions and, not satisfied with these efforts, he translated Frederick Grimke's *Consideration upon the nature and tendency of free institutions,*[132] and Francis Lieber's *On civil liberty and self-government.*[133] González made these two authors known in Spanish America. William Whatley Pierson, in his article on foreign influence on Venezuelan political thought, says that he found copies of Grimke in many bookshops and private libraries, and that the historians and lawyers gave him a high testimony as to the importance of the book. "Many estimated it as more significant than the classic work of Mill on *Representative government."* It is curious that this book should have enjoyed such popularity in Spanish America when it was little known in the United States. On the other hand, Lieber, who was a personal friend of Ticknor and the author of *Letters to*

---

[131] *Ibid.,* pp. 42-44.

[132] Frederick Grimke, a member of a distinguished family of American liberals, first published his book, *Considerations upon the nature and tendency of free institutions,* in Cincinnati, 1848; a second edition appeared in 1852; there are several editions of the Spanish translation *Naturaleza y tendencia de las instituciones libres por Federico Grimke,* 2d. ed. Paris and Mexico, 1887.

[133] Francis Lieber, the author of many books on America, first published his work in Philadelphia, 1853; a second ed. in 2 vols. appeared in Philadelphia, 1859; a third edition in 1874; the Spanish translation, *La libertad civil y el gobierno propio* por el Doctor Francisco Lieber, was published in Paris and México, 1889.

a gentleman in Germany, recording the prosperity and freedom of the New World, was well known in this country.[134]

In Argentina, JUAN BAUTISTA ALBERDI (1810-1884) believed that the solution to the problems of Spanish America was to be found in modernization.

When he was only seventeen (1837), he was obliged to seek safety from Rosas' tyranny by fleeing to Montevideo. He contributed to the review *Muera Rosas,* one of the many periodicals edited for the purpose of attacking the tyrant. In 1843 he went to Europe. This trip had much to do with determining his mature point of view. Upon his return he wrote his *Bases para la organización de la República Argentina,* a critical examination of the history of Argentina along with suggestions for a suitable government for the country that had a great influence upon the members of the convention that voted the constitution of 1853.[135]

It seems that Alberdi became interested in the United States while, still in his youth. Robertson in his book *Hispanic American relations with the United States* says that among Alberdi's favorite writers as a youth was Judge Story and the authors of *The Federalist.* "Alberdi, who seems to have had only a slight knowledge of English, apparently became acquainted with Story's *Commentaries on the Constitution* and *The Federalist* through French editions of those works. It is also possible that he increased his knowledge of the political ideals of North America during his residence in Chile; for gold hunters on their way to or from California occasionally sojourned in Valparaiso; and a Spanish edition of the Constitution of California was published there in 1850."[136] These readings, however, only constituted the beginning of an interest that was to last Alberdi's entire lifetime. A prolific reader, he was acquainted with most of the important works written about the United States during his day. Tocqueville's *Democracy,* his favorite work on this subject, he quotes and paraphrases constantly throughout his writings.

His appreciation of the United States is decidedly utopian. In his book *El crimen de la guerra,* in which he condemns all violence as the main obstacle to the progress of humanity, he states that the happiness of man comes from security and industry, as has been proven in the United States. Alberdi's heroes are those great men who have contributed to material progress and spiritual freedom, such as the inventors Franklin and Fulton.[137] If Washington is great it is not because of the part he played in the war of independence, "the glory of Washington is not that of war, but of liberty."[138] In his book *La Revolución de Mayo* he states that democracy does

---

[134] He was at one time a professor at Columbia University.

[135] Coester, *The literary history of Spanish America,* p. 121.

[136] Robertson, *Hispanic American relations with the United States,* p. 89.

[137] Juan B. Alberdi, *El crimen de la guerra,* Buenos Aires, 1915, p. 258.

[138] *Ibid.,* pp. 262-263.

not belong to any one nation, it is the patrimony of humanity as a whole. The May Revolution of Argentina, the French Revolution and the War of Independence in the United States are all legitimate sisters.[139]

Alberdi is of the opinion that Argentina should imitate the United States, particularly New England. "The foundation of New England," says he paraphrasing Tocqueville, "was a novel spectacle, and all the circumstances attending it were singular and original. The settlers who established themselves on her shores all belonged to the more independent classes of their native country... The other colonies had been founded by adventurers without families: the immigrants of New England brought with them the best elements of order and morality... But what specially distinguished them above the others was the aim of their undertaking. They had not been obliged by necessity to leave their country; the social position they abandoned was one to be regretted, and their means of subsistence was certain... Their object was the triumph of an idea." This ideal was political and religious liberty. "In this sense the settlers of Massachusetts were not mere immigrants, but pilgrims. They did not emigrate for the sake of gold or subsistence but they were impelled by an excellent purpose, that of escaping all oppression, whether civil or religious."[140]

As a product of this environment he cites William Wheelwright, and with this purpose in mind he wrote La vida de William Wheelwright.[141] Alberdi's thesis is that men are the product of the society in which they are born and trained, as well as the family and the school. "The life of William Wheelwright forms a part of the history and progress of South America during the last fifty years. The disinterested character of his services for the public welfare reveals the compatriot of Washington and Franklin. He is the personification of his country acclimated in South America, and work like his is the best and surest method the rival republic of the North can employ to destroy the relics of a despotism which has so retarded the progress of our own States. Our rulers fear such an invasion more than an armed conquest. They prefer to copy the written laws of the United States, rather than receive those laws embodied in the manners and customs of its citizens. Nothwithstanding their great magnitude, the services Wheelwright has rendered to the countries of Spanish America have cost neither blood nor tears, nor treasure paid by the government in the form of compensation."[142] Alberdi believes that to study and reproduce such men was the best way to introduce in Spanish America the civilization of the United States; in

---

139 Alberdi, La Revolución de Mayo, pp. 119-120, 126.

140 Alberdi, Life of William Wheelwright, pp. 12-13.

141 La vida y los trabajos industriales de William Wheelwright en la América del Sud, París, 1876. It was translated into English: Life and industrial labors of William Wheelwright in South America, translation by Caleb Cushing, Boston, 1877.

142 Ibid., pp. 1-2.

other words, "the liberty and progress of the Anglo-Saxons for the benefit of the Latin race."[143]

In Venezuela, JESUS MUNOZ TEBAR, historian and sociologist, in his book, *El personalismo i el legalismo: Estudio político* New York, 1891 expressed similar opinions. As in the case of González, he believed that the character of men depended on the education they received and that by education the customs of a nation could be changed. He advises that the arbitrary individualism of the Spanish Americans be controlled for the common good, that personalism or *caudillismo* be substituted by civil justice. The model for these changes was to be the United States.

In essence the ideas of the above-mentioned authors had not progressed much since Rocafuerte. He, too, believed that the solution to the problems of Spanish America consisted in establishing North American institutions and changing the customs to go with the new pattern. It took political leaders until the end of the nineteenth century to come to the realization of the fact that states are built not by theories but on facts: geographical features, type of people, traditional culture, as Toynbee would say, shaped by moral challenges; that civilizations respond to historic forces that up to now have proven uncontrollable by man; that we can contribute to the progress of civilization but that once it is put into motion we know not where it goes, and even if we did we cannot control its course.

3. Literary Men

As a literary subject, the United States does not play an important part in the pure literature of Spanish America. The closest thing we have to it are descriptions by the travellers to the North American landmarks; of these Niagara Falls continues to be the most popular one. As we have already seen, much was written on this subject, but, besides the prose descriptions that we have already mentioned, there is an excellent poem by Juan Antonio Pérez Bonalde, "El poema del Niagara," published in New York, 1883, that rivals Heredia's in dramatic splendor. Also of literary value are the descriptions of life in the large American cities, a topic that has always been of interest to the Spanish Americans.

Literature concerning the great men of America, now seen more from a distance, became less political and more literary. Washington and Franklin still retained their popularity, but they were slowly being supplanted by Lincoln. JUAN MONTALVO (1832-1889), the leading Spanish American essayist of his day, wrote his famous essay "Washington and Bolivar", a subject often discussed during the previous era. Montalvo manages, however, to give it a new quality. Written in a beautiful "castizo" Spanish, it has lost all flavor of frontier literature. It is no longer the revolutionist who

---

[143] *Ibid.*, p. 205.

speaks. In his place we find the artist, who now, having plenty of time at his disposal, models his work with care and is more interested in its beauty than in the didactic, or moral value of his exposition.

Washington and Bolívar

Washington's fame does not rest so much on military exploits as on the result of the work he accomplished both with success and good judgment. The fame of Bolívar goes hand in hand with the noise of arms, and in the splendor which that radiant figure gives off, we see the forces of tyranny fall and fade away; bugles sound, horses neigh, everything centered around this South American is warlike. Washington presents himself to our memory and imagination first as a great citizen, then as a warrior, first philosopher then a general. Washington might well be in the Roman Senate by the side of old Papirius Cursor, and in being a former monarch he might well be Augustus, that calm and reposed man who delights in sitting between Horace and Virgil, while all nations revolve reverently around his throne. Between Washington and Bolívar there is a similarity of purpose, namely freedom for their country and the establishment of democracy. In the endless difficulties that the one had to overcome and the ease with which the other saw his task completed lies the difference between these two men. Bolívar, in several periods of the warfare, had no outside aid to fall back on, nor did he know where to find that aid. His great love of country, the high sense of honor working in his heart, his vivid and fruitful imagination and the marvelous activity that made up his character enabled him to make possible the impossible and gave him the power of turning nothingness into a reality. He is like a man inspired by Providence, who breaks a rock with a rod and a torrent of crystalline water issues forth. He treads the earth and thousands of fighters come from out of nowhere to follow in his path.

The North Americans were rich, powerful and civilized even before their independence from England. If they had lacked their leader, one hundred Washingtons would have volunteered to fill the vacancy. Many notable and worthy men surrounded Washington. There are Madison, Jefferson, and Benjamin Franklin who not only snatched the lightning from the sky but also snatched the power from the hands of tyrants. And these and all the others, how great and numerous, were all united in a common cause. Each contributing to the immense torrent that overran the armies and enemy fleets and destroyed the English power. This was not the case with Bolívar. He had to subdue his officers, had to fight and overcome his own countrymen, and had to struggle against many elements opposed to independence, at the same time that he fought against the Spanish hosts and conquered them or was conquered. The work of Bolívar was more difficult and for the same reason is more praiseworthy.

Washington is generally considered a person who deserves a great deal of respect: Bolívar was a man of eminence and splendor. The former founded a land which has become one of the greatest in the world. The latter also founded an important country, which, however, did not become one of the major nations. Washington's successors, who were truly great citizens, never thought of dismembering the nation for their own personal benefit, while Bolívar's companions destroyed Colombia and took for themselves all possible plunder, insane with ambition and tyranny. In mythology, Saturn devoured his children. We have seen and we are seeing certain children devour their mother. If it were not that Páez, whose memory should be cherished, took part in this crime, I would make an excellent exposition of how our great land was destroyed . . . Washington, less ambitious but also less magnanimous, was more modest but less lofty than Bolívar. The first having finished his work and having refused the presidency of a third term, gave his authority in the government to another and retired to a life of privacy, still loved by his friends and possessing no enemies. A truly rare man indeed! Bolívar by dubious means took over the authority of the government for a third time, and died hated and persecuted by his subjects. Time has erased this episode from our minds, and today we see only the splendor that surrounds the greatest of all South Americans. Washington and Bolívar, fortunate characters that are the glory of the New World and the honor of the human race, let us place them along with the other great men of all races and all times.[144]

Salvador Camacho Roldán, of Colombia; Manuel Corchado, of Puerto Rico; Enrique Piñeyro, of Cuba; and Domingo Faustino Sarmiento, of Argentina are among the many who wrote on the life of Lincoln.[145]

Though the United States did not enjoy popularity as a literary subject, criticism of American letters and translations of American poetry, on the other hand, were more abundant. Surprisingly enough, this literature was written by Spanish Americans not in their own countries but in the United States and Spain, a phenomenon that would be interesting to analyze.

Of the storytellers Washington Irving was much admired. He is the first of this group of authors that was interested in reconstructing our Spanish past.[146] Speaking of him, Domingo del Monte y Aponte, Cuban poet and bibliographer, who was born in Maracaibo (Venezuela) says: "Anglo-American literature, more varied and abundant than we suspect hereabouts, has many valuable works wherein one notes the fondness with which its most gifted writers treat Spanish subjects. Mr. Irving himself, aside from his works on Spanish history, has written the *Tales of the Alhambra*, purely peninsular in their inspiration and worthy, by the

---

144 Juan Montalvo, *Siete tratados,* Ambato, Ecuador, 1942-43, pp. 141-144.
145 See bibliography.
146 Washington Irving was first translated into Spanish in Spain: *Historia de la vida y viajes de Cristóbal Colón, por Washington Irving. Traducida al castellano por D. José García de Villalta.* Madrid, 1833-34; The first American translation appears in México: *Vida y Viajes de Cristóbal Colón por Washington Irving,* México, 1853; another is: *Viajes y descubrimientos de los compañeros de Colón,* Madrid, 1854. Most of Irving's works, however, were read in English.

vividness of native color which marks their beautiful pictures, of being placed beside the *Guerras civiles de Granada* of Ginés Pérez de Hita."[147]

Longfellow was perhaps the best known of the poets. His romantic poems had great appeal to the Spanish American temperament. "A poet as truly inspired as he is erudite and whose poetic talent had been worthily recognized in England," says del Monte, 'he has cultivated Spanish literature as well as the literatures of the north of Europe; and his lyre has been able to repeat in English, without disfiguring them, some of the greatest tones of the Castilian muse." See for instance his *Spanish Student*, his *Outre Mer* and his translation of the *Coplas* of Jorge Manrique.[148]

We shall never know the names of all the Spanish Americans who visited Longfellow nor of the translations of his poems that were never published, but we can be certain that there were many. There are definite indications that he made it a point to keep in contact with the Spanish speaking countries. During his stay in Spain he made friendships that he cultivated throughout his lifetime, and in his home at Cambridge he would often entertain Spanish Americans who made the trip there to meet him. In October, 1866, Eusebio Guiteras, a Cuban author of books on travel, published in the review *Liceo Matanzas* an account of a visit he paid to Longfellow, in which he tells of the friendly reception given to him.[149] We definitely know that he was acquainted with Mendive, Irizarri, Sarmiento[150] and Miralla; it is also probable that he knew most of the distinguished Spanish Americans who resided in New York at that time.

Translations of his works into Spanish first appeared in 1871. On this date Carlos Morla Vicuña translated "Evangeline" which, according to Professor Ferguson, was published in New York and is the first of its

---

[147] Domingo del Monte y Aponte (article taken from *Revista de Ciencias, Literatura y Artes*, Sevilla, 1856, vol. II) quoted in John De Lancey Ferguson, *American Literature in Spain*, p. 151-155.

[148] *Loc. cit.*

[149] Eusebio Guiteras, "Una visita a Longfellow", *Liceo Matanzas*, Oct., 1866.

[150] Sarmiento writes to Mrs. Mann, Boston, Sept. 15, 1865, "Pero desde que me vine de Concord mi vida ha sido un continuo paseo gracias a V. misma que me procuró la relación de Mr. Gould, quien me ha hospedado en su casa i puéstome en contacto con Mr. Hill, Longfellow y cuantos personages notables hay en Cambridge. Ayer pasé todo el día con Mr. George Emerson, y puede V. imaginarse cuan gratos momentos pasaría con este partriarca de la educación...Otro Mr. Longfellow que sabe y habla perfectamente bien el castellano...Ahora voi a ver a Mr. Ticknor que me ha buscado y escrito una carta..." "Cartas de Sarmiento," *Boletín de la Academia Argentina de Letras*, 1936, IV, 346-347. Charles C. Chanman relates that José Toribio Medina, the famous bibliographer, translated Longfellow's "Evangeline". Medina tells that he almost became an American. He and a friend took rooms with a private family in Philadelphia in 1876, and the two daughters of the famliy were so attractive that they never left the house for a single night. The friend married one of the two daughters and Medina was never sure why he had not married the other. "A 'Recuerdo' of José Toribio Medina", *The Hispanic American Historical Review*, II, 525.

kind in Spanish.[151] After this, translations became so numerous that we lose track of them. Among the best known are those by the Cuban poet Mendive, published in the *Mundo Nuevo,* a review edited in New York by Enrique Piñeyro; and those of F. S. Amy, a Puerto Rican, the author of *Ecos y notas,* a book dealing with Longfellow, Whittier and the other American poets of this day, published in Ponce (1884).

James Fenimore Cooper at one time enjoyed a great vogue throughout the Spanish-speaking world.[152] Most children, and grownups, too, were initiated into the mysteries of the North American continent by reading *The last of the Mohicans* or *The deerslayer.* "Neither the present genera-tion", writes Rafael M. de Labra in the *Revista de España,* April 1879, "which knows by heart the novels of Dumas the younger and the entertain-ing works of Alphonse Karr, nor that earlier one which grew up with *The Count of Monte Cristo, The mysteries of Paris,* the griefs of *Père Goriot* and the passion of *Indiana,* will be able to remember the days, already remote, when the Spanish press used to fill its 'folletines' with the maritime novels of Fenimore Cooper, alternating with the famous descriptions of Walter Scott. The vogue of the Scottish novelist and the American writer, whose likenesses are evident and of whom comparative studies have so often been made, was extraordinary about 1840, and for a long time the influence of both writers made itself felt in the whole of Continental Europe, and, in our Spain, caused the appearance of a succession of novelists and a list of 'mountain and sea', historical and tragic novels, which for the good of literature and even for the honor of their country were so devoured by the romantic fury of its contemporaries . . ."[153]

Labra was a Cuban and, although at this time he was writing from Spain, his attitude toward Cooper may be considered representative of the country of his birth.

Admiration for Prescott seems to have been general throughout Spanish America. "The good faith and diligence with which he has examined our ancient documents" says del Monte, "the ability with which he has been able to understand and interpret them despite the fact that he is a foreigner and a citizen of a democratic republic, and the impartiality of his judgments, being mindful in passing them only of the noble magistracy of the his-torian, place him in the rank of the Robertsons and the Gibbons, and make him worthy of the popularity he has won at home and abroad."[154] Del

---

[151] *Ibid.,* pp. 109-110, 140-42.

[152] Because of the analogy that existed between Cooper's North America and Sar-miento's Argentina, Sarmiento was a great admirer of this author. "I que me hagan el gusto de encuadernarme media pasta una edición completa de las novelas de Cooper i otra de las de Dickens para mi propio uso i pasarme la cuenta." Sarmiento to Mrs. Mann, N. Y., June 30, 1868 "Cartas" *op. cit.,* 1935, III, 380-381.

[153] Rafael M. de Labra (*Revista de España,* April, 1879, vol. 67) in Ferguson, *op. cit.,* pp. 48-50.

[154] Del Monte, *Loc. cit.*

Monte was not alone in this attitude. On July 30, 1893, the review *La Ilustración* of Madrid published the results of a symposium of Spanish authors and public men on the value of Prescott's work. Upon this occasion, Julio Betancourt, Colombian Ambassador to Madrid, after complaining of the "Black Legend" unjustly created by historians against Spain, says that Prescott is an exception who deserves the highest praise for his fidelity to the truth of history.[155]

When Vicuña Mackenna visited Boston, he found that Prescott, Everett, and Ticknor lived here among other noteworthy people. He had known the three by reputation, but was particularly interested in meeting the first, "the classical and likeable genius who had painted the epic of our conquest with masterful art." Curtis obtained an appointment for him with the distinguished man, and one afernoon he went to his house on Beacon Street. A servant ushered him into a spacious library, and in a few minutes there came in a gentleman, of pleasant appearance, who approached him with much grace and greeted him in French. Vicuña describes Prescott as a man of about sixty but whose physical appearance and bearing made him seem younger. He was tall and well-built, and his face was animated by two large green eyes whose weakness in no way diminished their brilliance. A handsome forehead and a head already greying gave him a graceful, world- ly look, a venerable tint of thoughtfulness and knowledge. Their conversation began in French and continued in English and Spanish. Prescott preferred to hear Vicuña speak in his own language, which he knew well, but be- cause of lack of practice did not speak fluently. He told him that since he was very young he had had a liking for Spanish literature and for the ex- ploits of the Castilians in America. Out of this interest were born the works on Mexico and Peru. He said that he was not concerned with the conquest of Chile because there was not much material on this subject and that there was the poem *The Araucana* that covered the period excellently.[156]

Comparing the two Americas, Prescott told Vicuña that Spanish coun- tries lived in the past while the United States lived in the present. "You have a past so beautiful that you may well be excused your forgetfulness of the present; we, on the contrary, that have so little tradition are in the pro- cess of creating some for the future, for that we are at present working."[157]

He asked Vicuña about Mr. Wheelwright, to whom the Pacific owes so much. They then proceeded to discuss Cortés, whose admirable character, according to Prescott, was the opposite of that of Pizarro, astute and fero- cious. As he was busy at the moment writing the life of Philip II, he did not show him his new essays. Speaking of the death of Charles I, Prescott

[155] Quoted in Ferguson, *op. cit.*, p. 156.
[156] Benjamín Vicuña Mackenna "Páginas de mi diario," *Obras completas,* I, 159-160.
[157] *Loc. cit.*

said that he had evidence that it was more grief than venom that had made him leave the side of the somber Philip.[158]

The library of Mr. Prescott was a historical museum. All his documents on Peru, Mexico, and the kingdom of Isabel, that must have cost a fortune, were there in good order. He showed Vicuña relics of different heroes whom he had popularized, a piece of lace of the collar in which Cortés was buried, given to him by Lucas Alamán. At the entrance of his study there was a copy of the one original picture of Pizarro, to be found in the Cathedral of Valladolid, and another of Columbus copied by Madrazo. In a folder he had letters from Isabel and Ferdinand, a note of Charles V to the Emperor Maximilian when he was only a child of fifteen, and some scribblings of Gonzalo de Córdova.[159]

On the following day Vicuña received a note from Prescott inviting him to visit his study, located on the top floor of his house and completely surrounded by large glass casements in order to have a strong enough light to aid his eyes now almost without vision. He could work only one hour of the day. The rest of the time he spent listening to the reading of his documents by a reader who recited the Spanish perfectly but did not understand it. He showed Vicuña a special blackboard on which he wrote, and from which it was later copied by his assistant. "The quantity of patient rectification and research that are in the work of this great man are infinite."[160]

Prescott, not content with presenting to Vicuña a volume of his essays as a keepsake, took out his pencil and wrote without looking at the paper: "I hope the day will come when my history of Peru shall be translated into the beautiful Castilian on the other side of the Andes, as it has been in Mexico—W. H. Prescott." Prescott, who at twenty was already a lawyer, spent ten years in classical readings, which must have produced his fine, clear and brilliant style, and ten years in writing his scholarly work *The history of the reign of Isabel and Ferdinand*. He spent no less than eight years on his two other works about Spanish America. He was the father of three grown sons and possessed a considerable fortune. "As a historian," says Vicuña, "he is without doubt the most highly reputed that America has produced." The Chilean observed his bust by the side of Washington Irving's, and Prescott told him of his great enthusiasm for that fine writer. Crossed above a door Vicuña saw two swords, one that of his grandfather, General Prescott, who was Commander-in-Chief of the American troops in the first battle of Bunker Hill, the other that of his wife's grandfather, who opposed General Prescott in that same battle on the English side.[161]

Vicuña took leave of Mr. Prescott, having added to his admiration

---

158 *Loc. cit.*
159 *Loc cit.*
160 *Ibid.,* p. 161.
161 *Loc. cit.*

for his talent and agreeable memory of his kindness, which was especially evident in this case because of his being a Spanish American, "a people that," as Prescott said, "it could not be difficult for us to like," even if he had described their ancestors Almagro, Pizarro, Valdivia, Carvajal, as not very amiable people.[162]

Of all the Spanish American authors, only Sarmiento seems to question Prescott's greatness.[163] This might well be due to the fact that he did not share Sarmiento's prejudice against the past. Motley's *Rise of the Dutch Republic* was more to Sarmiento's liking.[164]

Historical investigation on the part of the North American authors was not limited to political subjects. George Ticknor writes his *History of Spanish Literature,* that was to enjoy five English editions and was to be translated into French, German, Italian and Spanish. This great work won the unanimous admiration of the Spanish Americans. Sarmiento calls Ticknor the greatest erudite in the field of Spanish American literature.[165] Irizarri wished to be given the opportunity of translating Ticknor's history. And Bello,[166] the great Spanish American grammarian, wrote an article, "Observaciones sobre la historia de la literatura española," in which he praises Ticknor's ability.

In his correspondence with Gayangos, Ticknor himself modestly gives some indications as to how his *History* was first received and of the trouble he had discouraging his admirers from translating it. "I continue to receive assurances from England and from different parts of the United States," he will write in March, 1850, "that the book is well considered. Among the rest, there have been favorable notices of it in a Havana newspaper, and in the *Revisor,* a Spanish review, printed at New York. Indeed a Spanish translation is announced there, which I understand is to be undertaken by Don Antonio José de Irizarri; a person entirely unknown to me—the editor of the *Revisor.*"[167] And a few days later (March 18) he will add: "since I wrote you last, I have received a letter from the gentlemen in New York, who think of making a Spanish translation of my work. I find they are señor Purroy, a lawyer of that city educated there, and Irizarri, the editor of *El Revisor,* a political and literary review, recently transferred to New York from Curaçao. Both I believe are natives of Venezuela, and Purroy is, I am told, a respectable man. I have written to them, to discourage them from their undertaking, and told of your translation, and how much I expected

---

162 *Loc. cit.*
163 Sarmiento "Discurso de Rhode Island", *Obras,* XXI, 214.
164 *Ibid.,* p. 215.
165 Sarmiento, *Obras,* XXI, 215-216.
166 Andrés Bello, "Observaciones sobre la historía de la literatura española" *Universidad de Chile, Anales,* Santiago, 1852-55.
167 Ticknor to Gayangos, Boston, March 5, 1850, in Clara Louisa Penny, *George Ticknor, Letters to Pascual de Gayangos,* p. 199.

to have my work enriched and improved in your hands."[168]   Purroy and Irizarri were not induced to abandon their project until Ticknor visited Purroy and explained to him clearly and sincerely the impracticability of the whole matter.[169]

Vicuña Mackenna also would have liked to know Ticknor, and if it had not been for a sudden indisposition on his part, he would have had the opportunity in Mr. Prescott's house. Curtis, however, brought him to another notable American, the celebrated linguist and preacher, Theodore Parker. Vicuña describes him as a clergyman without any fixed religion, a great preacher and an impassioned enemy of slavery. He had mastered seventeen languages (among others Spanish, but he did not understand Vicuña) and was the owner of the best private library in Boston.

> He is a man sixty years old, small, erect in figure and colossal in his ideas and aspirations. We were only with him a half hour, and a quarter of it he occupied in asking Curtis questions about the Indians in California and about the islands of the Pacific. The other quarter he spent asking me the same questions about the Araucanians in almost the same words. He seemed to me on the whole an insignificant man, vain and somewhat fidgety, as they say in England, not to repeat the word 'humbug' of the Yankees. Miss Isabella Curtis (a sister of Curtis) was a passionate enthusiast of Mr. Parker, but I took notice that the latter was not very friendly toward Prescott, probably because of religious differences. Mr. Parker told me that he had published some half dozen volumes, and he gave me a booklet about the 'Free-Soilers' in which I found truly eloquent and philosophic pages.[170]

To my knowledge, the first comprehensive study of the literature of the United States by a Spanish American was that of the Cuban DOMINGO DEL MONTE Y APONTE, (1804-1854) in an essay republished in Seville, in the *Revista de Ciencias, Literatura y Arte,* in 1856. Del Monte, whom we have quoted repeatedly in this study,   gave an excellent estimate of the literary situation in contemporary United States. This work was followed in 1861 by JUAN CLEMENTE ZENEA'S 1832-1871) *Sobre la literatura de los Estados Unidos.*[171] Zenea was a Cuban who had lived for many years in the United States and was the editor of several reviews published in Spanish in this country; taking advantage of the different studies and monographs in both Spanish and English, that had preceded him, he was able to give us a complete and objective picture of American literature from its beginnings to his day. For the purpose of studying the attitude of the Spanish Americans, however, the shorter and more personal essays are of greater

---

168 *Ibid.,* p. 204.

169 *Ibid.,* p. 206.

170 Vicuña Mackenna, *op. cit.,* p. 162.

171 This book was first published in the review *La América* of Madrid and later reprinted as a book, Habana, 1861.

value. Typical of these is Vicuña Mackenna's brief sketch of the American literary scene of 1853.[172]

Boston may well be the Athens of America, but it is lacking the seven sages of Greece. Great talents are indeed few that can be produced in a country in which there is almost only a single profession, commerce and industry. Of modern reputation, Prescott, Bancroft (the author of the *History of the United States* not yet finished, and former ambassador and minister) and Jared Spark, the popular author of the *Life of Washington,* are the only historians of European fame. Edward Everett, who they tell me is the most learned man in the United States, and who has been a teacher, orator, journalist, author, statesman, and recent ambassador to London, is. like Ticknor, a critic and well known literary man. However, the most celebrated and popular writers are Washington Irving and Fenimore Cooper, both of whom have died recently. Mrs. Beecher Stowe has won a high position as the author of the well-known *Uncle Tom,* the modern work about which there has been more humbug than any other; it has been translated even into Persian, and a London printer put into circulation 10,000 copies of the book in a cheap popular edition. The greatest talent of the Americans is to be found in journalism, in the numerous newspapers and gazettes that are to be found in every town. There is indeed a powerful legion of poets, but among them only Bryant, the poet of enthusiasm and art, Longfellow, the singer of Nature, and Margaret Fuller, the George Sand of America, are the top poets. Then come Emerson, Poe, Halleck, Dana, Miss Kirkland and also a Miss Frances Sergent, about whom I have heard no one speak except the reviews of the country.

Herman Melville, the author of *Moby Dick* and the excellent short story *Benito Cereno* — in my opinion the best story by an American on a Spanish subject — seems to have been unknown in Spanish Ameria.

Most Spanish Americans agree on the fact that the newspaper editorials represented the type of literature most typically American. They describe this literary genre as essentially popular and democratic. The newspaper reporter they see as one of the most characteristic products of the American psychology. "This type, the reporter", says Prieto, "deserves a special description, he is the most active part, the source of all news in a newspaper. He is astute and versatile, and an excellent example of American acceleration."[173]

For the most part, the Spanish American authors were attracted to those North Americans who in turn were interested in them. Washington Irving, Longfellow, Bryant,[174] Everett, Prescott, T i c k n o r, were the object of great admiration in Spanish America, but others who were equally great were practically unknown.

---

172 Vicuña Mackenna, *op. cit.,* p. 162-163.

173 Guillermo Prieto, *Viaje a los Estados Unidos,* pp. 53-54.

174 Bryant at one time visited Spanish America and published a memoir of his journey.

IV

DOMINGO FAUSTINO SARMIENTO

In the Spanish American literature of the nineteenth century there is one man who towers above all the others, the Argentinian Domingo Faustino Sarmiento. He was a man who belonged completely to his epoch, and therefore similar in many aspects to his contemporaries, but he possessed a personality that lent everything he did an extraordinary vitality and the stamp of originality. For this reason he occupies a position all his own in whatever aspect of his work one studies. With regard to the subject of this study, Sarmiento possesses many points in common with the other political writers of the period we have been examining, but he is unique in the sense that concern with the United States held the foreground all his life long, whereas for the others it was a matter of secondary consideration. The fundamental problem that preoccupied all Spanish American political thinkers subsequent to the Independence was that of incorporating their respective countries into the stream of modern European culture. This was Sarmiento's great concern, too; but ever present in him was the idea of the need to create an American culture in each of these countries, and the United States represented the culture of America that was at one and the same time the most American and the most European. Thus as he laid the groundwork for modern Argentina, which he, more than anybody else, shaped, he did not look upon the United States as something foreign, but as something closely related. He was never blind to the profound differences between the two Americas, but no one contributed so much as he to the idea of the unity amidst the diversity of America. This is the source of the originality of his ideas with regard to both Argentina and the United States.

1. Early Days (1811-1853)

Sarmiento was born in 1811, the first year of the movement for the independence of Argentina, and it may be said that he grew up with his country; and as he died in 1888, his life also closes with the end of the formative period of Spanish America and the coming of the Modern Age.

In the history of Argentina, these seventy-seven years of his life fall into two distinct parts: the first, an era of instability and dictatorship up to 1853; the second, an era of peace and material progress that follows Mitre's presidency.

To explain how Argentina passed from a feudal, primitive state to a modern and democratic nation is to tell the life history of this man of remarkable vision, who was able to see in advance what Argentina was to be in the next thirty years, at a time when it was the opposite of all he hoped and prophesied. This statesman and author was in himself a whole world of thought and action, undoubtedly the greatest South American figure of his epoch, as Bolívar had been of the previous.

His real name was Faustino Valentín Sarmiento, but due to some family tradition his friends started calling him Domingo Faustino and the name stayed. His parents represented middle class, provincial Argentina. His father was an honest, hard-working, patriotic man but with no other attributes that might have made him outstanding, even in the not too progressive province of San Juan. His mother, all kindness and abnegation, was the staunch pillar of the modest home. The peaceful existence of his early days has been told to us by Sarmiento himself in *Recuerdos de provincia*,[1] one of his finest literary productions, and in several very interesting autobiographical letters to Mrs. Horace Mann.[2]

As he himself used to boast with pride, he was "a self-made man." With the exception of his uncle, the priest José de Oro, from whom he obtained many of his ideals and interests, Sarmiento grew up alone. This in no way discouraged or handicapped him; on the contrary, he was always characterized by possessing definite aims and ambitions, almost prophetic in view of his later life.

He was greatly interested in foreign languages. He studied English and spoke French well, and although his culture was more European than American, the book that was to have the greatest effect upon him, as a man, was Benjamin Franklin's *Autobiography*.

He used to say that by founding a newspaper and a reading society Benjamin Franklin had done more for the emancipation of North America than an entire army.[3]

In 1826, he went with his uncle who was exiled to San Luis. The following years we find him working in his aunt's store in San Juan; later he leaves for Chile on business. In 1830, shocked by the atrocities commited by the 'caudillos', he joins the Unitarians and fights in the ranks of Nicolás Vega against the same man whom he has immortalized with his pen, Facundo Quiroga. Sarmiento and his companions were finally defeated in the Battle of Chanón in 1831. After this he fled to Chile, where he worked as a teacher, clerk, salesman and miner. This was the beginning of his exile that was to last, off and on, for twenty years. During this time, Sarmiento showed incredible energy and activity: he founded schools, published gazettes, gave speeches on vital issues and identified himself with the intellectual and

---

[1] Santiago de Chile, 1850.

[2] "Cartas de Sarmiento", *Boletín de la Academia Argentina de Letras*, 1935-1936, III-IV, nos. 6-14.

[3] "Mercurio", July 10, 1841, *Obras*, I, 70.

political life of the countries where he resided as if they had been his own. He also published *Facundo*,[4] which was to give him universal fame.

But before going any further, so that we may understand the real significance of this great man, let us survey the existing conditions of the Argentine of his day.

On the 25th of May, 1810, when the people of Buenos Aires declared their independence from José Bonaparte, then ruler of the mother country, the new nation was confronted by grave problems. The liberal creoles had automatically associated the ideal of independence with the liberal European ideas of the eighteenth century, and since the best model of this type which they had before them, the French Constitution, was Unitarian, they naturally assumed that the government of Argentina should likewise be Unitarian. This was an unfortunate selection, as the political theories of these men did not coincide with the national reality.

At this time the city of Buenos Aires was little more than a large village. The entire population of Argentina probably did not exceed six hundred thousand inhabitants. The roads were bad, and communications between the different provinces extremely difficult. With the coming of international commerce, Buenos Aires found itself more and more, as time went on, attached to foreign ideological and economic interests that were in many ways incompatible with those of the interior provinces. It is thus that the rivalry between the two sections started.

Mariano Moreno and Rivadavia were aware of the problem but did not attach much importance to it. Being essentially rationalists they pointed out the many weaknesses of the Federal system and let it go at that. They and their companions did not stop to consider that the same institutions and practices that meant liberty for the European, for the gaucho and his peculiar type of civilization meant slavery.[5] They did not realize, as Sarmiento did later on, that Argentina required a government that would protect the interests of both Buenos Aires and the provinces, and that the European shoe did not always fit the Argentinian foot. Led by capable and realistic leaders, the provinces fought back and finally imposed themselves with Rosas' dictatorship that lasted until 1853.

Such was the condition of Argentina when Sarmiento came into the picture, torn between two political factions, the Unitarians and the Federalists, and dominated by a reactionary dictatorship that obstructed the progress of the nation.

Sarmiento, essentially a realist, sensing the magnitude of the problem,

---

4 Santiago, 1845; English translation: *Facundo: Life in the Argentine Republic in the days of the tyrants; or Civilization and barbarism*, trans. by Mrs. Horace Mann, New York, 1868.

5 This disproportion is the theme for Argentina's main literary masterpiece, the *Martín Fierro* by Hernández.

did not come to any hasty conclusions as to its solution. He first approached it by analyzing the culture of his own people, as in *Facundo* and his articles in the newspapers of Chile, always maintaining a progressive point of view and displaying great interest in the newest political and economic ideas. In his early articles of the *Mercurio* and the *Nacional,* he frequently referred to the institutions, the men, and the ideas of the United States. Here are to be found the germs of many of the notions on education, libraries, newspapers, and government that made him famous in later years.[6] Later, aided by the Chilean government, he visited Europe and the United States and carefully compared conditions in these countries with those existing in the Spanish America of his day.

2. First Visit To The United States, 1848

He first went to France,[7] 1845, where he was given a hearty welcome. His book *Facundo* had preceded him and had been read with interest as an explanation of what Europeans, from their point of view, considered merely uprisings. Although mistakenly, both England and France continued to look upon Argentina because of its small population as offering easy possibilities of conquest and, therefore, of vital interest to them. Sarmiento was disappointed by what he saw there. In reality it proved to be the antithesis of what, in view of its political theorists, he had expected. No liberty existed, and reactionaries were in power. From there he continued on to Spain,[8] which he found in the throes of political disorder similar, so he declares, to that of Argentina itself. Next he went to Morocco,[9] Italy,[10] and finally to the United States.

Seeing this country as he did, after his travels in Europe, he was well prepared to make comparisons and to evaluate American progress at its true worth. Unlike most of his predecessors, he viewed the United States not as an ideal, but as a reality, its virtues together with its defects, a country in which the political principles of liberty and justice were not a matter for theory, but were actually being put into successful operation. He likewise observed that many of the existing circumstances of this nation, such as climate, territory and frontier background, coincided with those of Argentina. The United States, therefore, became for him a model, and he continued to write about it the rest of his life.[11]

---

6 *Mercurio, June* 10, 1841, *Obras,* I, 70 (on Benjamin Franklin); August 3, 1841, *Obras,* I, 100 (Costumbres Yankees); March 20, 1842, *Obras,* I, 178-180 (Washington, biography): *Obras,* II, 336 (Public librares in U. S.); *Obras,* II, 208 (Emancipation) *Obras,* II, 248 (Education).

7 Sarmiento, "Viajes," *Obras,* V, 88.

8. *Ibid.,* p. 146.

9 *Ibid.,* p. 196.

10 *Ibid.,* p. 234.

11 Sarmiento, "Argirópolis", *Obras,* XIII.

At the end of August, 1847, Sarmiento arrived in New York, after having passed through London and Liverpool.[12] The impression that the United States made upon him was tremendous. He had anticipated the new nation in all its strength and youth, but the true and living reality he saw before him exceeded all his calculations. His funds, in the meantime, diminished daily, but his eagerness to understand increased unendingly as he saw more of the country. His thirst for America was never quenched. This republic was such as he had dreamed: rich, just, free enterprising, educated. "God has finally wished that there should be found united in one lone die, in one lone nation, virgin land to allow the people to multiply without fear of misery, iron to complement human energy, coal to move engines, woods to supply lumber . . . , popular education to make each individual of the nation more productive, freedom of faith . . . , political freedom . . . , in short, the republic, strong and growing like a new star upon the sky."[13] His admiration was unbounded. From every point of comparison the United States measured greater than any of the other countries he had seen. Confronted with economic realities, however, he decided to reduce his stay to two months; during this short time he intended to visit the principal cities and to become acquainted with the American system of education.[14]

Indeed, it may well be said that he possessed a greater insight into the United States than any other Spanish American of his day. He sees this country, and rightfully so, as the promised land of abundance. Shortly after his arrival he writes to his friend Montt:

If God were to commission me with the forming of a great republic, I would not undertake such a serious project except on condition that he give me at least these fundamentals: space without known limits in order that some day two hundred million inhabitants could be satisfied there; coasts dotted with gulfs and bays, a terrain varied yet not presenting difficulties to the railroads and canals which have to cross the state in all directions; and as I would never agree to do without railroads, there would have to be enough coal and iron so that by the year 4751 the mines could still be exploited just as they were in the beginning. There should be plenty of timber; I myself would be in charge of giving opportune direction to the navigable rivers which would traverse the country in all directions, be converted into lakes, empty into all the oceans and thus connect all the climates, so that the products of the poles would travel directly to the tropical countries, and vice versa. Then, for future purposes, I would ask that everywhere there be plenty of marble, granite, porphyry and other hard stones without which nations cannot leave their footprints on a forgetful land. "Land of Cockaigne" a Frenchman will say. "The Isle of Barataria" the Spaniard will point out. Fools! It is the United States which God has formed,

---

12 Sarmiento, "Viajes", *Obras,* V, 333; *Ibid.,* 425.
13 *Ibid.,* p. 386.
14 *Ibid.,* pp. 423-424.

and I would swear that upon creating this bit of the world he knew very well that by the nineteenth century, the people being trampled—enslaved and dying of hunger in other places—would all come to join here and avenge humanity, for so many years of suffering, by their example.[15]

As a result of this first trip and for the purpose of making the United States known in Spanish America, Sarmiento wrote *Viajes por Europa, Africa y América,* first published in 1849. His observations are given in the form of a letter to Valentín Alsina and are not only a description of this country but also an interpretation of the relations, or a comparison between the United States and Europe and Spanish America. The style of writing he uses is definitely influenced by the romanticism of the epoch. Sarmiento sees everything dramatically. The United States presented to him "el espectáculo de un drama nuevo" without precedent. This romantic attitude, however, in no way deformed his interpretation of the realities that surround him; on the contrary, he was able to discern clearly that which is really great and of permanent endurance within the national character. His judgment was based on human values, free from prejudice, and universal in scope.

The principal object of his trip was to visit Horace Mann, the great reformer of primary education, who, like Sarmiento, had travelled to the different countries of Europe in search of new methods of education. He was living at the time in Newton East, a small town outside of Boston. Following the example of other travellers, Sarmiento made this trip by way of Niagara Falls, and once in Boston he spent hours talking with Mr. Mann on subjects of common interest. Sarmiento describes him as a man who possessed the rare virtues, in both his acts and in his writings, of prudence and profound knowledge.[16]

Fortune favored Sarmiento. Upon his return to New York, he met a Señor Santiago Arcos who, though not wealthy, was better off than he, and they both pooled their money for the trip home.[17] From Boston Sarmiento was to go to Washington by way of Philadelphia and Baltimore, and eventually return to Harrisburg where he was to meet Sr. Arcos in the United States Hotel. Things did not turn out according to plan, as often happens. There was no such establishment in that city, and when Sarmiento, despondent at finding himself penniless in a strange town, tried in vain to make himself understood by the hotel clerks, a blank expression came over their faces. To the amazement of all those present, Sarmiento, losing his patience after several days of waiting, went into a rage that might have well been understood in any of the Spanish countries but not in Harrisburg. "Yankees are not accustomed to the manifestations of southern passions," says Sarmiento. The hotel proprietor looked at him in dismay as he heard him curs-

---

15 *Ibid.,* pp. 335-336.
16 *Ibid.,* p. 446, 450.
17 *Ibid.,* p. 426.

ing excitedly in a foreign tongue. Finally, signaling Sarmiento to stop for
a moment, he went running to the street, "probably in search of a constable."
Minutes later, he returned accompanied by an individual with a pen behind
his ear, who coldly inquired, first in English, then in French, and later
with an occasional word in Spanish, about the excitement that the innkeeper
had reported. The man listened to Sarmiento without moving a muscle, and
when he had finished he said to him in French: "The only thing I can do
is to pay your hotel bill and your expenses as far as Pittsburgh, provided
that, when you reach that city, you pay in the Merchant's Manufacturing
Bank." Sarmiento could give no guarantee that the money would be returned, but the man did not seem to be much concerned about this.[18]

Sarmiento waited in case Arcos might arrive. Arcos never did, but his
newly formed friend brought him several books in Spanish, French and
Italian for his amusement. The following day he gave Sarmiento twenty
dollars, much more than he needed for so short a trip. Arcos was finally
discovered in Pittsburgh[19] and the two continued together the rest of the
voyage.

During this first trip Sarmiento was interested in the various methods
of travel, the hotels, the numerous large and prosperous cities, the people
in general, and the development of the Far West.

The river boats fascinated him.

They are floating palaces, three stories in height, with galleries and roofs
for promenades. Gold shines in the capitals and architraves of the thousand
columns which, as in the Isaac Newton, flank monstrous halls capable of
containing the senate and the house of representatives. Artistically draped
hangings of damask hide staterooms for five hundred passengers, and there
is a colossal dining-room with an endless table of polished mahogany and
service of porcelain and plate for a thousand guests. This boat can carry
two thousand passengers; it has seven hundred and fifty beds, two hundred
private cabins; it measures three hundred and forty-one feet in length,
eighty-five in width, and it carries one thousand, four hundred and fifty
tons of cargo in addition.[20]

The hotels in America were to the nineteenth century what the cathed-
rals had been for the thirteenth. The hotel Saint Charles, in New Orleans,
which raised its proud head over the surrounding hills and woods, the Saint
Charles, which had reminded him of Saint Peter's in Rome, was nothing
but an inn. "Behold the sovereign people which builds for itself palaces
under the roofs of which to lay its head for a night; behold the worship
granted to man, as man, and the marvels of art employed, lavished, to glorify

---

[18] *Ibid.*, pp. **447-479.**
[19] *Ibid.*, p. **481.**
[20] *Ibid.*, p. **347.**

the popular masses."[21] Arcos—Sarmiento's companion, who, up to then had displayed indifference toward democracy—after passing through the inner streets which give communication to hundreds of rooms, decorated with all the gradations of luxury exacted by the diverse condition of the guests, and which extended fabulous distances, remarked, "I am now converted...through the intercession of Saint Charles, now I believe in the republic; I believe in democracy; I believe in everything. I pardon the Puritans, even the one who was eating raw tomato sauce straight with the point of his knife and before the soup. Everything should be pardoned the people who raise monuments to the dining-room and crown the kitchen with a cupola like this."[22]

Sarmiento's own primary interest lay in the progress and superiority of the United States over Europe as seen in the way all the newest developments of sciences and material well-being were at the disposal of the entire population. He visited in all twenty-one states, and although he did not consider them perfect, he deemed them further along the road than any nation in Europe. To him the typical life of the United States was to be seen in the American village with all its parts functioning in perfect order. He never ceased to marvel at its miniature structure, like that of a little state, with bank, church, school, newspaper, census, etc. This was in great contrast with his own Argentina where a great disparity existed between the city of Buenos Aires and the rest of the population, almost entirely rural.[23]

The wealth and size of the American cities fascinated him. He looked upon them with envy, and hoped that some day there would be similar ones in his own country.

New York he describes as the center of North American activity, the point of debarkation for European immigrants, and therefore the least American city in the Union in its appearance and customs. "Whole quarters have very narrow and dirty streets bordered with houses of miserable appearance. Pigs are necessary personages in the streets, where they hide and where no one disputes with them their rights to citizenship. Broadway is located in the center of the most beautiful part of this city...It was built by a bond issue, as are all the great North American enterprises. On Broadway there are beautiful private homes, a white marble bazaar believed to be unrivaled in Europe, and, under construction, a theater for Italian opera. In one hour I counted on Broadway four hundred and eighty carriages...At night, *Hernani* was being given in a theater improvised in Castle Garden."[24]

Buffalo was a frontier town, located at the eastern end of Lake Erie. It was the line of navigation for Chicago and the west. Due to the large number

---

[21] *Ibid.*, p. 352.
[22] *Ibid.*, pp. 353-354
[23] *Ibid.*, p. 342.
[24] *Ibid.*, p. 425.

of transients that passed daily through this city, it had become too small for the number of its inhabitants.[25]

The dramatic splendor of Niagara Falls appealed to his romantic spirit. Inspired by its beauty Sarmiento declaims:

> Flow on for ever, in thy glorious robe
> Of terror and beauty. God hath set
> His rainbow on thy forehead; and the cloud
> Mantled around thy feet. Awe he doth give
> Thy voice, a thunder, power to speak to Him
> Eternally bidding the lip of man
> Keep silence; and on thine altar pour
> Incense of awe-struck praise.[26]

Boston, founded on a peninsula connected to the continent by a mile long isthmus, represented for Sarmiento the epitome of American culture and tradition. "In Boston that famous law of 1676 was formulated, the law of general and obligatory education which was a prelude to the habilitation of human kind. In Boston the colonists assembled in meetings and resolved not to pay the duty on tea, to abstain from the use of this infusion and to throw into the sea the boxes of tea in the warehouse. In Boston the public schools are converted into temples, such is the magnificence of their architecture. Each living being pays a dollar a year to educate the children of his fellowmen, and every poor child annually consumes seven dollars of public income in his education. In Boston is the seat and center of the religion of Unitarianism that tends to unite in a common center all the subdivisions of sect and raise belief to the order of religious and moral philosophy. From Boston, finally, set out those crowds of colonizers who bear to the Far West the institution, knowledge, and habit of government, the Yankee spirit, and the manual arts which preside over the possessing of the land. Four lines of steamers bind it to Europe. A railroad runs along the coast as far as Portland in Maine; another, to Concord, puts it into communication with the state of New Hampshire; another, with Troy and its tributary lines and canals; three with New York, which are completed by lines of navigation by sea or by Long Island Sound. Its hotels are the pride of the United States, and the Tremont Hotel is considered superior to all in elegance and comfort."[27]

Sarmiento's comments on the various characteristics of American life indicate how well he observed and how he was able to perceive the deep significance underlying seemingly small and unimportant details and customs.

---

[25] *Ibid.*, p. 431.
[26] Written by an unidentified young lady.
[27] *Ibid.*, p. 444.

He remarked that in the United States everyone lived in his own house.[28]
Manufacturing was extensive, from kitchen utensils to coaches, and these
products were in general use by all. Everyone had watches, a high standard
of dress prevailed, even on the part of the working classes.[29] The signboards
were really works of art with great attention being paid to spelling and to
the formation of the letters.[30] All Americans had a rough, direct manner,
but one that Sarmiento considered at least partly deliberate to encourage
democratic spirit.[31] Love for prosperity and the spirit of enterprise were inherent in the national character. The United States had taken the best of
all civilization and had improved on it, so much so, that the general aspect
of well-being on the part of all seemed even monotonous.[32]

The progress of the United States was not due, as so many had thought,
to its great size but to spiritual strength. Skill and self-reliance were a
national fetish.[33] "The Yankee is his own keeper", says Sarmiento, "and if
he wants to kill himself, no one will prevent it. If he runs after the train to
catch it, and if he dares to give a leap and hang from a rail, escaping the
wheels, he is at liberty to do so; if the rascally paperboy, driven by the
desire to sell one more copy, has waited until the train is proceeding at full
speed and then jumps off, all will applaud the skill with which he lands
steadily and continues on his way afoot. This is the way the character of
the nation is formed and how one uses liberty. Perhaps there are a few more
victims and accidents, but, on the other hand, they are free men and not
disciplined prisoners . . . The child who wishes to take the railroad, steamer,
or canal boat, the bachelor who goes to pay a visit two hundred leagues
away, never meets anyone to ask them with what object, with what permission they leave the paternal fold. They are making use of their liberty
and their right to move about. As a result of this the Yankee child horrifies
the European by his assurance, his cautious prudence, his knowledge of
life at ten years of age."[34]

Liberty was by no means limited to men. It was also enjoyed by
women. The North Americans had created for themselves customs which
had neither example nor antecedent on this earth. "The unmarried woman,"
says Sarmiento, "is as free as a butterfly until the moment of entering the
domestic cocoon for the fulfilment of her social functions with matrimony.
Before this period she travels alone, she strolls through the streets of the
cities, and publicly carries on chaste yet untrammelled love affairs under the
indifferent eye of her parents. She receives people who have not been in-

---

28 *Ibid.*, p. 342.
29 *Ibid.*, pp. 344, 360.
30 *Ibid.*, p. 343.
31 *Ibid.*, p. 358.
32 *Ibid.*, p. 346.
33 *Ibid.*, p. 361.
34 *Ibid.*, p. 365.

troduced to her family, and at two in the morning, she returns home from a dance accompanied by the man with whom she has waltzed exclusively all night."[35]

The freedom enjoyed by the people of this country was never due to moral laxness. He describes the American character as possessing firm moral convictions, shaped by religious exercises.

There also existed in the United States a democratic attitude toward life in general that Sarmiento describes as having the qualities of "moral consciousness."[36] This exquisite virtue was shared by all regardless of their social or economic position. The American was far from polished, but he was good-natured and kind. If four individuals sat around a table they would infallibly put their eight feet upon it. "I have seen seven Yankee dandies in amicable discussion, seated as follows: two with their feet on the table, one with them on the cushion of an adjacent chair, another with his passed over the arm of his own chair, another with both heels supported on the edge of the cushion of his own chair, so as to rest his chin between both knees, another embracing, or rather wrapping his legs around the back of the chair, just as we do to support our arms."[37] But this familiar behavior of the Americans Sarmiento does not condemn as a defect; on the contrary, for him it is the natural behavior of man in a free state. The president of the United States was not above such familiarities. Two or three days of the year he received without ceremony those who wished to see him. "On July 4," says Sarmiento, "Lafayette square is filled with the carriages of the visitors on that day of congratulations; these alight from the carriage, and after them, the coachman who entrusts the care of the horses to some boy in exchange for a few cents. On those days, the president is on real exhibition. The coachman opens a passageway through the multitude, his hobnailed shoes resounding on the marble floor; he arrives in the presence of the president and stretches out to him a calloused hand which grasps his strongly and shakes it, looking into his face all the while and laughing at him with a good-natured, provocative, and satisfied expression; he then returns to his horses, turning around from time to time to cast a glance at the president, to obtain a last peep of pleasure and felicitation. Poor president of the democracy! . . ."[38] "The Europeans make fun of the rough manners of the Americans, more put on than real, and the Yankees, because of a spirit of contradiction, become obstinate about the matter, and pretend that it is the prerogative of liberty and the American spirit to behave as they chose. Without wanting to defend such habits or even justify them, I would like to say that, after having visited the leading

---

35 *Ibid.*, pp. 380, 383.
36 *Ibid.*, p. 358.
37 *Ibid.*, p. 358.
38 *Ibid.*, p. 458.

nations of Christendom, I came to the conclusion that the only cultured people that exists in the world, the last product of modern civilization, is the North Americans."[39]

The only defect he found at this time with American culture was its materialism and unscrupulousness when it came to business matters and money.[40]

When he left to return to Chile he went confused and a little saddened. Many of his illusions had been destroyed and others, which he never would have suspected, had been born. He had seen the great monuments of Europe, of France, of Europe was exquisite and eternal, but in the United States he had just perceived another culture younger and more vigorous. He had seen a great spectacle for him hitherto unknown. In this new state there was happiness and grandeur, and here it was shared by all from the highest to the lowliest citizen. In truth, the United States was an earthly paradise, a utopian dream come true. Sarmiento's thoughts would then wander back to his own people and to the chaos that kept them in a state of bondage. He could think of many reasons to explain the prosperity of the North American republic, and the anarchy of Argentina, but one in particular kept coming back to him with added strength: education. Nothing was as important as culture, which in his opinion was the primary virtue of this nation. Without education neither free people nor democratic institutions could possibly exist. Ignorance and intellectual notions divorced from the existing realities were the evils of Argentina, and he made up his mind that he would dedicate the rest of his life, if necessary, to overcome them both.

The leading characters in this Argentinian drama were the "gauchos", whom Sarmiento called his "enemigos amigos," and the intellectuals of Buenos Aires, his "amigos enemigos."

On the one side, as José Luis Romero has pointed out, was a peasant or semi-rural group, politically inexperienced, whose simple thoughts and ideals, nurtured on a vigorous although elementary democratic sentiment, fluctuated between the aspiration to uncontrolled freedom and a reversion to homage and subjection to an efficient leader, in whom they saw the reflection of their own ideals and virtues. They did not hesitate to defend these ideals even with arms because they believed that they were incompatible with those of the city bourgeoisie. The members of this group, as we have seen, were known as the Federalists.

On the other side, were the educated groups, usually urban, to whom emancipation and a central representative organization appeared synonymous. As the crisis deepened, this second group, being essentially theoretical and

---

[39] *Ibid.*, pp. 359, 360.
[40] *Ibid.*, p. 387.

abstract, refused to recognize the existing realities that surrounded them. They tried to justify their position with academic arguments that the "gauchos" could not possibly understand, and thus helped to widen the cleavage between the two parties.

During his voyage through the United States Sarmiento had come to the realization that these two sides were not necessarily incompatible, that both had two mutual aims, independence and democracy, and that it was necessary to employ conciliatory political reforms in order to save the nation.

There were many Unitarians who believed that the only possible solution was to subdue by violence those whom they considered uncontrollable groups, and they did not hesitate to resort to arms or to negotiate for foreign protection. Sarmiento might have shared this point of view at one time in his life, but after his return from the United States he had the conviction that the rural masses and their leaders represented a reality which it was useless to deny and had to be reckoned with in order to find a solution to the national problems.

For the purpose of bringing these two groups together Sarmiento wrote *Argirópolis,* sponsoring the federal government and accepting the political and economic demands of the provinces. In this book Sarmiento made a favorable comparison between the potential possibilities of Argentina and the actual conditions of the United States of that day. He explained that changes along the lines of the federal government would in no way jeopardize the interests of the city of Buenos Aires, but, on the contrary, would bring peace and prosperity to the entire nation. In order to overcome any other differences that might arise in the future, Sarmiento proposed creating a new national capital located in a position acceptable to both sides. He also recommended building railroads, canals, a public school system and the sponsoring of European immigration. Every one of these issues was in one way or another influenced by what he had seen in the United States and their ultimate objective was to create in Argentina conditions similar to those existing here.

The conciliation between the Unitarians and the Federalists was not accomplished in a day. Rosas was defeated in 1852 and a federal constitution was written in 1853, but actual peace did not come until 1862 with Mitre's presidency.

With the triumph of the allied or liberal party Sarmiento was made governor of the province of San Juan, (1862-1864) and was able to put into practice many of the notions he had acquired during his trips and meditations. He founded the community of Chivilcoi, a social experiment that was later to serve as a model for all of Argentina. In a letter to Mrs. Horace Mann of May 20, 1866, he tells how the entire thing came about. "The system of distribution of public lands which the Spaniards left us," explains Sarmiento, "is the cause of the many wars and general backwardness of the country. Each property is one or two leagues in dimension and there are some royal grants as large as seventy leagues. In California there was a great deal of this. There were about forty leagues in the possession of squatters, proprietors without title. I took it upon myself to introduce here the North American system of dividing the land into lots of two hundred units each, with broad roads, fifty feet wide, running through them, and to sell them cheap so that the farmers would have land, which they did not at this time, since this country was laid out for the grazing of cattle. As a result a rural, agricultural district was formed made up of immigrants and other hard-working people who are very happy today. The town, designed with broad streets like those I had seen in North America, is beautiful."[41] Years later, when he was made president of the republic, he was asked what his platform was and Sarmiento answered with one word: "Chivilcoi."

In 1865 he was appointed Argentinian Ambassador to the United States for Mitre's government and remained in this country for the next three years.

3. Second Visit To The United States, 1865-1868

On May 15th, 1865, the new Argentine Ambassador to the United States, Domingo Faustino Sarmiento, disembarked in New York, almost twenty years after his departure, and with his customary exuberance rediscovers the United States. "I marvel at the amazing changes that have taken place during these twenty years in this section of the country," he remarked. "What power!" "What riches!"[42]

Sarmiento was too frank and outspoken to make a good diplomat; personally, however, he did more to foster good relations than had an entire century of diplomacy. His friends were many and of all kinds, including teachers, scientists, senators and even revolutionists, and his duties, most of them self-imposed, most unorthodox for an ambassador. There was no university or important college that he did not visit. He attended teachers' conventions. "I am invited to the reunion for superintendents of all schools of the South," he writes on January 23, 1865, "and I will disseminate throughout America whatever resolutions we take."[43] And although the English he spoke was a jargon he had learned from reading the commercial posters of Valparaíso, when it came to matters of education he always found a way of understanding and making himself understood. He sent back to Argentina everything imaginable: instruments of all kinds, books, manuals, maps, statues, paintings, even a piano. He made arrangements with two publishing houses, Appleton and Scribner, to print books

---

[41] Sarmiento, "Cartas", IV, 299-300.
[42] *Ibid.*, p. 474.
[43] *Ibid.*, p. 83.

and maps in Spanish.[44] He himself undertook the task of translating the *Agriculturist*[45] and got permission from his government to reprint the works of Horace Mann for Spanish American consumption.[46] He proposed the building of a system of public libraries to be supplied with books in Spanish from the United States.

If I succeed in interesting America in my ideas, and two thousand libraries are founded, then the booksellers of Boston and New York will be able to publish in Spanish all books deserving of fame, and thus will open the gates of Spanish America, at present closed to liberty and to thought, to science and the republic...[47]

He defended feminism, and even intervened in North American politics.[48] He pointed out the dangers that isolation from Europe and Spanish America represented for the United States.

The more transcendental side of his activities is excellently summarized in a letter from Mrs. Horace Mann to Governor Andrews of Massachusetts.[49]

I am a stranger to you, writes Mrs. Mann, but nevertheless I address you on the principle that every man and woman in Massachusetts ought to give you a little pleasure, if possible. I believe you have seen Mr. Sarmiento, our Minister from the Argentine Republic, but I doubt if you know what a remarkable and interesting man he is. He has spent his life in endeavoring to elevate the Argentine Republic politically and educationally and has the most genuine love of our institutions, which he has been the chief means of seeing planted there. He knows all about you, and what you have done, and why, as well as any Massachusetts man and appreciates it all at its true value. Indeed I doubt if many Massachusetts men look at the influence of their own State in civilizing the rest of the country with the insight that he does. He looks upon us in our ideal rather than in what we have actually attained—he sees what will be the result when the best purposes of our best men shall have been realized, for his enthusiasm for the United States has been stimulated to a poetical appreciation, if I may so speak, by all that he has suffered in seeing the disadvantages which his own beautiful country has encountered in their efforts after Independence.

He visited me yesterday with his interesting young secretary Batholomero [sic] Mitre, son of the President of the Republic, and handed me a Spanish paper in which is printed a letter he wrote to Chile after he heard of your project of sending women to humanize Barhington Territory. I begged him to leave it that I might translate it and send it to you, for it will surely be agreeable after all the harsh things that have been said about your missionary ship. His Secretary told me it had been printed in all the

44 *Ibid*. p. 95.
45 *Ibid.*, p. 114.
46 *Ibid.*, p. 93.
47 *Ibid.*, p. 115.
48 Sarmiento "Cartas", III, 396.
49 Sarmiento "Cartas", IV, 649-652.

newspapers of Chili. I, hope it will be printed in one of our Boston papers, and for that purpose I have put a little heading to it. If you send it to a paper, please remit to him (and to me) a copy of it.

I wish the suggestion he makes that six hundred school mistresses sent to the Argentine republic would do great good there, could be the basis of introducing the study of Spanish into our public schools. It ought to be done, for those are surely sister Republics, and Mr. Sarmiento has such influence with the home government that I do not doubt he would secure great facilities, even grants of land which are so marvellously productive there, to such an emigration of women. If you were still to be Governor I should dwell much upon this. Mr. Sarmiento has just written a life of Lincoln for his own countrymen and has promised to furnish it in unlimited quantities from the N. York press if they will diffuse it. It is admirably written. I have translated the Introduction which I hope to publish somewhere. If I had money, I would print it, with extracts from the book, and a fine discourse by him which will be read tomorrow before the Historical Society of Providence—and which I have just helped to translate for the purpose. I think they would do more toward enlisting public interest in S. America than any theirs [sic] that any one else could say. He is preparing a history of education in S. America to be put into English and to be published here if he can caerful [sic] confident that it will be read, I am somewhat acquainted with this subject, for I knew Mr. Sarmiento when he visited this country in 1846 and learnt from my husband the details of the Common School System of Massachusetts, which he afterward established in Chili and in the Argentine Republic.

I did not expect to write so long a letter, but it is with the hope of interesting you that I say all this. I think I shall put one sentence out of this letter into my heading, which you will please excuse.

Although Governor Andrews did not come to Sarmiento's aid as Mrs. Mann had suggested in her letter, nevertheless the program of sending American school teachers to South America and the construction of an astronomical observatory in Córdoba to be directed by an American scientist went on as planned.

Sarmiento was at first very concerned with the original success of this venture. He feared that the American girls would not take to the new environment. On April 13, 1866, he writes to Mrs. Horace Mann:[50]

I am not only much occupied with the idea of procuring persons who will completely fulfill their mission, but that the promises which I have made shall be abundantly redeemed, in order that a first *disenchantment* may not close the door to future efforts. Of this I cannot be completely sure without receiving from there replies to the repeated letters which I have written, accompanying your own which I sent home in order to give greater weight to my suggestions.

---

[50] Sarmiento to Mrs. Mann, New York, April 13, 1866, *Ibid.*, pp. 596-602.

First, we must consider the nature of the Schools.

1. The Sarmiento School is for males, and might consist of the two sexes, but in no case for women entirely. A director of this, whether man or woman, would be sure of a thousand dollars annually, perhaps more: a house and a sum of perhaps three hundred dollars for provision, preelluding [sic] any discussion which might arise from any other arrangement.

2. There is besides a College of ladies which my sister at present has the direction of. This might be put under the direction of another lady with the same or perhaps other advantages. Either or both could then open other classes in English or give lessons outside of their respective Schools.

3. A contract should be made for three years in order that there might be full time to terminate the course of study in various branches.

Two teachers of equal grade in the same establishment would at present be too many, because there are young people there who could fill the places of assistants.

The direction of each establishment would be confided entirely to the Principal in order that she might regulate them in her own way.

There are boarding-school-pupils in the Ladies College, and my sister or my daughter would be ready to serve as matrons for that and for the other establishment if the two sexes are admitted. (You perceive that I am answering your enquiries in order.)

There are buildings or arrangements for each lady to live in her own establishment.

The social situation they would occupy would be very distinguished, even better than here, if I may so speak without being misunderstood, from the prestige that would accompany them by the powerful recommendations which would introduce them, and from their being Northamericans and people of fine education. Their acquaintances would be of the first families of the country.

The rout [sic] which is altogether the preferable one would be from N. York to Buenos Ayres and from there to San Juan by Stagecoach which crosses the Pampas in ten days with every security, respect and careful attention. In Buenos Ayres they could stay a month or more in the house of one of my friends, an [sic] a delicious country seat and in the bosom of a family if they prefer it, and which would be best in order that they may become familiar with the Spanish language.

The route by Chile is enormously expensive; the Cordillera cannot be passed till December. But they should find a friendly house and family in Valparaiso!

A sailing vessel would be the best mode of transportation because it would go directly to Buenos Ayres, while the Steamers from N.Y. only go to Rio Janeiro from which another vessel goes to B.A. The passage by Steam would cost $400.00 each—by sailing vessel $100.00 each. The contract should commence when they leave here. This would be a good precedent and would relieve our friends there from too many obligations.

In regard to the prejudices of the country which they would have to combat or consult none occurs to me of any importance.

If they are Catholics they would give religious instruction accordingly. If they are not Catholics, I will make it known and they will not be molested. They are a people full of fanaticism and will be surprised like persons of a nation that holds other ideas, but they are without the spirit of propagandism.

The clemate [sic] is extremely healthy [sic]. There is much heat in Summer, as much or more than in N. York and it is cold in winter. For their personal convenience it would be well for the ladies to take such furniture as they are accustomed to use. Provision is easy to be procured, and cheap. Meat, bread and every thing else are abundant, delicious fruits, fine peaches, grapes and all fruits any other of any temperate climate, oranges, flowers, vegetables, and in quantities without price. (Mr. S. once told me that the most delicious grapes were fifty cents a ton, and that peaches had no money value at all—our squashes he despises because they are so inferior to theirs M.M.) In regard to vegetables, an order sent to the Normal School Estate would furnish them daily with all they could want. It is indispensable to teach the use of sewing machines of which they have four.

The books of instruction I have sent from here and they can take such as they need.

It is a thing yet to be decided there whether the teaching shall be in English or in Spanish. I think it will be necessary to use the English in some high classes when it has been taught in the lower ones. There are English Colleges in Buenos Ayres in which the lessons are taught in English or at least the pupils are obliged to talk English among themselves. I incline to have English popularized. But we must not forget that the Sarmiento School is the prencipal [sic] object, and the master must adapt himself to the School, and not the School to the qualities they may happen to be met with in a master. This school and the college for ladies once provided with Principals a necessary development will introduce other teachers of both sexes and the Normal School of which I have spoken before as one of my desiderata, and of which I frequently confer with my government, I hope for immediate replies to the numerous letters I have written upon this subject to the Minister of Instruction of the National Government and to the Governor of San Juan.

Will they be satisfactory? I often ask myself. Will they sympathize with the passionate interest I feel upon this important matter? I can be sure of nothing. The papers from Buenos Ayres lament that since I came away nothing has been done there to sustain and advance education.

I will now tell you something which may be useful. San Juan is a province of the interior with good manners and excellent aspirations for improvement, but behindhand in buildings, in conveniences and in comfort. A stranger might feel shocked by a thousand trifles, by the relative inferiority of the common people who are ignorant and uncleanly, by customs to which he is not habituated, by a homesickness which will make every thing appear desagreeable [sic], unless he is possessed of a spirit superior to all these things and feels that his mission is precisely to change the state of things.

Persons placed thus in special circumstances by contrast, which they may not fulfill as they ought, are the cause of many misfortunes and disappointments in South America. I will give one example. Desiring to develop the industry of the mines, I solicited in Chile a metallurgist. What would be the situation of the one they sent me may be inferred from the circumstance that he asked $100.00 a month to transport himself to San Juan. There I made him inspector of mines, major of volunteers, Chief of a mining company, and sent him to England with money, recommendations, letters and honors which gave him the same position in his own country. He married there, thanks to his respectable situation, a rich and educated lady. He returned insufferable, exigeante [sic], taking airs upon himself in every way over me then Governor and creator of this fantasma, as of others. At last he became a millionaire without ever having shown any gratitude or deference to me whatever. Much entered into this, personal character and even race, but a long experience of analogous cases has shown me that without individual perversity, this abuse arises from the exceptional position in which persons so situated are placed who cannot cope with difficulties inherent in circumstances and life, and who think they can alter the world to conforme [sic] it to their habits.

If I had desired the services of therse [sic] ladies for Buenos Ayres, I should not have dwelt so much upon these considerations, for if there, and if they did not suit to fulfill their engagements, they could open a College for ladies on their own account, and make much money. In Buenos Ayres, a rich and civilized city as full of comfort and conveniences as the best of cities here, they pay for education, above all for that of females, for which the Schools of foreigners are preferred and even demanded, and those of north americans recommended by me could be especially sought. If I were there I should demand female teachers for the public schools of Buenos Ayres, and all would go well, with these suggestions which I have made in answer to your questions, you can consult with the ladies, and remembering that there are two destinct [sic] Schools, propose to them that they should draw up a form of contract as they would desire it and sent it to me that I may see if their conditions can be met and give security for their fulfillment. I have informed my government that I am taking these steps and of the possibility that I may subscribe to an agreement with the suggestions which they have made to me and which are sufficient to guarantee it even if I do not receive more complete authority from them.

Sarmiento was particularly interested in having the teachers know Spanish[51] With this purpose in mind, as well as the general good of inter-American relations, he had proposed time and again to American educators that Spanish be taught in our schools.[52] He was elated whenever an American teacher knowing Spanish came to see him.

---

[51] *Ibid.*, pp. 116-118.
[52] *Ibid.*, p. 464.

He had hoped to build an American University and to make Mrs. Mann's son its president. "Wouldn't it be a wonderful moral effect to have the son of Horace Mann, a graduate of the University of Cambridge, in charge of this reform."[53]

Sarmiento's efforts were not in vain; American schools with American teachers, as well as an observatory in Córdoba directed by the American scientist Mr. Gould, were eventually built in Argentina and played a significant part in the development of the nation.

As to Sarmiento's literary works, mentioned in Mrs. Mann's letter to Governor Andrews, they all dealt with a common theme — inter-American relations.

His *Life of Lincoln*, intended for Spanish American consumption, had didactic rather than literary aspirations. "The text of this work," he writes to Mrs. Mann, "is not worth translating, for only the final chapters and a few explanatory observations necessary for the South American reader are actually mine. The rest I have obtained from several biographies that I consulted."[54] Yet in spite of Sarmiento's negative appraisal of his own work—a rare thing, indeed, for he was notoriously self-possessed—Mrs. Mann found it to be excellent and insisted on translating it. There were others who shared this same opinion, and it was not hard to persuade him to have a second edition made in 1866.[55]

The History of Education in South America that Mrs. Mann mentions was originally to be published in English and, according to Sarmiento's own words, it was intended to interest the people of the United States in the Spanish American countries. "Now that the unfortunate tendencies toward slavery, annexation, and conquest have changed, I would like to point the way to the American philanthropists of extending the republican form of government,"[56] he writes on September 28, 1865.

And in another letter written on November 25, 1865, he says:

I have decided not to send to Mr. Allen, who seems like such a nice person, the *Anales de Educación* because I am waiting until I can send with it and with other books of mine concerning education, the manuscript of the introduction that I have already written for a book I have in mind, History of Education in South America in relation to the republican institutions. The reason I am doing this is to consult his better judgment and to solicit its publication in his review; because I would not risk publishing the book in English if I could not be sure beforehand that some friends of education would prepare the public to receive it favorably. This will be the best way of making these countries known, I won't say favorably, but in a manner that would awaken the interest of the North Americans, judging them with

53 *Ibid.,* p. 118.
54 *Ibid.,* p. 468.
55 *Ibid.,* p. 93.
56 *Ibid.,* pp. 453-454.

less severity after knowing the difficulties against which they fight. The motive of half our revolutions is to achieve the progress into which the United States has initiated the world. We made ourselves independent following the impulse given by the independence of the United States. Half of the republics, Mexico, Central America, Colombia, the Republic of Argentina have involved themselves in revolutions in order to become federalist states like the United States. The freedom of worship, a North American doctrine and institution, and dispossessing the Catholic church of its secular domination ... have caused us torrents of blood. And when they see us enveloped in the dust of so much disorder not only do they abandon but scorn us.[57]

The history of education in Spanish America, however, was a subject of little interest to the people of the United States, and Sarmiento's friends convinced him of the many difficulties this literary project would encounter. Instead, with the material gathered for this book, along with other that he had been accumulating for years, he wrote, in Spanish, *Las escuelas, base de la prosperidad de la república en los Estados Unidos,* published in New York in 1866.

Sarmiento's *Rhode Island speech,* which was translated into English by Mrs. Mann and published under the title *North and South American discourse,* is of particular interest to us because it is the first attempt by an American, of either hemisphere, to give the gist of the relations between the Spanish and the Anglo-Saxon peoples; and to this day it is comparable to anything written along these lines, even if the facts in some cases are incorrect.

Sarmiento started his lecture by discussing the historical background of these two peoples, giving particular emphasis to the moral, cultural tendencies of the Puritans as against the rapacity of the Spaniards. He then points out that it was the example of the United States that was primarily responsible for the emancipation of the Spanish American countries. From that he goes on to the Monroe Doctrine, which he believes could have been a good thing if it had been handled in the right spirit, but unfortunately it was being misused. "The Monroe Doctrine lost its sanctity and ceased to be a protective barrier of separation to become in itself a threat."[58] "Who was to believe that there would come a day when the republic would cast shadows all around itself: slavery to the South, conquest to the West, a menace to the North and a challenge to Europe ..."[59]

He knew all of America, North and South, had common origins, and he points to the fact that this reality was appreciated in this country by the great inter-Americanists: Breckenridge, Irving, Prescott, Motley, Ticknor,

---

[57] *Ibid.,* pp. 349-350.
[58] Sarmiento, "Discurso de Rhode Island", *Obras,* XXI, 207.
[59] *Ibid.,* p. 209.

Cooper, Longfellow, Arnold, Brown and others. Sarmiento in general is optimistic in regard to the future relations of the two peoples.

A work of primary importance that Mrs. Mann does not mention in her letter to Governor Andrews is Sarmiento's review *Ambas Américas* which appeared for the first time in May, 1867. Its purpose was to diffuse new ideas on education and foster the coming of international arbitration. The success of this review was relative. On June 11, 1867, Sarmiento writes: "I have just finished sending *Ambas Américas* all over the continent, but since everyone is at war, it would not surprise me if it didn't receive any support."[60] By September it still had less than 100 subscribers. In a letter he writes: "In Venezuela, Nueva Granada, Ecuador, Perú and México it is the first time that a review dealing entirely on educational matters is in circulation. This seed will give fruit later on but at present it is costing me $500.00."[61] And in another letter a few days later he writes again: "I believe that I will have to wait until I am president to accomplish my work, acting first and talking later."[62] Young Mitre used to say in friendly jest that Sarmiento with *Ambas Américas* had put both hemispheres to sleep.

Sarmiento's friendship with Mrs. Mann is one of the most beautiful chapters in his life. Mr. Horace Mann had died in 1859, six years before Sarmiento's second arrival in this country. His widow had retired to live with her children in Concord, a rustic Puritan town not far from the learned city of Boston. Mary Mann was at this time sixty years old, but she courageously continued to work on intellectual tasks. She had hardly seen Sarmiento during her husband's lifetime, but she knew his spirit and admired him. With unostentatious kindness she opened many doors to her friend, and led him around like a good fairy with an invisible hand. Few people have understood Sarmiento better than this foreign woman. It was Mrs. Mann who selected the teachers that were to be sent to Argentina and it was she who interested Mr. Gould, director and organizer of the Astronomical Observatory of Córdoba, to take part in this venture. It was through her that Sarmiento met Brown, Arnold, Longfellow, Ticknor, Emerson, Barnard, and many other leading American citizens of the day. And it was also through her intervention that the trustees of the University of Michigan were moved to grant Sarmiento an honorary doctor's degree.

Sarmiento has written his impressions of this extraordinary woman in a letter which he sent to his friend Aurelia Vélez.

> Mrs. Mann has taken me in as one of the family with the hospitality of New England, where everyone has the spirit of brotherliness, with the affection and the regard of an old friend. She knows French and Spanish

---

[60] Sarmiento, "Cartas", IV, 357.

[61] *Ibid.*, p. 332.

[62] *Ibid.*, p. 326.

and takes pleasure in translating to me. I impose on her. She has three older sons who study . . .

Mary Mann is my "Angel Viejo". My heart is attracted to her (there is a spiritual attraction). Oh! in the midst of so many disillusions and treasons, the consolation of having been loved is comforting to me, how they all loved me, you, your father, Aberastain, Posse, Mary Mann, and the others. The last-mentioned is a victim of a fascination which perhaps springs from an overabundance of motherly love, or perhaps it is brought about because she finds in me an admirer and continuer of her husband. We have seen each other only four times in two years, but we write frequently.

She lives for me, to aid me, to make me worth something. The first thing she asks when anyone approaches her is: Do you know about the Argentine Minister? Then begins the eulogy. Through her I have come in contact with the best of people, and been introduced to the most notable persons.

I know that a certain article in a magazine is hers because there is in it the same material as is in my letters. She would like to translate all my works. She admires my *Viajes,* and in speaking of my *Recuerdos de Provincia* says she has never before read descriptions which equal them. My biography takes up all of the time which her other duties leave her.[63]

Mrs. Mann in turn writes to Juana Manso, another heroic and self-sacrificing soul who for many years had been a devoted follower of Sarmiento:

I am very much interested in Señor Sarmiento's plans to send New England school teachers over to his country to introduce some of our methods of teaching and innoculate his countrymen with our zeal for education. I shall try to persuade some of our scholars and exceptional educators to go, and I myself would also go if I were younger . . . You will marvel at my confession that I have been presumptuous enough to have begun writing the biography of our illustrious friend, Señor Sarmiento . . . I should like to become more fully acquainted with the views of such a man as he on every subject, because he is so profound an historian that his less learned compatriots would be able to obtain from him all the knowledge that they now lack. I have already outlined his superb life and now I can devote myself to a consideration of his masterpieces and works that I have collected; I have become so absorbed in my delightful task that I have decided not to end my study after I have published all the feats that make up his biography . . . With regard to intellectual culture, I have never encountered a more remarkable case than that of Señor Sarmiento, who at such an early age has through his imagination traversed the ends of the earth, and who has understood the politics of all the nations of the world as well as the exact reasons for their specific cultures and prosperity. What a pity that such a man should ever grow old! He should live on for many more generations in order to impart to the world all the wisdom and knowledge that his keen

---

[63] Quoted in Eduardo Correas, *Andanzas de un civilizador,* Mendoza, 1944, pp. 15-16.

mind possesses. My beloved husband used to say that he would like to live for a hundred years, thinking, writing, and teaching. It seemed to him that sixty-three years of work was not nearly enough.[64]

In the meantime Sarmiento had been writing numerous letters to Mrs. Mann concerning the custom of certain American universities of giving honorary degrees to distinguished persons. "You tell me" writes Sarmiento on April 6, 1867, "that colleges here are in the habit of granting some persons with degrees... If Mr. Hill or some other person would do the same for me, with a degree in law, since I hold one in Humanities from the University of Chile; you have no idea what an effect this would have in my country, where everything concerning the United States is held with high regard, and of course the college of Harvard is well known. This honorary title, because of coming from such a favored university, would be the straw that would break the camel's back, as far as my opponents are concerned."[65] Mrs. Mann never gave a direct answer to this and other petitions, but finally one day Sarmiento received a letter from Mr. Barnard inviting him to attend the commencement exercises at the University of Michigan, in Ann Arbor, to be awarded an honorary degree, which was one of the greatest satisfactions of his life.

4. President Of Argentina

"They write me from my country," tells Sarmiento in January 1867, "that I am the only possible candidate for the presidency, and according to all logic I am of the same opinion, but the real world does not work this way; there are the politicians to contend with . . ."

Sarmiento's chances were much better, indeed, than this statement would indicate. His residence in the United States, the prestige that he enjoyed in American educational centers, and the actual value of his lifetime work, all tended to give him in the eyes of his compatriots tremendous political stature. In the interval of his absence he had been remembered for his good qualities rather than his violent temperament, his extreme frankness, and his great energy that was feared by many.

When Rivadavia, in a way his predecessor in the work of organizing the country, returned from England, he brought with him English ideas pertaining to economics, immigration and government. His models had been European. Sarmiento, in his turn, was now bringing something new, the American practical genius and the spirit of the "Yankee go ahead." His particular brand of importation was to be American.[66] did not mean at all that he was anti-Spanish, as has been charged. His

---

64 (In Spanish) *Ibid.,* p. 17.
65 Sarmiento, "Cartas", IV, 321-322.
66 *Ibid.,* p. 305.

When he was asked what his presidential platform was, he replied laconically: "to teach how to read."[67]

His program, of course, was to be much more intensive and complex than this phrase would indicate, but it portrays the spirit of the man. He was essentially practical and realistic. On another occasion, about this same period, confronted by a group of pedantic adversaries who wanted to know if he had ever actually worked for a doctor's degree, Sarmiento answered: "No, but I planted a tree in the middle of the Pampa." In Argentina there were many men who had doctor's degrees, but only Sarmiento had thought of planting a tree where there had never been one before. He was a realist surrounded by theoretical rationalists of the French school. He believed that actions spoke louder than words. As a matter of common education, he intended to introduce his fellow countrymen to the ideas of government which he had seen carried out successfully in the United States and which he had been advocating for many years.[68]

The eminent men of Argentina continued to sincerely believe, on the one hand, in the theories of the Spanish colony; on the other, in the imported French revolutionary ideas which, according to Sarmiento's own words, had caused so much useless disturbance in Europe and in America "without succeeding in establishing anything in almost a century, unless it is despotism." "In the midst of that general backwardness and disorder, which seems to be their normal condition, there are those who believe that they have liberal institutions more advanced than those of the United States. My plan would be to attain in practice the high level which the United States have achieved, by following closely in their footsteps."[69]

One of his first actions in office was to call a meeting of the educators, then few in number, to see about improving the educational system. This was followed by a series of vital improvements. He began to construct the canals and railroads, which had interested him so much in the United States. He ordered the first national census, and set out to solve the many problems of immigration peculiar to his own country. And of course, he built the schools and the Córdoba observatory he previously had planned.

It is characteristic of Sarmiento's great insight that he did not believe that the United States should be slavishly imitated by Spanish America. He recognized that the coming of independence had not altered the fundamental fact that the people of Spanish America were still Spaniards. He recognized, too, that Spain had had a different industrial and political organization from that of France or England. What he wished, because he saw that Spain was retarded in comparison with these two countries, was to shake off the Spanish influence and in a way begin to Europeanize. This

---

[67] *Loc. cit.*
[68] *Ibid.,* p. 315.
[69] *Ibid.,* pp. 315-316.

great admiration for the United States sprung from the fact that it had done just this — taken the best that Europe had to offer and erected on this groundwork a nation truly great and outstandingly progressive, creative and adaptable.

An important contribution to the development of this great state had been European immigration, which indirectly made possible the development of the West.

Where do these men come from?, he first wrote in 1848, European immigration figures second in these successive migrations. The old or adult states are giving birth to the new ones that are appearing. The "Indian hater", possessed by a peculiar aversion for the Indians, pushes ahead; always spreading, like the members of a strange instinctive sect, whose only dogma is to pursue the savage, whose only appetite is the extermination of the indigenous races. No one has sent him; alone with his rifle and dogs, he goes to the woods to hunt the savages, putting them to flight and making them abandon the hunting grounds of their fathers. Then comes the squatters, misanthropes, who seek solitude for a dwelling place, danger for emotions and the labor of clearing the forest as a solace. At a distance follow the pioneers, opening the forest, sowing the land, and scattering themselves over a broad area. Next come the capitalist impresarios, with immigrants for peons, founding cities and villages as the topography of the land advises. Upon the heels of these groups there follow to take their immediate place the young industrial, mechanical, permanent settlers, breaking with the old states to seek and create its fortune.[70]

There was no place where the ingenuity of the North American was more evident than in the manner in which he took possession of and developed the new lands that were to give him and his family a livelihood. And the South Americans had much to learn from them.[71]

Wherever the United States puts its hand nations rise as if by enchantment. The State of Ohio was incorporated into the Union with 50,000 inhabitants in 1802, and by 1840 it had a million and a half, that is to say, in forty years it had equaled the population of Chile that has been in existence for 300 years... California and Oregon will have in less than ten years the population of Chile...[72]

The spectacle of the rapid development of the Far West... actually makes me sick, when I think of how far behind them we are, possessing similar conditions.[73]

Sarmiento believed that the same could be done in Spanish America. Now that he was president, the time for comparisons and words was over.

70 Sarmiento, "Viajes", *Obras,* V, 394.

71 *Ibid.,* p. 368.

72 Sarmiento, *Obras,* XXIII, 88.

73 Sarmiento, "Cartas", III, 83.

Now was the time for action, and Sarmiento set himself to put into effect the many ideas he had written about in previous years.

Immigration brought to Argentina an increasing number of foreigners from the various European countries, and even from Asia, who desired to be incorporated into the new scheme of life that the American countries had to offer. "To make America" was not only to enrich oneself; it was also to live in a new way, to leave behind the caste system, to be promoted in social category, to realize a new chance of life that only seemed possible to those who had the courage to break away from the customs that they, and their fathers before them, had practised for centuries. The change in attitude was almost immediate. With the crossing of "the great pond," many of the evils of the old continent were left behind. America, whether Argentina or the United States, meant new hope.

The mythical land that Columbus had described as a paradise of abundance; that Thomas More had used as the setting for his *Utopia;* that Campanella deals with in his *City of the Sun;* the land of Cipango and the Seven Golden Cities of Cibola; the great experiment of man, as conceived by Benjamin Franklin, Jefferson, and Lincoln; America, the hope of the human race; with Sarmiento's presidency this poetic blend of truth and fiction was once again to become a reality on this continent.

In 1874 Sarmiento's presidency ended. During these years of feverish activity he had not forgotten his American friends; his letters were less frequent, but he continued to inform them of events in his native land.

The struggle was not yet over. Many victories had been won, but age-old prejudices continued to crop up with renewed force. On October the second, 1884, he writes to Mrs. Mann from Buenos Aires:

The country is agitated by what they call a religious affair; that is, an uprising of the Catholic clergymen who are asking that the catechism be taught in the public schools. One of the clergymen from Córdoba declared that the Normal School for Women was Protestant because the teacher, one of the many North Americans that you and I had sent, is Protestant, and he has excommunicated the girls who might attend this school and take instruction from the teachers provided by the government. The government has removed him from his position as clergyman but a bishop of Salta made a similar declaration. He ordered the doors of the church to be closed to all girls who attended these schools, In Catamarca another of these incidents has taken place, so that the Normal School for Women will actually be closed for lack of attendance, and perhaps the young North American teachers will have to return to their country . . . This country has fallen after such long efforts, into the hands of bold generals without principles, and the people have shown themselves indifferent to the loss of the republican order, in exchange for the wealth being developed due to loans which pay for the cost of railroads and other enterprises. Public education has made little progress because the people in power are against it, and the townspeople too indifferent to pay for it. A school census was ordered, and now it is seen that there are fewer people who have schooling than before.[74]

Despite the pessimism of this letter, Sarmiento knew full well that his life venture had been a success. He possessed a clear historic consciousness of his own worth. In a "Political Testament" he wrote on the page of an album, he summarizes for us the part he played in the development of Spanish America.

No one will ever relate in fewer words a longer life. I have lived in many countries, but never as a traveller; wherever I have lived, I have always shared the intimate life of my host. I leave behind me a permanent trail in the field of education. The buildings and schools I have constructed will mark the path I followed throughout America. I fought against the barbarism of the "caudillos", in the name of wholesome practical ideas; and, when I was called to execute my program, if all the promises were not fulfilled, at least I am responsible for whatever advances have been accomplished in this part of America. I have spun like the caterpillar my rough cocoon; and, without reaching the state of a butterfly, I shall still live to see my thread used by those who follow me. Born in poverty, reared in the struggle for existence, more than my own that of my country, toughened to hardships, and adhering to all that which I believed good—my perseverence was finally crowned by success. I have been to all the civilized nations of the world, and I have enjoyed, within the modest scale of my country and my times, a good share of earthly honors. I have been favored by many of the great men of my day. I have written a little that is good along with a great deal that is mediocre. And without material wealth—for which I had never strived, since it was heavy baggage in a life of constant struggle I am now waiting for a good bodily death, for my political one will be that which I long since anticipated. My only wish has been to leave as my heritage thousands of people in a more enlightened condition, our country in peace, our institutions secure, the land crossed by railroads, and the rivers and canals covered with boats, so that everyone may participate in the feast of life, which I have enjoyed only in stolen moments. Amen.

---

[74] Quoted in Correas, *Andanzas de un civilizador,* p. 29.

V

CONCLUSIONS

1. Inter-American Relations Up To 1890

Since the very beginning of inter-American relations there have been two primary problems on which the different attitudes of Spanish American authors toward the United States have hinged. First, should the Spanish nations of America look toward the United States as their model? Second, did the United States represent a menace to the existence of these nations? During the periods of independence and formation the relations between the two Americas varied in intensity, but the fundamental problems governing the attitudes of the writers remained consistent throughout the two epochs. Underlying these two problems was the complex pattern of the cultures of the two peoples, comprising both negative and positive factors; on the one hand, prejudices and differences centuries old; on the other, geographic, historic and psychological similarities that bred a common continental consciousness.

The notion of "America the model" dates back to long before the independence of Spanish America and, as we have seen in this study, had European antecedents. Once on the American continent, however, this idea developed along original lines. Spanish American writers studied conditions in the United States and wrote numerous works advocating the American democratic way of life. What had democracy done for the common man? This was one of the questions they were trying to answer.

This group of Spanish Americans, made up of authors such as Rocafuerte, Mier, Torres, Pazo, Nariño, Henríquez, and others, believed that democracy in the United States had given the common man a sense of dignity and of responsibility toward society hitherto unheard of among the peoples of other nations. Along with this moral condition there went a general improvement in material wealth and in the standards of living. All men were equal before the law. Women and children enjoyed a privileged position in society. Moral standards were remarkably high. The schools, the churches and the courts were the pillars of the temple of democracy. Its apostolic ideals were freedom of faith and freedom of speech. The national heroes were not those of war but of peace. The happiness of the United States consisted not so much in the enjoyment of pleasures as in the absence of sorrow.

Most advocates of independence were of the opinion that once republican institutions were established they would automatically produce in Spanish America the same conditions that prevailed in the United States.

Unfortunately this was not the case. Independence was attained and the constitutions of the different nations formulated, but conditions did not improve. During the course of the nineteenth century, Spanish American writers were dismayed to discover that the political theories sponsored by the liberals did not coincide with the different national realities, and that the institutions they had created were little more than worthless. They then inverted the process. Men such as Lastarria, Alberdi, González, Muñoz Tébar, Salazar, decided to change the habits and customs of the people through education so as to make North Americans institutions possible. In other words, the institutions became a goal in themselves. There were Spanish Americans, such as Alamán and Egaña, who saw a flaw in this way of thinking. They recommended, as Bolívar and Rodríguez had during the previous era, that the United States be imitated in principle, but that Spanish America create its own systems, according to the existing conditions of each particular nation, thinking that the important thing was not the institutions but the quality of the culture as a whole.

About the middle of the century, Sarmiento came to the realization that Argentina possessed conditions analogous to those of the United States and that this country was destined to have a future similar to that of its northern neighbor. On the strength of this conviction he opened the doors of Argentina to the historic forces of the nineteenth century. Railroads and canals were constructed, making possible easy communication over great distances. The public school system was initiated. Land was given to thousands of settlers that arrived yearly from the different European countries. Sarmiento and those who followed him had been able to take from the United States those elements that were useful to them and integrate them in their own civilization. Sarmiento was the first to realize that nations are not built on theories but on facts — geographic features, type of people, traditional culture, and so forth.

The idea that the United States represented a threat to the existence of the Spanish American nations is likewise prior to their independence. Fear of the United States was not limited to a fear of military invasion; the Spanish Americans feared that their culture or way of life, would also disappear, if not in whole at least in part. What would be the consequences of the freedom of faith? Could morality prosper in Spanish America without an established church? Many Spanish Americans believed that the United States was a soulless nation, with suicidal tendencies, not liberal at all but indifferent when it came to religious matters. They also associated religious freedom with the imperialistic ambitions of the United States. In Mexico after the war of 1848, Protestants were considered traitors to the nation. Writers like Egaña believed that a national religion would bring stability and order whereas a diversity of religions would eventually bring chaos.

They feared the consequences of political democracy. Lucas Alamán was of the opinion that democracy would destroy the established hierarchies and interests, and would automatically bring anarchy, violence and destruction. Many believed that democracy at its best would eventually degenerate into the tyranny of the majority. For similar reasons they were against the Federalist system. They wanted a highly centralized government that would insure internal order and would protect the nation from foreign invasion. They disapproved of a society which they said was dominated by women and children. And last, but not least, they believed the United States to be a utilitarian, materialistic nation incapable of producing arts or sciences. If New England in a way had contributed along these lines to world civilization, it was because of its aristocratic inclinations. The arts could not possibly prosper in a society committed to the doctrine of equality.

Both groups, those who admired and those who feared the United States, respected and understood the greatness of this nation. The truth is, that the two interpretations are not incompatible. Both groups found sufficient proof to substantiate their opinions, and in order to understand the true nature of the attitude of Spanish America, both schools of thought must be taken into account. Each should be considered as a part of the whole.

Both groups shared a great admiration for the American heroes. Among the most discussed were Benjamin Franklin, the father of science; wise and affable George Washington, called to nurse the new republic in his arms; John Adams, the second president, the organizer and statesman that was to guide the nation through its adolescence; Jefferson, the first democrat and the man who did most to shape the moral character of the nation; Madison, the first to recognize Spanish American independence; Monroe, the sponsor of the two continent theory; Webster and Clay, the friends of the new republics; Jackson, the Indian hunter; Lincoln, the new apostle of democracy; Grant, the hero of the Civil War.

2. A New Epoch

The date of Sarmiento's death (1888) marks the close of one epoch and the beginning of another in the attitude of Spanish American writers toward the United States. By reason of his extraordinary personality he occupies a unique position in the formative period of the American nations, which include the United States. During this period the note common to both Americas is that of indifference and isolation. They coincide in their centripetal concentration on their own pressing internal problems, and in their separate orientation toward Europe, as we have already pointed out. The Spanish American writers we have studied are political writers who take into account the United States along with Europe in the formulation of their political ideas, or travelers who regard the United States as a land remote and different from their own. Sarmiento alone in the two

Americas is aware of the continental significance of America, and his life-work was guided by this idea. Shortly before his death, in the last speech he delivered on May 30, 1887, in Asunción, Paraguay, at the end, after expressing the desire that the flags of Argentina, Chile, Uruguay and Paraguay—the Spanish-American countries that had been the scene of his labors—should be his shroud, in his last words he affirmed anew his unswerving attitude toward the United States and his ideal of continental solidarity:

> Chance has been kind enough on this occasion to put me beside His Excellency, the Minister of the United States, who has chosen to honor this act with his presence, for it was in his country that I studied the reasons for that nation's extraordinary development, and the bases of its liberties, in order to apply them to our lands. Thus the two extremes of America are linked in a single thought, and are moved by the hope that all the rest will soon follow in this great movement.[1]

In 1889, the year after Sarmiento's death, the First International Conference of American States met in Washington, and in 1890 the Pan-American Union was founded. At that time there was living in the United States, where he spent fourteen years, (from 1881 to 1895), the man who, as we see over the perspective of years, came to occupy the pre-eminent place in the history of Spanish American tought and literature that Sarmiento had held in the preceding epoch, the Cuban, José Martí. Martí, who likewise was gifted with prophetic vision and a universal breadth of outlook, was the initiator and creator of a new epoch, which begins with the literary revolution that goes by the name of Modernismo, and which was to become the line of demarcation between the nineteenth and twentieth centuries.

In his late years Sarmiento had read in *La Nación* the articles of the young Cuban and had sensed before anyone else the unique personality of the man. "There is nothing in Spanish to compare with Martí's bellows, and after Victor Hugo, France can offer nothing like his metal resonance", he wrote to Paul Groussac.[2] Despite his admiration for Martí's qualities as man and writer, there was a profound discrepancy between the two with regard to the United States. Martí knew the United States better than Sarmiento because of the years he had lived in the country, and he was, without doubt, the first Spanish American who knew it in all the aspects of its culture. He disseminated this knowledge in Spanish America through the articles he contributed regularly to *La Nación* of Buenos Aires, which, collected in the edition of his complete works (Editorial Trópico), occupy fourteen volumes entitled *Escenas norteamericans,* and three entitled *Norteamericanos.* Sarmiento voices his dissent in these words:

---

[1] *Discursos populares,* Buenos Aires, 1927, pp. 245-246.
[2] Sarmiento, *Obras,* XLVI, 175-176.

I would wish that Martí might give us less Martí, less of the Latin, less of the Spaniard in race, and less of the South American, and a little more of the Yankee, the new type of modern man . . . He should be our eye viewing the movement of mankind where it is swiftest, most intellectual, freest, best directed toward society's high purposes, in order that he might communicate this to us, to correct our missteps and show us the right road.[3]

There was always present in Sarmiento the idea which had prevailed from the time of the Independence and throughout the nineteenth century in the progressive and liberal spirits of Spanish America, namely, to regard the United States as the model, guide, and elder brother in the great family of American nations. To be sure, during all this period, from the days of the Independence, there had co-existed another attitude, that of those who saw in the United States a future threat to the weaker, disorganized nations to the South. The attitude of Martí, which was to be that of the epoch which begins with him, was new; it was neither the one nor the other, but rather both together, and was based on a deeper, truer unity. Martí summed up in a phrase, written in 1889, this union of love and fear: "We love the land of Lincoln, but we fear the land of Cutting."[4] Before this, in 1884, he had voiced, though with reservations, the fear that the United States might become an imperialist nation:

The nation which has been the home of liberty must not—God forbid!— become the dragon on which conquest mounts, nor the new tomb of mankind, in the manner of those despotic or corrupt nations which have degraded or dominated the world.[5]

This fear was to grow and be confirmed in later years until it led him to the conviction that the internal growth of the United States would lead, inexorably and inevitably, to a new phase of expansion beyond its frontiers and into the Spanish American nations to the south, which would constitute the gravest danger for the future of these nations. In 1884 he had already seen the difficulties of establishing inter-American friendship because of the ignorance and contempt of the United States toward what he begins to call "our America"—a term that was to become general throughout the epoch that followed:

The contempt of this powerful neighbor, who is ignorant of her, is the greatest danger our America faces, and there is no time to be lost, *for the day of the visit is at hand,* (the italics are mine), in this neighbor's knowing her, knowing her soon, so she may not feel contempt for her.[6]

In 1889, when the First International Conference of American States was held in Washington, he judged the United States to be "a nation that

---

[3] *Loc. cit.*

[4] *Obras completas,* II, 65.

[5] *Ibid.,* XVI, 187.

[6] *Ibid.,* p. 21.

is beginning to regard liberty as its sole privilege, and invoke it to deprive other nations of theirs."[7]

And in 1892 he stated:

> Beyond doubt the hour has come for this country, egged on by protectionism, to bring into the open its latent spirit of aggression.[8]

With regard to the intervention of the United States in his native Cuba, for whose independence he fought uninterruptedly and in the end laid down his life, he considered this the greatest menace to his country and to all Spanish America. Above all the motives that led him to fight and die for the independence of Cuba was that of "preventing in time the United States from extending their power over the Antilles, and falling, with this added strength, upon our lands of America."[9]

Underlying this attitude of Martí's was the conviction of a deep, radical difference that existed between the two Americas:

> There are two nations in America, and only two, whose souls differ greatly by reason of their origins, antecedents and habits, and whose only resemblance is their fundamental human identity. On the one hand is our America...on the other the America which is not ours, whose enmity it is neither prudent nor practical to encourage, and whose friendship, maintaining a firm decorum and wise independence, it is useful and not impossible to win.[10]

We have analyzed Martí's[11] attitude toward the United States at some length because the ideas he expressed between 1883 and 1895 mark the beginning of a new epoch and the end of the one we have been studying. These ideas were later to develop to an amazing degree and spread throughout the Spanish-speaking world to become one of the basic, ever-present themes of Spanish American literature. The study of this new epoch which, with changes and variations, comes down to the present, lies without the plan of this work and would demand as much space as that we have devoted to the preceding epochs, up to 1890.

The situation subsequent to 1890 differed from that which, in its varying phases, existed in the eighteenth and nineteenth centuries, as did the attitude of the two Americas toward each other. Our sole object, in concluding this study, is to justify the chronological limits we have set as the end of an epoch in the history of inter-American relations. We are of the opinion that José Martí, who stands between the two epochs, the last representative of the nineteenth century and the first forerunner of the twentieth century, is the outstanding figure who typifies the crisis of

---

[7] *Ibid.*, XXI, 50.

[8] *Ibid.*, II, 92.

[9] *Ibid.*, VIII, 270.

[10] *Ibid.*, XIX, 199.

[11] For Martí see Andrés Iduarte, *Martí, escritor*, México, 1945.

the century which, in world ideology and in the history of America, marks the beginning of the contemporary period.

Martí was the interpreter of the United States to Spanish American readers to whom he revealed, with affection and admiration, the values of North American civilization at the moment this reached the peak of its complete national development. But it was this moment that troubled him, because he realized that once this country had achieved internal integration, its superabundance of strength would inevitably lead to its expansion beyond the limits of its own frontiers. Martí, who was living in the United States, foresaw this necessary, unavoidable transformation of the country as it emerged from its isolation to gradually enter upon all manner of international activities, and among these, in the front rank, those having to do with the neighboring countries of this continent. His prophetic words were quickly followed by facts which bore them out, and which it is unnecessary to examine here as they are so numerous and familiar.

Martí lived to see the organization of the Pan-American Union in 1890, but he died in 1895 on the battle-field fighting for the independence of his native Cuba. He did not live to see the war of the United States with Spain in 1898, the first of the series of armed interventions of the United States in Spanish America which succeeded one another in different countries up to the change initiated under the Good Neighbor Policy.

Although Martí could not know the episodes of many kinds, political, military, economic and others, that characterized the relations between the Unied States and Spanish America during this period, they were observed by all the Spanish Americans who had heard his prophetic words. And from 1898 on, Spanish American writers, almost without exception, have taken them to heart, have expanded upon them, under the stimulus of the events that were taking place, and which they interpreted in phrases which have since become stereotyped, such as "el peligro yanqui", "el imperialismo del dólar", and others of the same nature.

Among the earliest to adopt this new attitude was a contemporary of Martí, like himself a West Indian, Eugenio María de Hostos, the greatest intellectual figure of Puerto Rico, and a thinker and educator of continental stature in the second half of the nineteenth century. In his later years Hostos was gravely concerned over the future of his island, annexed to the United States in 1898.

But those who raised this new attitude to the level of primary importance, which it was to occupy in the minds of Spanish Americans in general from then on, were the two outstanding representatives of *modernismo,* the poet Rubén Darío, and the essayist José Enrique Rodó. The latter published in 1900 his famous essay *Ariel,* in which, addressing himself to the youth of Spanish America as teacher and guide, he endeavored to define the essence of Spanish American culture as contrasted with the Anglo-

American of the United States. Rubén Darío, who had sung Walt Whitman and Edgar Allen Poe, and whose complex poetry was strongly influenced by these two North American poets, from 1898 on developed the theme of the United States vis-a-vis Spanish America to its highest poetic expression. In ringing verses which all Spanish Americans know by heart, he sounded the tocsin of the imminent threat of absorption by the United States.

> ¿Seremos entregados a los bárbaros fieros?
> ¿Tántos millones de hombres hablaremos inglés?

And in his famous ode to Theodore Roosevelt he also presents the fundamental contrast between the two cultures.

Both Darío and Rodó, in the face of the common danger they saw in the North, advocated the spiritual union of the Spanish American nations among themselves and with Spain at the time that the latter, in 1898, had lost the last vestiges of her colonial empire. In rolling hexameters Rubén Darío proclaimed the unity of the nations of Spanish America, "sangre de Hispania fecunda"; and Rodó defined the "Magna Patria": "Patria es, para los hispanoamericanos, la América española."

These concepts, in which the relation with the United States had become the fundamental problem, and practically the *raison d'être* of Spanish America, spread like wild-fire throughout the Spanish-speaking world of America, and there is hardly a writer after 1900 who has not dealt with this theme. The multiplicity of facets of this rich and diversified literature, and the evolution of this attitude over the long space of fifty years, in Spanish America as in the United States, would require a detailed study of its own. In this study we have attempted to analyze the preceding epoch as a necessary preliminary step to the understanding of a problem which from its beginnings has increasingly developed into a matter of essential and vital concern for both Americas.

Not to conclude this study on a pessimistic note, we would like to add that the spirit of inter-American relations was soon to change. Mr. Root's speeches in Spanish America, Wilson's Mobile Address of 1913, Hoover's trip south of the border, and Franklin D. Roosevelt's article on the American Foreign Policy published in the review *Foreign Affairs*[12] in 1928 were all indications that Yankee Imperialism was to be short-lived, and that another epoch of a more liberal nature was to come into existence, that of the Good Neighbor Policy.

---

[12] Franklin D. Roosevelt, "Our Foreign Policy: A Democratic view," *Foreign Affairs*. VI, Oct. 1927-July 1928.

BIBLIOGRAPHY

I. SPANISH AMERICAN WRITERS

"Carta de un patriota." Apéndice, in Mier, *Memoria político-instructiva.* Philadelphia, 1821, p. 122.

Carta de un Americano al Español sobre su número XIX. Londres, 1812. (This pamphlet is signed V. C. R. and is addressed to J. M. Blanco White).

Segunda carta de un Americano al Español sobre su número XIX. Contestación a su respuesta dada en el número XXVI. Londres, 1812.

Cartas de un Americano sobre las ventajas de los gobiernos federativos. London, 1826.

Diálogo sobre la independencia de la América española. Philadelphia, 1812.

Historia concisa de los Estados Unidos desde el descubrimiento de América hasta el año de 1807. Philadelphia, 1812.

Inchiquin, The Jesuit letters, during a late residence in the United States of America: Being a fragment of a private correspondence accidentally discovered in Europe, containing a favorable view of the manners, literature and state of society of the United States and a refutation of many of the aspersions cast upon this country by former residents and tourists. By some unknown foreigner. New York, 1810.

"La intolerancia político-religiosa, vindicada, o refutación del discurso que en favor de la tolerancia religiosa, publicó don Guillermo Burke, en la Gazeta de Caracas, del martes 19 de Febrero de 1811, No. 20 por la R. y P. Universidad de Caracas." In: Blanco y Azpurúa, *Documentos,* III, 61-102.

Manual de un republicano para el uso de un pueblo libre. Philadelphia, 1812.

"Proclama anónima a los habitantes de la Florida a quienes se exhorta contra el Gobierno Español para hacerse Ciudadanos de los Estados Unidos" (Signed "El Amigo del Pueblo"). Ms. Department of Archives and History, Jackson, Mississippi.

Ahumada y Centurión, José de. *La abolición de la esclavitud en países de colonización europea.* Madrid, 1870.

Ahumada y Centurión, José de. *Memoria histórico-política de la Isla de Cuba.* Habana, 1874.

Alamán, Lucas. *Historia de México, desde los primeros movimientos que prepararon su Independencia en el año de 1808 hasta le época presente.* México, 1849-1852, 5 vols.

Alamán, Lucas. *Semblanzas e Ideario.* México, 1939. (Biblioteca del Estudiante Universitario, vol. 8).

Alberdi, Juan Bautista. *Autobiografía.* Buenos Aires, 1927.

Alberdi, Juan Bautista. *El crimen de la guerra.* Buenos Aires, 1915.

Alberdi, Juan Bautista. *La revolución de Mayo.* Buenos Aires, 1925.

Alberdi, Juan Bautista. *Life and industrial labors of William Wheelright in South America.* Transl. by Caleb Cushing. Boston, 1877.

Alcaraz, Ramón. *Apuntes para la historia de la guerra entre México y los Estados Unidos.* México, 1848.

Alcedo y Bexarano, Antonio de. Biblioteca Americana. Catálogo de los autores que han escrito de la América en diferentes idiomas, y noticia de su vida y patria, años en que, vivieron y obras que escriberon, 1807. (Ms. New York Public Library).

Alcedo y Bexarano, Antonio de. *Diccionario geográfico-histórico de las Indias Occidentales o América.* Madrid, 1786-1789, 5 vols.

Alcedo y Bexarano, Antonio de. *The geographical and historical dictionary of America and the West Indies.* Containing an entire translation of the Spanish work, with large additions, and campilations from modern voyages and travels, and from original and authentic information, by G. A. Thompson. London, 1819.

Alcedo y Bexarano, Antonio de. *Vocabulario de las voces provinciales de la América, usadas en el diccionario geográfico.* Madrid, 1789.

Alcedo y Bexarano, Antonio de. *Medicina doméstica; ó, tratado completo del método de precaver y curar las enfermedades con el régimen y medicinas simples y un apéndice que contiene la farmacopea necesaria para el uso de un particular.* Escrito en inglés por Jorge Buchan, traducido al castellano por A. de Alcedo. Madrid, 1818.

Alcedo y Herrera, Dionysio de. *Aviso histórico político, geográfico, con las noticias más particulares del Perú, Tierra-Firme, Chile y Nuevo Reino de Granada, en la relación de los sucesos de 205 años por la cronología de los adelantados, presidentes, gobernadores y virreyes de aquel reyno meridional, desde el año 1535 hasta el de 1740. Y razón de todo lo obrado por los ingleses en aquellos reynos por las costas de los mares del norte, y del sur, sin deferencia entre los tiempos de paz y de la guerra desde el año 1567 hasta el de 1739, por don . . . Dionysio de Alcedo y Herrera,* Madrid, 1740. (Reprinted under the title: *Piraterías y agresiones de los ingleses y otros pueblos de Europa en la América española; desde el siglo XVI hasta el XVIII, deducidas de las obras de D. Dionysio de Alcedo y Herrera; publícalos D. Justo Zaragoza,* Madrid, 1883).

Alvarez de Toledo, José. *Manifiesto o satisfacción pundonorosa a todos los buenos españoles de Europa y a todos los pueblos de América, por un diputado de las Cortes reunidas en Cádiz* (A. de Toledo). Philadelphia, 1812.

Alzate, José Antonio. *Gaceta de literatura de México,,* vols. I-III, México, 1893. (Reprint of the edition of Puebla, 1831).

Amunátegui, Miguel Luis. *Camilo Henríquez.* Santiago de Chile, 1889.

Amy, F. J. *Ecos y notas.* Ponce, 1884.

Antepara, José María. *South American emancipation. Documents historical and explanatory.* London, 1810.

Arango y Parreño, Francisco. *Obras.* Habana, 1888, 2 vols.

Arroyo de Anda. "Discurso". In: Alberto Bianchi, *Los Estados Unidos.* México, 1887, p. 94-95.

Artigas, José: Acevedo, Eduardo. *José Artigas: su obra cívica.* Montevideo, 1909.

Badía, J. *Cartas sobre los bancos de los Estados Unidos*. Matanzas, 1840.

Barros Arana, Diego. *Historia de América*. Santiago de Chile, 1908, 2 vols.

Belgrano, Manuel. *Despedida de Washington al pueblo de los Estados Unidos*. Traducción con una introducción en el año 1813 por el Gral. Manuel Belgrano. Pról. por Bartolomé Mitre. Buenos Aires, 1902.

Bello, Andrés. "Observaciones sobre la historia de la literatura española de Jorge Ticknor". (*Obras completas*, VI, 281-436).

Bianchi, Alberto G. *De México a Roma y de Roma a Barcelona*. Barcelona, 1901.

Bianchi, Alberto G. *Los Estados Unidos*. México, 1887.

Bilbao, Francisco. *Iniciativa de la América; idea de un congreso federal de las repúblicas*. Paris, 1856.

Blanchet, Emilio. *Estados Unidos, apuntes históricos*. Matanzas, 1911.

Blanchet, Emilio. "La ciudad de Washington". *Nuevo País*, Habana, Agosto 9, 1899.

Bocanegra, José María de. *Disertación apologética del sistema federal*. México, 1825.

Bocanegra, José María de. *Memorias para la historia de México independiente, 1822-1846*. México, 1892-1897, 2 vols.

Bolívar, Simón. *Cartas de Bolívar, 1799-1822*. Buenos Aires, 1913.

Bolívar, Simón. *Cartas de Bolívar, 1823-24-25*. Madrid, 1921.

Bolívar, Simón. "Contestación de un Americano Meridional a un Caballero de esta Isla." In: Blanco y Azpurúa, *Documentos*, V, 336.

Bolívar, Simón: *Memorias del General O'Leary*. Caracas, 1871-1888.

Bolívar, Simón: Mancini. *Bolívar et l'émancipation des colonies espagnoles*. Paris, 1912.

Bolívar, Simón: Monsalve, J. D. *El ideal político del Libertador Simón Bolívar*. Madrid, 1916.

Bolívar, Simón: O'Leary, D. F. *Bolívar y La emancipación de Sur-América*. Madrid, 1915.

Bolívar, Simón: O'Leary, D. F. *Ultimos años de la vida pública de Bolívar*. Madrid, 1916.

Bulnes, Francisco. *Sobre el hemisferio del norte. Once mil leguas*. México, 1875.

Bustamante, Carlos María. *El nuevo Bernal Díaz del Castillo, o sea historia de la invasión de los Anglo-Americanos en México*. México, 1847, 2 vols.

Bustamante, Carlos María. *Historia del Emperador D. Agustín de Iturbide hasta su muerte, y sus consecuencias; y establecimiento de la república popular federal*. México, 1846.

Caballero, Manuel. "Discurso." In: Bianchi, *Los Estados Unidos*. México, 1887.

Caballero, Manuel. *México en Chicago*. [México], 1893.

Cabrera y Bosch, Raimundo. *Cartas a Gorín. Impresiones de viaje*. Habana, 1892.

Cabrera y Bosch, Raimundo. *Los Estados Unidos, con notas, aplicaciones y comentarios*. Habana, 1889.

Camacho, Simón (Nazareno). *Cosas de los Estados Unidos*. New York, 1864.

Camacho Roldán, Salvador. *Abrahán Lincoln*. New York, 1925.

Camacho Roldán, Salvador. *Notas de viajes (Colombia y Estados Unidos)*. Bogotá, 1890.

Cardona S., Adalberto de. *De México a Nueva York. Guía para el viajero en que se describen las principales ciudades de México y los Estados Unidos del Norte.* Con profusión de grabados. San Francisco, 1890.

Carrasco, Albano. *Comentario sobre la constitución política de 1833.* Valparaíso, 1858.

Carrera, J. M.: Varas Velázquez, Miguel. *Don José Miguel Carrera en los Estados Unidos.* Santiago de Chile, 1912.

Castro, Vicente. "Una vista a la penitenciaria de Filadelfia". In: *Revista de la Habana,* 1855.

Céspedes, José M. *La doctrina de Monroe.* Habana, 1893.

Corchado, Manuel. *Abrahán Lincoln.* Barcelona, 1868.

Egaña, Juan de. *Memoria política.* Caracas, 1829.

Frías, José de. "Cartas sobre los Estados Unidos", *El Album,* 1839.

Gómez, Antonio. "Ensayo político, contra las reflecciones del señor William Burke, sobre el tolerantismo, en la Gazeta de 19 de febrero último". Caracas, 2 de marzo de 1811. In: Blanco y Azpurúa, *Documentos,* III, 46-61.

Gorostiza, Manuel Eduardo de. *Cartilla política.* Londres, 1833.

Gorostiza, Manuel Eduardo de. *Dictamen leído el 3 de junio de 1840 en el Consejo de Gobierno sobre la cuestión de Tejas.* México, 1844.

Gorostiza, Manuel Eduardo de. *Examination and review of a pamphlet printed and secretly circulated by M. E. A., late envoy extraorainary from Mexico . . .* Washington, 1837.

Guiteras, Eusebio *Un invierno en Nueva York.* Barcelona, 1885.

Guiteras, Eusebio. "Una visita a Longfellow." In:*Liceo Matanzas,* Oct. 1866.

Gutiérrez, Felipe S. *Viaje por México, los Estados Unidos, Europa y Sud-América.* México, 1882; 1883; 1885.

Gutiérrez de Lara, José Bernardo: "Diary of José Bernardo Gutiérrez de Lara," edited by E. West. *American Historical Review,* XXXIV, 1928, 55-77, 281-294.

Gutiérrez de Lara, José Bernardo: Estrada, Genaro. "El primer diplomático de la revolución de la independencia," *Revista Mexicana de Derecho Nacional,* México, I, 1919, 272-277.

Henríquez, Camilo. "Ejemplo memorable." In: Collier and Cruz, *La primera misión a los Estados Unidos de América en Chile,* pp. 66-69. Reprinted from *La Aurora de Chile,* no. 17, July 4, 1812.

Henríquez, Camilo. "Himno patriótico." In: Collier and Cruz, *La primera misión de los Estados Unidos en Chile.* Santiago, 1926, p. 61-63. Reprinted from *La Aurora de Chile,* no. 23, July 16, 1812.

Henríquez, Camilo. *La Aurora de Chile.* Santiago de Chile, 1812-1813. (Editor).

Henríquez, Camilo. "Noticias relativas a la guerra actual de los Estados Unidos con la Gran Bretaña. Extracto del Mensaje del Presidente (James Madison) de los Estados Unidos al congreso el 4 de noviembre, 1812." In: *Colección de historiadores y documentos relativos a la independencia de Chile.* Santiago de Chile, 1910, XXIV, 300-309. Reprinted from the *Monitor Araucano,* no. 45, July 20, 1813.

Henríquez, Camilo. "Semanario Republicano", no. 1, October 30, 1813. No. 3,

Nov. 13, 1813. In: *Colección de historiadores y documentos relativos a la Independencia de Chile,* XXIV, 113-115 y 137.

Heredia, José M. de. "Cartas sobre los Estados Unidos." In: *El Iris.* 1826, y *La Moda y Recreo Semanal,* 1829.

Heredia, José M. de: *The Odes of Bello, Olmedo and Heredia. Introduction by Elijah Clarence Hills.* New York, 1920.

Irisarri, Antonio José de (Dionisio Terrasa y Rejón). *Semanario Republicano de Chile,* 1813-1814.

Irisarri, Antonio José de (Dionisio Terrasa y Rejón): Donoso, Ricardo. *Antonio José de Irisarri.* Santiago, 1934.

José Amor de la Patria [seudónimo] [Attributed to Martínez de Rosas]. "Catequismo político cristiano". *Coleccion de historiadores y documentos inéditos relativos a la independencia de Chile,* XVIII, 116-125. Santiago de Chile, 1910.

Lastarria, José Victorino. *La América.* Madrid, 1917.

Lastarria, José Victorino. *Obras completas.* Santiago de Chile, 1906-1907.

Lombardo, Alberto. *Los Estados Unidos (Notas y episodios de viaje).* México, 1884.

López de Santa Ana, Antonio. *Mi historia militar y política.* México, 1905.

López Portillo y Rojas, José. *Egipto y Palestina. Apuntes de viaje.* México, 1874.

Loyola, Bernabé. *Doce episodios de la vida de Bernabé Loyola.* 1876.

Martínez, Ignacio. *Recuerdos de un viaje en América, Europa y Africa.* Paris, 1884.

Martínez, Melchor. *Memoria histórica sobre la revolución de Chile, desde el cautiverio de Fernando VII hasta 1814.* Valparaíso, 1848.

Meza, Ramón. "Hacia el Niágara". *Habana Elegante,* 1888-1889.

Mier, José Servando Teresa de. *Discurso que el día 13 de Dic. del presente año de 1823 pronunció el Dr. J. S. T. de Mier.* México, 1823.

Mier, José Servando Teresa de. *Memoria político-instructiva.* Philadelphia, 1821; 1822.

Mier, José Servando Teresa de. *Profecía política.* México, 1842.

Mier, José Servando Teresa de. Puede ser libre la Nueva España. Ms. in García Collection, University of Texas.

Mier, Juan Bernardo. Letter to José S. T. de Mier, June 21, 1822. Ms. in García Collection, University of Texas.

Mier y Terán, Manuel de. *Diario de viage de la Comisión de límites que puso el Gobierno de la República bajo lo dirección del Excmo. Sr. General de Division Don M. M. y T.* Mexico, 1850.

Milla, José. *Un viaje al otro mundo pasando por otras partes.* Guatemala, 1936, 3 vols.

Miralla, José Antonio: Labougle, Eduardo. *José Antonio Miralla, precursor de la independencia de Cuba.* Buenos Aires, 1924.

Miranda, Francisco de. *Archivo del General Miranda.* Caracas, 1929-1933, 14 vols.

Miranda, Francisco de: Robertson, W. S. *The diary of Francisco de Miranda's tour of the United States, 1783-1784.* Spanish text with introd. and notes. New York, Hispanic Society of America, 1928.

Miranda, Francisco de: Robertson, W. S. *Life of Miranda.* Chapel Hill, N. C., 1929, 2 vols.

Montalvo, Juan. "Washington y Bolívar." In: *Siete Tratados,* Ambato, Ecuador, 1942-43, **V,** 141-144.

Montenegro Colón, Feliciano. *Geografía general.* Caracas, 1833-37.

Moreno, Mariano. *Escritos políticos y económicos.* Buenos Aires, 1915.

Moreno, Mariano. *Vida y memorias.* Londres, 1812.

Nariño, Antonio. "Derechos del hombre". In: *Biblioteca de Historia Nacional,* Bogotá, 1903, II, 80.

Nariño, Antonio. "Los derechos del hombre en sociedad." In: Blanco y Azpurúa, *Documentos,* I, 235.

Ochoa, E. de. "Un paseo por América [1844]." In: *Miscelánea.* Madrid, 1867.

Páez, Ramón. *Ambas Américas.* New York, 1872.

Palacio Fajardo, Manuel. *Outline of the Revolution in Spanish America, or an account of the origin, progress and actual state of the war carried on between Spain and Spanish America . . .* by a South American. New York, 1817.

Pantoja, Domingo de. *Los Estados Unidos.* Buenos Aires, 1893.

Pazos Kanki, Vicente. *Compendio de la historia de los Estados Unidos de América, puesto en castellano por un indio de la ciudad de la Paz.* Paris, 1825.

Pazos Kanki, Vicente. *The exposition, remonstrance and protest of Don Vicente Pazos, commissioner on behalf of the republican agents established at Amelia island in Florida, under the authority and in behalf of the independent state of South America; with an appendix. Presented to the executive of the United States, on the ninth day of February, 1818.* Translated from the Spanish. Philadelphia, 1818.

Pazos Kanki, Vicente. *Letters on the United Provinces of South America, addressed to the Hon. Henry Clay, speaker of the House of representatives in the U. S.* By Don Vicente Pazos. Translated from the Spanish by Platt. H. Crosby, esq. New York: Printed by J. Seymour, 49 John Street. London. By J. Miller, Bow-Street, Covent Garden. 1819.

Pazos Kanki, Vicente. *Memorias histórico-políticas de don Vicente Pazos.* Vol. I. Londres, 1834.

Pérez Bonalde, J. A. *El poema del Niágara.* New York, 1883.

Pérez Bonalde, J. A. *Ritmos.* New York, 1880.

Pérez Rosales, Vicente. *Recuerdos del pasado (1814-1860).* Santiago de Chile, 1910.

Pérez Rosales, Vicente: Feliú Cruz, Guillermo. *Vicente Pérez Rosales Ensayo crítico.* Santiago de Chile, 1946.

Piñeyro, Enrique. *El Nuevo Mundo.* Nueva York, 1872-1875.

Pombo, Miguel de. *Constitución de los Estados Unidos.* Santa Fe de Bogotá, 1811.

Portugal, José María de Jesús. *Impresiones religiosas de un viaje a Tierra Santa, pasando por Nueva York, Paris y algunas ciudades de Italia.* Asientos, 1887.

Presas, José. *Juicio imparcial sobre las principales causas de la revolución de la América española, etc.* Burdeos, 1828.

Prieto, Guillermo. *Viaje a los Estados Unidos,* por Fidel. **México, 1877-1878.**

Prieto, Guillermo. *Memorias de mis tiempos, 1828 a 1840.* México-Paris, 1906.

Puglio, James. *El desengaño del hombre.* Philadelphia, 1794.

Quesada, Vicente Gaspar. *Recuerdos de mi vida diplomática; misión en Estados Unidos. (1885-1892)*. Buenos Aires, 1904.

Quijano. *Discurso sobre la insurrección de América que escribe el Dr. . . . Q.* Guadalajara, 1814.

Ramírez, José Fernando. *México durante su guerra con los Estados Unidos.* México, 1905.

Reyes, José María. *Breve reseña histórica de la emigración de los pueblos en el continente americano y especialmente en el territorio de la República Mexicana.* México, 1881.

Reynal, Rafael. *Viaje por los Estados Unidos del Norte, dedicado a los jóvenes mexicanos de ambos secsos.* Cincinnati, 1834.

Roa Bárcena, José María. *Norte América en México.* México, 1902.

Roa Bárcena, José María. *Recuerdos de la invasión norte-americana, 1846-1848. Por un joven de entonces.* México, 1883. Second edition, México, 1902, 2 vols.

Rocafuerte, Vicente. *Ensayo sobre la tolerancia religiosa.* México, 1831.

Rocafuerte, Vicente. *El sistema colombiano es el que más conviene a la América independiente.* Nueva York, 1823.

Rocafuerte, Vicente. *Ensayo político.* New York, 1823.

Rocafuerte, Vicente. *Ideas necesarias a todo pueblo que quiere ser libre.* Philadelphia, 1821.

Rocafuerte, Vicente. *La revolución de México.* Philadelphia, 1822.

Rodríguez, Simón. "El libertador del mediodía." In: Lozano y Lozano, *El maestro del libertador.* Paris, n. d.

Rodríguez, Simón: Lozano y Lozano, Fabio. *El maestro del libertador.* Paris, n.d.

Rodríguez Otero, Ricardo. *Impresiones y recuerdos de mi viaje a los Estados de Nueva York, Nueva Jersey y Pensylvania.* Sagua Grande, 1887.

Rojas, Francisco de. *Poema épico, la rendición de Panzacola y conquista de la Florida occidental por el conde de Gálvez. Componíalo el comisario de guerra. D. Francisco de Rojas y Rocha.* México, 1785.

Rosa, Luis de la. *Impresiones de un viaje de México a Washington en octubre y noviembre de 1848.* New York, 1848.

Roscio, Juan Germán. *El triunfo de la libertad sobre el despotismo, en la confesión de un pecador arrepentido de sus errores políticos.* Filadelfia, 1817; — 1821; — Oajaca, 1828.

Saco, José Antonio. *Contra la anexión.* Habana, 1928.

Saco, José Antonio. *Historia de la esclavitud de los indios en el nuevo mundo.* Habana, 1883.

Saco, José Antonio. *Historia de la esclavitud desde los tiempos remotos hasta nuestros días.* Paris-Barcelona, 1875-1877.

Saco, José Antonio. *Historia de la raza africana en el nuevo mundo.* Barcelona, 1879-1893.

Saco, José Antonio. *Paralelo entre la isla de Cuba y algunas colonias inglesas.* Madrid, 1837.

Sagra, Ramón. *Cinco meses en los Estados Unidos de la América del Norte, desde el 20 de abril al 23 de septiembre de 1835. Diario de viaje.* Paris, 1837.

Sagra, Ramón. *Memoria para servir de introducción a la horticultura cubana.* Nueva York, 1827.

Salazar, José María. *Observaciones sobre las reformas políticas de Colombia.* Filadelfia, 1828.

San Carlos de Pedroso, Marquesa de. *Les Américains chez eux.* Paris, 1890.

Sánchez Somoano, José. *Costumbres yankees, viajes por la América del Norte.* México, 1894.

Sarmiento, D. Faustino. *Ambas Américas.* New York, 1867-68.

Sarmiento, D. Faustino. "Cartas de Sarmiento [a Mrs. Horace Mann]." *Boletín de la Academia Argentina de Letras,* Buenos Aires, 1935-1936, III-IV, nos. 6-14.

Sarmiento, D. Faustino. *North and South America. A discourse delivered before the Rhode Island Historical Society, December 27, 1865.* Providence, 1866.

Sarmiento, D. Faustino. *Obras.* Santiago de Chile, 1885-1903, 52 vols.

Sarmiento, D. Faustino. *Vida de Abrán Lincoln.* New York, 1866.

Sarmiento, D. Faustino: Correas, Eduardo. *Andanzas de un civilizador.* Mendoza, 1944.

Sarmiento, D. Faustino: Nichols, Madaline. "A United States tour by Sarmiento in 1847." *The Hispanic American Historical Review.* XVI, 1936, 190-212.

Sierra, Justo. *En tierra yankee (Notas a todo vapor).* México, 1898.

Sierra O'Reilly, Justo. *Diario de nuestro viaje a los Estados Unidos. (La pretendida anexión de Yucatán).* Pról. y notas de H. Pérez Martínez. México, 1938.

Sierra O'Reilly, Justo: Menéndez, Carlos R. *El Dr. don Justo Sierra O'Reilly.* México, 1939.

Tanco Armero, Nicolás. *Viaje de Nueva Granada a China y de China a Francia.* Paris, 1961.

Torre, José María de la. *Viaje agrícola-industrial a los Estados Unidos,* 1848.

Torres, Manuel de. *La naturaleza descubierta en su modo de enseñar las lenguas a los hombres, etc. Las lenguas española e inglesa.* Philadelphia, 1811, 2 vols.

Trelles, Carlos Manuel. "Los Estados Unidos como potencia intelectual." *Revista Cubana,* Habana, mayo a octubre, 1894.

Varela, Félix. *El expositor católico.* Baltimore.

Varela, *El Mensajero Semanal.* Philadelphia.

Varela, Félix. *El Observador Habanero.* Philadelphia, 1823.

Vicuña Mackenna, Benjamín. *A sketch of Chili, expressly prepared for the use of emigrants from the United States and Europe* ... New York, 1866.

Vicuña Mackenna, Benjamín. *Diez meses de misión a los Estados Unidos de Norte América.* Santiago, 1867.

Vicuña Mackenna, Benjamín. *Francisco Moyen: or the inquisition as it was in South America* ... *Tr. from the Spanish* ... *by J. W. Duffy.* London, 1869.

Vicuña Mackenna, Benjamín. *La Argentina en el año 1855.* Buenos Aires, 1936.

Vicuña Mackenna, Benjamín. *Obras completas.* Santiago, 1936.

Vicuña Mackenna, Benjamín. "Páginas de mi diario durante tres años de viaje: 1853-1854-1855." *Obras completas,* vol. I-II.

Vidaurre, Manuel Lorenzo. *Cartas americanas, políticas y morales que contienen muchas reflexiones sobre la guerra civil de las Américas.* Philadelphia, 1823.

Vidaurre, Manuel Lorenzo. *Efectos de las facciones en los gobiernos nacientes. Principios fundamentales del gobierno democrático constitucional representativo.* Boston, 1828.

Vigunt, G. F. de. "Paseo por Nueva York." *Revista Habanera,* 1861.

Vizcardo y Guzmán, Juan Pablo. "Lettre aux Espagnols-Américains." *Archivo del General Miranda,* XV, 321-342.

Zambrana, Ramón. "Baracoa y de Filadelfia a Baltimore.' *Revista del Pueblo,* Habana, Abril y Mayo 1865.

Zavala, Lorenzo. *Viaje a los Estados Unidos del Norte de América.* Paris, 1834.

Zeballos, Estanislao S. *La concurrencia universal y la agricultura en ambas Américas.* Washington, 1894.

Zenea, Juan Clemente. *Sobre la literatura de los Estados Unidos.* New York, 1861.

Zenea, Juan Clemente: Gómez Carbonell, María. *Estudio crítico biográfico de Juan Clemente Zenea.* Habana, 1926.

2. WORKS OF REFERENCE

Diario de las operaciones contra la plaza de Panzacola concluídas por las armas de S. M. C. baxo las órdenes del Mariscal de Campo D. Bernardo de Gálvez. (Apparently printed at Madrid about 1781).

Documentos de que hasta ahora se compone el expediente que principiaron las Cortes extraordinarias sobre el tráfico y esclavitud de los negros. Madrid, 1814.

Historia de la administración del Lord North, primer ministro de Inglaterra, y de la guerra de la América septentrional hasta la paz, por P. P. de A. Madrid, 1806.

Manifiesto del consulado sobre la guerra entre los Estados Unidos y la Gran Bretaña. Habana, 1812.

Observations sur la Virginie traduites de l'anglais par André Moreller. Paris, 1786.

Política de los Estados Unidos explicada por los mismos Norte-Americanos. Cádiz, 1852.

Quadro comparativo de la extensión, comercio, y amonedación de los Estados Unidos del Norte, y de las Provincias-Unidas de le Nueva Granada al tiempo de su transformación política, según los cálculos de Brissot, Rochefoucauld y Homes. Spain, circa 1806.

Spanish archives, 1766-1805; Wisconsin Historical Society, Madison, Wis. [Photographic copies of official civil despatches of the governors of Louisiana to the Captain General of Cuba, from the Archives of the Indies at Seville, Spain.] *Wisconsin Historical Collection,* XVIII, 299-468.

The economic literature of Latin America. Cambridge, 1935-1936.

Tratado de amistad, límites y navegación concluído entre el rey (Carlos IV) y los Estados Unidos de América. Madrid, 1796.

Adams, John. *A defense of the constitution of the government of the United States of America, against the attack of Mr. Turgot in his letter to Dr. Price, dated the twenty-second day of March, 1778.* London, 1787.

Adams, John Quincy. *Memoirs of John Quincy Adams.* Philadelphia, 1874-1877.

Allier, Raoul. *La psychologie de la conversion chez les peuples non-civilisés . . .* Paris, 1925.

Alvarez, Francisco. *Noticia del establecimiento y población de las colonias inglesas en la América septentrional; religión, orden de gobierno, leyes y costumbres de sus naturales y habitantes; calidades de su clima, terreno, frutos, plantas y animales; y estado de su industria, artes, comercio y navegación.* Madrid, 1778.

Aranda, Pedro Pablo Abarca y Bolea, conde de. "Informe secreto de Aranda." (Sept. 3, 1783). In: Blanco y Azpurúa, *Documentos,* I, 186; also in Alamán, *Historia de México,* I, 145; English trans. in: Chandler, *Inter-American Acquaintances,* p. 4-5.

Arciniegas, Germán. *Caribbean: Sea of the New World.* New York, 1946.

Bancroft, Hubert Howe. *History of Central America.* San Francisco, 1883.

Bancroft, Hubert Howe. *History of Mexico.* San Francisco, 1882.

Bard, Harry Edwin. *Intellectual and cultural relations between the United States and the oher republics of America.* Washington, Carnegie Endowment for International Peace, 1914.

Barrera, Isaac. *Historia de la literatura hispanoamericana.* Quito, 1935.

Beard, Charles A. *The American spirit.* New York, 1942.

Belaúnde, Victor Andrés. *Bolívar and the political thought of the Spanish American revolution.* Baltimore, 1938.

Bermúdez, Alejandro. *Lucha de razas.* México, 1917.

Bernstein, Harry. "Las primeras relaciones entre New England y el mundo hispánico: 1700-1815." *Revista Hispánica Moderna.* V, 1939, 1-17.

Bernstein, Harry. "Some inter-American aspects of the Enlightenment." In: *Latin America and the Enlightenment,* p. 53-69.

Bernstein, Harry. *Origins of Inter-American interest, 1700-1812.* Philadelphia, 1945. [This important work should have been mentioned in the Introduction].

Blanco, José Félix, and Azpurúa, Ramón. *Documentos para la historia de la vida pública del Libertador de Colombia, Perú y Bolivia.* Caracas, 1875-78, 14 vols.

Blanco Fombona, Horacio. *Crímenes del imperialismo norteamericano.* México, 1927.

Blanco-White, José. *The Life of the Rev. Joseph Blanco White, written by himself, with portions of his correspondence.* Ed. by J. H. Thom. London, 1845, 3 vols.

Bolton, Herbert E. *History of the Americas.* Boston, 1935.

Brackenridge, H. M. *A voyage to South America.* London, 1820, 2 vols.

Brackenridge, H. M. *Early discoveries by Spaniards in New Mexico: containing an account of the castle of Cibola . . .* Pittsburgh, 1857.

Brackenridge, H. M. *Mexican letters written during the progress of the late war between the United States and Mexico . . .* Washington, 1850.

Brackenridge, H. M. "North American pamphlet on South American affairs." *Pamphleteer,* London, 1819.

THE UNITED STATES AS SEEN BY SPANISH AMERICAN WRITERS   211

Brackenridge, H. M. *South America.* Washington, 1817.

Brissot de Warville. *New travels in the United States of America. Performed in 1788.* Dublin, 1792.

Brooks, P. C. "Spanish royalists in the United States. 1809-1821." *Studies in Hispanic American Affairs,* vol. IV, Washington, 1936.

Brooks, Van Wyck. *The flowering of New England.* New York, 1936.

Brooks, Van Wyck. *The world of Washington Irving.* New York, 1944.

Browne, Waldo R. "A backward glance in history." *The Nation,* September 13, 1947.

Bullock, William. *Six month's residence and travels in Mexico.* London, 1824.

Burke, Wm. *Additional reasons for immediately emancipating Spanish America.* London, 1808.

Burke, Wm. *South American independence or the emancipation of South America, the glory and interest of England.* London, 1807.

Burke, Wm. "Los derechos de la América del sur y México." *Gazeta de Caracas,* of the following issues: November 23, 1810; December 7, 1810: December 21, 1810; February 19, 1811.

Campanella, Tommaso. *La città del sole, di Tommaso Campanella.* Traduzione dal latino. Lugano, G. Ruggia & C., 1836.

Carbia, Rómulo D. *Historia de la leyenda negra hispanoamericana.* Buenos Aires, 1943.

Carli, Giovanni Rinaldo. *Lettres américaines.* Paris, 1788.

Casas, Fray Bartolomé de las. *Historia de las Indias.* Madrid, 1875.

Carver, Jonathan. *Three years travels through the interior part of North America.* London, 1778.

Castañeda, Carlos F. "Some facts on our racial minorities." *The Pan-American,* October, 1944.

Castillo Nájera, Francisco. *Future relations between Mexico and the United States.* Washington, 1942.

Cejador y Frauca, Julio. *Historia de la lengua y literatura castellana.* Madrid, 1917.

Chacón y Calvo, José María. *El documento y la reconstrucción histórica.* La Habana, 1929.

Chandler, Charles Lyon. *Inter-American acquaintances.* Sewanee, Tennessee, 1915.

Chinard, Gilbert. *Bibliographie critique des ouvrages francais relatifs aux Etats Unis (1770-1800).* Paris.

Chinard, Gilbert. *Washington as the French knew him.* Princeton, 1940.

Clavigero, Francisco Saverio. *Storia antica del Messico.* Cesena, 1780-81.

Cobarrubias, José de. *Memorias históricas de la última guerra con la gran Bretaña desde el año 1774 hasta su conclusión. Tomo I. Estados Unidos de América. Años 1774 y 1775.* Madrid, 1783.

Coester, Alfred. *The literary history of Spanish America.* New York, 1929.

Coffin, Isaac F. *Diario de un joven norte-americano detenido en Chile durante el período revolucionario de 1817 a 1819, traducido del inglés por J. T. Medina.* Santiago, 1898.

Collier & Cruz. *La primera misión de los Estados Unidos de América en Chile.* Santiago de Chile, 1926.

Comettant, J. P. O. *Tres años en los Estados Unidos* (1852-55). *Traducida del francés.* Madrid, 1858.

Depons, François Raymond Joseph. *Voyage à la partie orientale de la Terre-Ferme dans l'Amérique méridionale fait pendant...1801-1804...* Paris, 1806.

Depons, François Raymond Joseph. *A voyage to the eastern part of Terra Firma, or the Spanish Main, in South America, during the years 1801, 1802, 1803, 1804.* New York, 1806. [Translated by Washington Irving.]

Drake, Sir Francis. *The world encompassed.* London, Hakluyt Collection, 1893.

Duane, William. *A visit to Colombia, in the years 1822 & 1823.* Philadelphia, 1826.

Duane, William. *The two Americas, Great Britain, and the Holy Alliance.* Washington, 1824.

Duponceau, P. S. *Breve reseña de la constitución de los Estados Unidos.* New York, 1848.

Englekirk, John E. *Edgar Allan Poe in Hispanic Literature.* New York, 1934.

Englekirk, John E. "Whitman in Spanish America." *Hispania,* November, 1942.

Esquivel Obregón, Toribio. *Influencia de España y los Estados Unidos sobre México.* Madrid, 1924.

Estrella Gutiérrez, Fermín & Emilio Suárez Calimano. *Historia de la literatura americana y argentina.* Buenos Aires, 1940.

Everett, Alexander H. *America, or a general survey of the political situation of the several powers of the western continent, with conjectures on their future prospects. By a citizen of the United States.* 1828. [A Spanish translation appears to have been printed at Northampton, Mass., this same year.]

Everett, Edward. "South America." *North American Review,* III, 1821, 432-443.

Fabela, Isidro. *Los Estados Unidos contra la libertad.* Barcelona, 1920.

Ferguson, John De Lancey. *American literature in Spain.* NewYork, 1916.

Fernández Mejía, Abigail de. *Historia de la literatura dominicana.* Ciudad Trujillo, 1937.

Fernández de Navarrete, M. *Colección de viajes y descubrimientos.* Madrid, 1829.

Ferrer del Río, Antonio. *Historia del reinado de Carlos III.* Madrid, 1856.

Fisher, Lillian Estelle. *The background of the revolution for the Mexican independence.* Boston, 1934.

Ford, Paul Leicester. *The writings of Thomas Jefferson.* New York, 1892-99.

Ford, Paul Leicester. *Works of Thomas Jefferson.* New York, 1904-05.

Foronda, Valentín de. "Apuntes ligeros sobre la América septentrional." Philadelphia, marzo 13, 1804. Ed. by José de Onís, *The Americas,* IV, 351-387.

Foronda, Valentín de. Correspondance, legajos 5633, 5634. (Library of Congress Division of Manuscripts).

Foronda, Valentín de. *Sobre lo que debe de hacer un príncipe que tenga colonias a gran distancia.* Philadelphia, 1803.

Forsyth, J. *Observaciones sobre la Memoria del señor. Onís, relativa a la negociación con los Estados Unidos.* Madrid, 1822, (Written in English. Translated into Spanish from the original manuscript, by Father Thomas Gough).

Franklin, Benjamin. *El libro del hombre de bien.* Opúsculos morales, económicos y políticos estractados de Benjamin Franklin. Barcelona, 1843. (There is another edition of 1867.)

Franklin, Benjamin. *Lo camí de la fortuna: consells brèus y senzills pera esser rich.* Barcelona, 1868.

Gaer, Joseph. *Bibliography of California literature, pre-gold rush period.* California, 1897.

Galiani, Ferdinando. *Correspondance inédite de l'abbé Ferdinand Galiani . . .* Paris, 1818.

Galiani, Ferdinando. *Dialogues sur le commerce des blés,* 5 vols. 1770.

Galiani, Ferdinando. *Diálogos sobre el comercio de trigo, atribuídos al Abate Galiani.* Madrid, 1775

Garcés de Marcilla, Pedro. *Vida de D. Benjamin Franklin sacada de documentos auténticos.* Madrid, 1798.

García Calderón, Francisco. *Latin America; its rise and progress.* London, 1913.

Gaxiola, José. *La frontera de la raza.* Madrid, 1917.

Gerbi, Antonello. *Viejas polémicas sobre el Nuevo Mundo.* Ciudad de los Reyes, 1946.

Goldberg, Isaac. *Studies in Spanish American literature.* New York, 1920.

Gómez Restrepo, Antonio. *Historia de la literatura colombiana.* Bogotá, 1938.

González, Manuel Pedro. "Intellectual relations between the United States and Spanish America." *The Civilization of the Americas,* Berkeley, 1938, p.

González, Manuel Pedro. "Las relaciones intelectuales entre los Estados Unidos e Hispanoamérica." *Universidad de la Habana,* 1939, VIII (no. 24-24), 84-110.

González Peña, C. *Historia de la literatura mexicana.* México, 1940.

Griffin, Charles C. *The United States and the disruption of the Spanish empire, 1810-1822.* New York, 1928.

Groussac, Paul. *Del Plata al Niágara.* Buenos Aires, 1897.

Guillén, Jorge. "George Ticknor, lover of culture." *More Books, The Bulletin of the Boston Public Library,* October, 1942.

Hanke, Lewis. *The first social experiment in America.* Cambridge, Mass., 1935.

Haring, Clarence H. *South America looks at the United States.* New York, 1928.

Hart, Francis Russell. *The disaster of Darien.* Boston, 1929.

Helman, Edith F. "Early interest in Spanish in New England (1815-1835)." *Hispania,* August, 1946, p. 339-351.

Henríquez-Ureña, Pedro. *Literary currents in Hispanic America.* Cambridge, Mass., 1945.

Hill, Roscoe R. *Descriptive catalogue of the documents relating to the history of the United States in the "Papeles procedentes de Cuba," deposited in the Archivo general de Indias at Seville.* Washington, 1916.

Howren, Alleine. "Causes and origin of the Decree of April 6, 1830." *The Southern Historical Quarterly,* XVI, 1913, 395-398.

Irving, Washington. *Historia de la vida y viajes de Cristóbal Colón.* Traducida al castellano por D. José García de Villalta. Madrid, 1833-34.

Irving, Washington. *Vida y viajes de Cristóbal Colón por Washington Irving.* México, 1853.

Irving, Washington. *Viajes y descubrimientos de los compañeros de Colón.* Madrid, 1854.

Jefferson, Thomas. *Notes on Virginia.* Paris, 1784-85.

Jefferson to Foronda, Monticello, October 4, 1809. Jefferson Papers, Library of Congress [acknowledges receipt of Spanish Constitution.] M. S.

Jiménez Rueda, J. *Historia de la literatura mexicana.* México, 1928.

Jones, H. M. *Ideas in America.* Cambridge, Mass., 1944.

Juan, Jorge, y Antonio de Ulloa. *Noticias secretas de América. London, 1826.* Madrid, 1917.

Juan, Jorge, y Antonio de Ulloa. *A voyage to South America,* 2 vols. London, 1806.

Kibbe, Pauline R. *Latin Americans in Texas.* Albuquerque, 1946.

Lanzos, Manuel. "Diario de que se ha llevado por el capitán del regimiento fijo Don Manuel Lanzos tocante a la sedición de los habitantes de este distrito al favor del comandante americano llamado Pope y su comisario de límites Andrés Elicot." Natchez, June 9, 1824. Department of Archives and History, Jackson, Miss.

Leavitt, Sturgis E. *Hispanic American literature in the United States.* Cambridge, Mass., 1932.

Leboucher, Odet Julien. *Historia de la última guerra entre la Inglaterra, los Estados Unidos de América. la Francia, España, y Holanda:desde 1775, hasta 1783.* Alcalá, 1793.

Leonard, Irving A. "A frontier library." *The Hispanic American Historical Review,* Feb. 1943.

Lewin, Boleslao. "El informe secreto de Aranda en 1783 sobre la independencia de las colonias españolas. El ambiente de la época y las dudas acerca de su autenticidad." *La Nación,* Buenos Aires, 8 Oct. 1944.

Lockey, Joseph Byrne. *Pan-Americanism. Its beginnings.* New York, 1920.

López, Marcial Antonio. *Descripción de los más célebres establecimientos penales de Europa y los Estados Unidos.* Valencia, 1832.

Lummis, Charles F. *The Spanish pioneers.* Chicago, 1899. Second edition: Chicago, 1925.—*Los exploradores españoles del siglo XVI. Vindicación de la acción colonizadora española en América,* Prólogo de Rafael Altamira. Barcelona, 1916.

Maggs Brothers. *Bibliotheca Americana,* part VI, Books on America in Spanish. London, 1927.

Marinello, Juan. *Literatura hispanoamericana.* México, 1937.

Martínez, José. "Report by Engineer José Martínez concerning the Americans and their explorations," New Orleans, Aug. 20, 1804. Missouri Historical Society.

Mather, Cotton. *Religión pura to which is added La fe del christiano; en veynte quatro artículos de La institución de Christo. An essay to convey religion into the Spanish Indies.* Boston, 1699.

Medina, J. T. *Biblioteca americana.* Santiago de Chile, 1888.

Medina, J. T. *Biblioteca hispanoamericana (1493-1818).* Santiago de Chile, 1898-1907, 7 vols.

Melfi, Domingo. *Estudios de la literatura chilena.* Santiago, 1938.

Molina, Juan Ignacio. *Compendio de la historia geográfica, natural y civil del Reyno de Chile.* Madrid, 1788-95, 2 vols.

Molina, Juan Ignacio. *The geographical, natural and civil history of Chili.* [Trans. by William Shaler & Richard Alsop]. Middletown, Conn., 1808.

Monaghan, Frank. *French travellers in the United States, 1765-1932.* New York, 1933.

More, Thomas. *Utopia,* originally printed in Latin, 1516. Tr. into English by Ralf Robinson . . . his 2d and rev. ed., 1556; preceded by the title and epistle of his first ed., 1551 . . . ed. by Edward Aber . . . London, A. Murray & Son, 1869.

Morison, Samuel Eliot and Commager, Henry S. *The growth of the American republic.* New York, 1942.

Morse, Jedidiah. *The American gazetteer.* Boston, 1797.

Moses, Bernard, *Spanish colonial literature in South America.* New York, 1922.

Moses, Bernard. *The establishment of the Spanish rule in America.* New York, 1895.

Muñoz, Juan Bautista. *Historia del Nuevo Mundo.* Tomo I. (Unico publicado). Madrid, 1793.

Muñoz, Juan Bautista. *The history of the New World,* vol. I (all published). London, 1797.

Napoleon, Joseph. "Instructions given by Joseph Napoleon to the commissary or principal agent appointed by him at Baltimore, M. Desmolard, and to others who furnished with his orders have gone to Spanish America for the purpose of exciting a revolution there." In: Palacio Fajardo, *Outline of the revolution in Spanish America,* London, 1817, p. 55-58.

Navarro y Lamarca, Carlos. *Compendio de la historia general de América.* Buenos Aires, 1910-1913. 7 vols.

Nevins, Allan. *American social history as recorded by British travellers.* New York, 1923.

Niles, John Milton. *A view of South America and Mexico, comprising their history, the political condition, geography, agriculture, commerce, . . .* New York, 1825.

Nogales y Méndez, Rafael de. *The looting of Nicaragua.* New York, 1928.

Nunn, Marshall. "Rubén Darío y los Estados Unidos." *América,* Habana, I, 1939, 61-64.

Onís, José de. "Valentín de Foronda's memoir on the United States of North America, 1804." *The Americas,* IV, 1948, 351-387.

Onís, José de. "Orígenes de las relaciones internacionales." *Revista de América,* Bogotá, XV, 1948 (no. 43-44), 106-114.

Onís, José de. "The letter of Francisco Iturri, S.J. (1789)." *The Americas,* VIII, 1951, 85-90.

Onís, José de. "Alcedo's Bibliotheca Americana." *The Hispanic American Historical Review,* XXXI, 1951, 530-541.

Onís, Luis de. "Aviso de Don Luis de Onís." In: Fray Melchor Martínez, *Revolución de Chile,* p. 42.

Onís, Luis de. Letter, Philadelphia, February 14, 1812. In: Blanco y Azpurúa, *Documentos,* III, 608.

Onís, Luis de. *Memoria sobre las negociaciones entre España y los Estados Unidos de América que dieron motivo al tratado de 1819. Con una noticia sobre la estadística de aquel país. Acompaña un apéndice, que contiene documentos importantes para mayor ilustración del asunto* ... Madrid, 1820; — Mexico, 1826.

Onís, Luis de. *Memoir upon the negotiations between Spain and the United States of America, which led to the treaty of 1819. Translated with notes by Tobias Watkins.* Baltimore, 1821.

Onís, Luis de. *Official correspondence between D. Luis de Onís and John Quincy Adams.* London, 1818.

Onís, Luis de [Verus]. *Observation on the conduct of our executive toward Spain.* Georgetown, D. C., Nov. 12, 1813.

Onís, Luis de [Verus]. *Observation on the existing difference between the government of Spain and the U. S.* Philadelphia, 1817.

Ortega, J. *Historia de la literatura colombiana.* Bogotá, 1934.

Osgood, Herbert L. *The American colonies in the eighteenth century.* Vol. IV. New York, 1924.

Oviedo y Romero, A. de. *Biografías de mexicanos célebres.* Paris-México, 1889.

Paine, Thomas. *La independencia de la costa firme, justificada por Thomas Paine treinta años há. Extracto de sus obras traducido del inglés al español por D. Manuel García de Sena.* Philadelphia, 1811.

Paine, Thomas. *Historia concisa de los Estados Unidos.* Philadelphia, 1812.

Palomeque, Alberto. *Orígenes de la diplomacia argentina.* Buenos Aires, 1905.

Pane, Remigio U. "Two hundred Latin American books in English translation: a bibliography." *Modern Language Journal*, XXVII, 1943, 593-604.

Para Pérez, C. *Historia de la primera república de Venezuela.* Caracas, 1939

Pedreira, Antonio S. *Hostos, ciudadano de América.* Madrid, 1932.

Pereyra, Carlos. *Bolívar y Washington: un paralelo imposible.* Madrid, 1915.

Pereyra, Carlos. *El mito de Monroe.* Madrid, 1914.

Pereyra, Carlos. *Historia de la América española,* 8 vols. Madrid, 1920-1926.

Pereyra, Carlos. *La constitución de los Estados Unidos como instrumento de dominación plutocrática.* Madrid, 1917.

Pereyra, Carlos. *La doctrina Monroe, el destino manifiesto y el imperialismo.* México, 1908.

Pérez, Luis Marino. *Guide to materials for American history in Cuban archives.* Washington, 1907.

Picón Salas, Mariano. *Formación y proceso de la literatura venezolana.* Caracas, 1941.

Picón Salas, Mariano. *De la Conquista a la Independencia.* México, 1944.

Piernas, Pedro. "Description of the Illinois country." *Wisconsin Historical Collection*, XVIII, 299-468.

Poinsett, J. R. *Exposición de la conducta política de los Estados Unidos.* México, 1827.

Poinsett, J. R. *Notes on Mexico, made in the autumn of 1822; accompanied by an historical sketch of the revolution.* London, 1825.

Poinsett, J. R. *Observaciones sobre las instrucciones que dió el presidente de los*

Estados Unidos . . . *a los representantes de aquella república en el Congreso de Panamá en 1826: sobre la conducta del señor Poinsett* . . . *y sobre nuestras relaciones con la América Española en general* . . . Filadelfia, 1830.

Posada, Eduardo. "Prefacio." *Biblioteca de Historia Nacional,* II. Bogotá, Colombia, 1917-1925.

Pratt, E. F. "Anglo-American commercial and political relations." *The Hispanic American Historical Review,* II.

Prescott, G. H. *Historia de la conquista de México,* 3 vols. New York, 1843.

Prescott, G. H. *Historia de los Reyes Católicos Fernando e Isabel.* Philadelphia, 1872.

Ramsay, David. *Jorge Washington: su vida, deducida de la que publicó M. David Ramsay.* Paris, 1819.

Ramsay, David. *The history of the American revolution.* Philadelphia, 1789.

Raleigh, Sir Walter. *The history of the world with the life and trial of the author.* London, 1687.

Raynal, G. T. *Histoire philosophique et politique des établissements et du commerce des européens dans les deux Indes.* Genève, 1780.

Raynal, G. T. *De los pueblos y gobiernos; colección de pensamientos extraídos de la historia filosófica de las dos Indias.* Londres, 1823.

Remos y Rubio, Juan J. *Historia de la literatura cubana.* Habana, 1938.

Rich, Obadiah. *A catalogue of books relating principally to America, arranged under the years in which they were printed.* London, 1832.

Rich, Obadiah. *A general view of the United States of America.* London, 1833.

Rich, Obadiah. *Bibliotheca americana nova.* London, 1835-1846. Vol. I, 1701-1800; vol. II, 1801-1844.

Rich, Obadiah. *Bibliotheca americana vetus.* London, 1845.

Rich, Obadiah. *Catalogue of a collection of manuscripts.* London, 1848.

Rippy, J. Fred. "Bolívar as viewed by contemporary diplomats of the United States." *The Hispanic American Historical Review,* XV, 1935, 287-297.

Rippy, J. Fred. *Historical evolution of Hispanic America.* New York, 1943.

Rippy, J. Fred. *Joel R. Poinsett, versatile American.* Durham, N. C., 1935.

Rippy, J. Fred. *Rivalry of the United States and Great Britain over Latin America.* Baltimore, 1929.

Robertson, James Alexander. *List of documents in Spanish archives relating to the history of the United States, which have been printed or of which transcripts are preserved in American libraries.* Washington, 1910.

Robertson, William. *History of America.* London, 1777.

Robertson, William S. *Hispanic American relations.* New York, 1923.

Robinson, William D. *Memoirs of the Mexican revolution: including a narrative of the expedition of General Xavier Mina* . . . Philadelphia, 1820.

Robledo, Alfonso. *Una lengua y una raza.* Bogotá, 1916

Robles, Juan. *Las dos razas.* México, 1922.

Rodó, José Enrique. *Ariel.* Chicago, 1929.

Rojas, Ricardo. *Historia de la literatura argentina.* Madrid, 1924.

Roosevelt, Franklin D. "Our foreign policy: a democratic view." *Foreign Affairs,* IV, Oct. 1927-July 1928.

Roux de Rochelle, J. B. G. *Historia de los Estados Unidos de América. Traducido al castellano.* Barcelona, 1841.

Rydjord, John. *Foreign interest in the independence of New Spain.* Durham, N. C., 1935.

Sabin, Joseph. *A dictionary of books relating to America, from its discovery to the present time.* New York, 1868-1936, 29 vols.

Sáenz, Vicente. "The peaceful penetration of the United States." *Current History,* XXVI, 913-918.

Salas S., Irma. "Las relaciones culturales entre Chile y los Estados Unidos." *Boletín de la Unión Panamericana,* 1940, p. 570-576.

Sánchez, Luis A. *Historia de la literatura americana.* Santiago, 1937.

Sánchez, Luis A. *La literatura del Perú.* Buenos Aires, 1939.

Sánchez, Luis A. *Un sudamericano en Norteamérica.* Santiago de Chile, 1942.

Sánchez, Luis A. *Vida y pasión de la cultura en América.* Santiago de Chile, 1935.

Sánchez Alonso, Benito. *Fuentes de la historia española e hispano-americana.* 2 vols. Madrid, 1927.

Shearer, James F. "Agustín de Letamendi: A Spanish expatriate in Charleston, S. C. (1825-1829)." *The South Carolina Historical and Genealogical Magazine,* XLIII, no. 1, 1942, 18-26.

Shearer, James F. "Pioneer publishers of textbooks for Hispanic America: the house of Appleton," *Hispania,* February, 1944.

Shepherd, William R. *Guide to the materials for the history of the United States in Spanish archives.* Washington, 1907.

[Smith, Adam]' Marqués de Condorcet. *Compendio de la obra inglesa intitulada Riqueza de las naciones.* Traducido con varias adiciones del original por D. Carlos Martínez de Irujo, Madrid, 1792.

Sosa, Francisco. *Biografías de mexicanos distinguidos.* México, 1884.

Spell, J. R. "An illustrious Spaniard in Philadelphia." *Hispanic Review,* Philadelphia, IV, 1936, 136-140.

Sprague, William Forrest. *Vicente Guerrero, Mexican liberator.* Chicago, 1939.

Stewart, Watt, and William French. "Influence of Horace Mann on the educational ideas of Domingo Faustino Sarmiento." *The Hispanic American Historical Review,* XX, 1940, 12-31.

Stewart, Watt, and William French. "The diplomatic services of John M. Forbes at Buenos Aires." *The Hispanic American Historical Review,* XIV, 202.

Teixidor, Felipe. *Viajeros mexicanos (siglos XIX-XX).* México, 1939.

Temperly, Harold William Vazeille. "The later American policy of George Canning." *American Historical Review,* XI, 1906.

Ticknor, George. *Historia de la literatura española, traducida al castellano, con adiciones y notas críticas, por D. Pascual de Gayangos y D. Enrique de Vedia.* Madrid, 1851-1856.

Ticknor, George. *Historia del origen, formación y adopción de la constitución de los Estados Unidos.* Trad. por J. M. Cantillo. Buenos Aires, 1866.

Ticknor, George. *Life, letters and journals.* London, 1876.

Tocqueville, Alexis de. *Democracy in America. Translated by Henry Reeve.* London, 1836.

Tocqueville, Alexis de. *De la démocratie en Amérique.* Paris, 1836.
Tocqueville, Alexis de. *De la démocratie en Amérique.* Paris, 1836.
Bustamante. Paris, 1836-37.
Torrente, Mariano. *Historia de la revolución hispano-americana.* 3 vols. Madrid, 1829.
Trelles, Carlos M. "Bibliografía de la segunda guerra de la independencia cubana y de la hispano-yankee." *Cuba y América,* Habana, 1902.
Trelles, Carlos M. *Biblioteca geográfica cubana.* Matanzas, 1920.
Trelles, Carlos M. *Estudio de la bibliografía cubana sobre la doctrina de Monroe.* Habana, 1922.
Trollope, Mrs. *Costumbres familiares de los americanos del norte. Obra escrita en inglés . . . y traducida por Juan Florán . . .* Paris, 1835.
Tuckerman, Henry J. *America and her commentators.* New York, 1864.
Vernon, Edward. *Original papers relating to the expedition to Carthagena.* London, 1744.
Vial, Pedro. "Journal of his voyage from Santa Fe to Saint Louis, 1792." In: Houck, *Spanish Regime,* I, 329-333. (Translation).
Walker, William. *The war in Nicaragua.* Mobile, 1860.
Walsh, Thomas. *Hispanic anthology.* New York, 1920.
Walton, William. *An appeal to the British nation on the affairs of South America.* London, 1819.
Walton, William. *Exposé of the dissensions in Spanish America.* London, 1814.
Walton, William. *Outline of the revolution in Spanish America.* New York, 1817.
Warren, Harris Gaylord. "The early revolutionary career of Juan Mariano Picornell." *The Hispanic American Historical Review,* February 1942.
Ward, Sir Henry G. *Mexico in 1827.* 2 vols. London, 1928. (Includes an "Account of Texas" by Gen. Wavel).
Whitaker, Arthur P. "José Silvestre Rebello." *The Hispanic American Historical Review,* XX, 1940.
Whitaker, Arthur P. *The United States and the independence of Latin America, 1800-1830.* Baltimore, 1941.
Whitaker, Arthur P. *Latin America and the Enlightenment.* New York, 1942.
White, Elizabeth Brett. *American opinion of France.* New York, 1927.
White, John W. "Uruguay, bulwark of Pan-Americanism." *The Inter-American Monthly,* November, 1942, p. 13.
Whitman, Iris Lilian. *Longfellow and Spain.* New York. 1927.
Wilgus, A. Curtis. *Histories and historians of Spanish America.* Washington, 1937.
Wilgus and d'Eça. *Outline history of Latin America.* New York, 1939.
Wright, Irene A. "Memorandum of index of documents in Madrid archives furnished to the library of Congress by Miss Irene A. Wright, Archivo Histórico Nacional, Madrid; Diplomatic Section; Correspondence of the Spanish legation in the United States, including supplementary notes in each legajo." Library of Congress Division of Manuscripts.
Yela Utrilla, Juan F. *España ante la guerra de la independencia de los Estados Unidos.* 2 vols. Lérida, 1925.
Zum Felde, Alberto. *Progreso intelectual del Uruguay.* Montevideo, 1930.

INDEX OF NAMES